Also by John Vaillant

The Golden Spruce

THE TIGER

THE
TIGER

A TRUE STORY OF VENGEANCE AND SURVIVAL

John Vaillant

ALFRED A. KNOPF | NEW YORK | TORONTO | 2010

THIS IS A BORZOI BOOK
PUBLISHED BY ALFRED A. KNOPF
AND ALFRED A. KNOPF CANADA

www.aaknopf.com
www.randomhouse.ca

Library of Congress Cataloging-in-Publication Data
Vaillant, John.
The tiger : a true story of venegeance and survival / by John
Vaillant.—1st ed.
p.   cm.
"A Borzoi Book."
ISBN 978-0-307-26893-8
1. Tiger hunting—Russia—Russian far east.   2. Tiger
attacks—Russia far east.   I. Title.
SK305.T5V35 2010
599.7560957'7—dc22   2010004068

Library and Archives Canada Cataloguing in Publication
Vaillant, John (John H.)
The tiger : a true story of vengeance and survival / John Vaillant.
ISBN 978-0-307-39714-0
1. Trush, Yuri—Travel—Russia (Federation)—Primorskii krai.
2. Markov, Vladimir, d. 1997.   3. Tiger hunting—Russia
(Federation)—Primorskii krai.   4. Hunters—Russia
(Federation)—Primorskii krai.   5. Primorskii krai (Russia)—
Description and travel.   I. Title.
SK305.T5V34 2010   799.2'775609577   C2009-906953-9

Manufactured in the United States of America

First Edition

The text and jacket paper this book is printed on comes from
well managed forest sources and complies with SFI
(Sustainable Forest Initiative) requirements.

To the memory of
Joanna and Ellis Settle

viriditas

In the taiga there are no witnesses.

V. K. ARSENIEV,
Dersu the Trapper

no easy bargain
Would be made in that place by any man

Beowulf

Contents

The Russian Far East

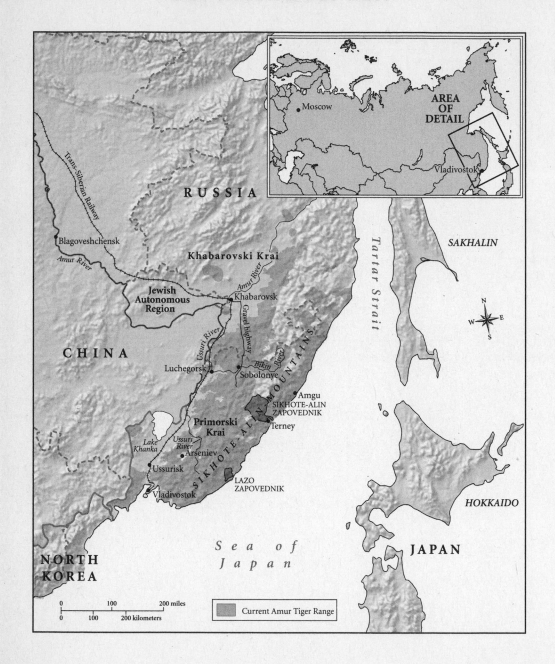

The Bikin River Valley

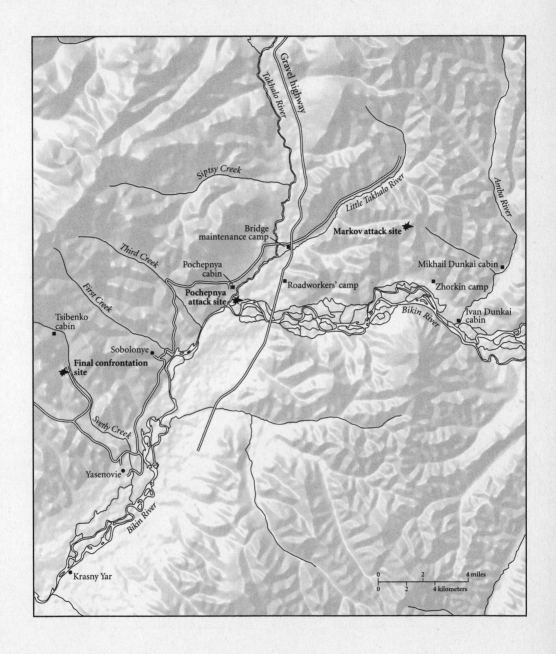

THE TIGER

Prologue

HANGING IN THE TREES, AS IF CAUGHT THERE, IS A SICKLE OF A MOON. Its wan light scatters shadows on the snow below, only obscuring further the forest that this man negotiates now as much by feel as by sight. He is on foot and on his own save for a single dog, which runs ahead, eager to be heading home at last. All around, the black trunks of oak, pine, and poplar soar into the dark above the scrub and deadfall, and their branches form a tattered canopy overhead. Slender birches, whiter than the snow, seem to emit a light of their own, but it is like the coat of an animal in winter: cold to the touch and for itself alone. All is quiet in this dormant, frozen world. It is so cold that spit will freeze before it lands; so cold that a tree, brittle as straw and unable to contain its expanding sap, may spontaneously explode. As they progress, man and dog alike leave behind a wake of heat, and the contrails of their breath hang in pale clouds above their tracks. Their scent stays close in the windless dark, but their footfalls carry and so, with every step, they announce themselves to the night.

Despite the bitter cold, the man wears rubber boots better suited to the rain; his clothes, too, are surprisingly light, considering that he has been out all day, searching. His gun has grown heavy on his shoulder, as have his rucksack and cartridge belt. But he knows this route like the back of his hand, and he is almost within sight of his cabin. Now, at last, he can allow himself the possibility of relief. Perhaps he imagines the lantern he will light and the fire he will build; perhaps he imagines the burdens he will soon lay down. The water in the kettle is certainly frozen, but the stove is thinly walled and soon it will glow fiercely against the cold and dark, just as his own body is doing now. Soon enough, there will be hot tea and a cigarette, followed by rice, meat, and more cigarettes. Maybe a shot or two of vodka, if there is any left. He savors this ritual and knows it by rote. Then, as the familiar angles take shape across the clearing, the dog collides with a scent as with a wall and stops short, growling. They are hunting partners and the man understands: someone is there by the cabin. The hackles on the dog's back and on his own neck rise together.

Together, they hear a rumble in the dark that seems to come from everywhere at once.

PART ONE

| | |

MARKOV

1

There are many people who don't believe this actually
happened. They think it's some phantasm of my
imagination. But it was real. There are the facts.

YURI ANATOLIEVICH TRUSH

SHORTLY AFTER DARK ON THE AFTERNOON OF DECEMBER 5, 1997, AN
urgent message was relayed to a man named Yuri Trush at his
home in Luchegorsk, a mid-sized mining town in Primorye Territory in Russia's Far East, not far from the Chinese border. Primorye (Pri-*mor*-ya) is, among other things, the last stronghold of
the Siberian tiger, and the official on the line had some disturbing
news: a man had been attacked near Sobolonye, a small logging
community located in the deep forest, sixty miles northeast of
Luchegorsk. Yuri Trush was the squad leader of an Inspection
Tiger unit, one of six in the territory whose purpose was to investigate forest crimes, specifically those involving tigers. Because
poachers were often involved, these included tiger attacks. As a
result, this situation—whatever it might entail—was now Trush's
problem and, right away, he began preparing for the trip to
Sobolonye.

———

Early the following morning—Saturday—Yuri Trush, along with
his squadmates Alexander Gorborukov and Sasha Lazurenko,
piled into a surplus army truck and rumbled north. Dressed in
insulated fatigues and camouflage, and armed with knives, pistols,

and semiautomatic rifles, the Tigers, as these inspectors are some-times called, looked less like game wardens than like some kind of wilderness SWAT team. Their twenty-year-old truck was nick-named a Kung, and it was the Russian army's four-ton equivalent to the Unimog and the Humvee. Gasoline-powered, with a winch, four-wheel-drive, and wide waist-high tires, it is a popular vehicle in Primorye's hinterlands. Along with a gun rack and brackets for extra fuel cans, this one had been modified to accommodate makeshift bunks, and was stocked with enough food to last four men a week. It was also equipped with a woodstove so that, even in the face of total mechanical failure, the crew could survive no matter where in the wilderness they happened to be.

After passing through the police checkpoint on the edge of town, the Tigers continued on up to a dirt road turnoff that led eastward along the Bikin (be-*keen*) River, a large and meandering waterway that flows through some of the most isolated country in northern Primorye. The temperature was well below freezing and the snow was deep, and this slowed the heavy truck's progress. It also allowed these men, all of whom were experienced hunters and former soldiers, many hours to ponder and discuss what might be awaiting them. It is safe to say that nothing in their experience could have prepared them for what they found there.

———

Primorye, which is also known as the Maritime Territory, is about the size of Washington state. Tucked into the southeast corner of Russia by the Sea of Japan, it is a thickly forested and mountain-ous region that combines the backwoods claustrophobia of Appalachia with the frontier roughness of the Yukon. Industry here is of the crudest kind: logging, mining, fishing, and hunting, all of which are complicated by poor wages, corrupt officials, thriving black markets—and some of the world's largest cats.

One of the many negative effects of perestroika and the reopening of the border between Russia and China has been a surge in tiger poaching. As the economy disintegrated and unem-ployment spread throughout the 1990s, professional poachers, businessmen, and ordinary citizens alike began taking advantage of the forest's wealth in all its forms. The tigers, because they are so rare and so valuable, have been particularly hard hit: their organs, blood, and bone are much sought after for use in traditional Chinese medicine. Some believe the tiger's whiskers will make them bulletproof and that its powdered bones will soothe their aches and pains. Others believe its penis will make them virile, and there are many—from Tokyo to Moscow—who will pay thousands of dollars for a tiger's skin.

Between 1992 and 1994, approximately one hundred tigers— roughly one quarter of the country's wild population—were killed. Most of them ended up in China. With financial assistance (and pressure) from international conservation agencies, the territorial government created Inspection Tiger in the hope of restoring some semblance of law and order to the forests of Primorye. Armed with guns, cameras, and broad police powers, these teams were charged with intercepting poachers and resolving a steadily increasing number of conflicts between tigers and human beings.

In many ways, Inspection Tiger's mandate resembles that of detectives on a narcotics detail, and so does the risk: the money is big, and the players are often desperate and dangerous individuals. Tigers are similar to drugs in that they are sold by the gram and the kilo, and their value increases according to the refinement of both product and seller. But there are some key differences: tigers can weigh six hundred pounds; they have been hunting large prey, including humans, for two million years; and they have a memory. For these reasons, tigers can be as dangerous to the people trying to protect them as they are to those who would profit from them.

The territory covered by Yuri Trush's Inspection Tiger unit in the mid-1990s was centered on the Bikin River. You can drive a truck on the Bikin in winter, but in summer it has a languid bayou feel. For many of the valley's jobless inhabitants, the laws imposed by the river and the forest are more relevant than those of the local government. While most residents here poach game simply to survive, there are those among them who are in it for the money.

———

In 1997, Inspection Tiger had been in existence for only three years; given the state of the Russian economy in the 1990s, its members were lucky to have jobs, particularly because they were paid in dollars by foreign conservation groups. Four hundred dollars a month was an enviable wage at that time, but a lot was expected in return. Whether they were doing routine checks of hunters' documents in the forest, searching suspect cars en route to the Chinese border, or setting up sting operations, most of the people Inspection Tiger dealt with were armed. As often as not, these encounters took place in remote areas where backup was simply not available, and they never knew what they were going to find.

Following perestroika, virtually everything in Russia went on sale, and vast quantities of military ordnance disappeared from local armories. In the course of their raids on the many anonymous hunting cabins that dot the forest here, Trush and his men confiscated plastic explosives, TNT, and 12mm (.50 caliber) machine guns, robbed from armored vehicles. Trush could not imagine what one would do with guns that size in the forest, but the explosives were easier to explain: they were used in creeks to kill fish en masse, or to blow bears out of their dens. The Asian market is less interested in the intact skins or carcasses of bears than it is in their paws and gall bladders; the paws go into soup, and the gall bladders are used for medicinal purposes. In Primorye, in the mid-1990s, life, for man and animal alike, was cheap, and corruption was widespread at every level of government. During these years, Trush made busts involving high-ranking police officers and members of parliament, and these were dangerous enemies for a person to have. Trush, however, was well suited to this work because he can be dangerous, too.

Trush stands about six-foot-two with long arms and legs and a broad chest. His eyes are colored, coincidentally, like the semi-precious stone tiger's eye, with black rings around the irises. They peer out from a frank and homely face framed by great, drooping brows. Though frail and sickly as a boy, Trush grew into a talented athlete with a commanding presence, a deep resonant voice, and an ability to remain composed under highly stressful circumstances. He is also immensely strong. As a young soldier in Kazakhstan, in the 1970s, Trush won a dozen regional kayaking championships for which he earned the Soviet rank Master of Sports, a distinction that meant he was eligible to compete at the national level. It was a serious undertaking: he wasn't just racing against Bulgarians and East Germans. "I was," he said, "defending the honor of the Military Forces of the USSR." In his mid-forties, when he joined Inspection Tiger, Trush won a territory-wide weightlifting competition three years running. This was not the kind of weightlifting one is likely to see in the Olympics; what Trush was doing looks more like a contest devised by bored artillerymen during the Napoleonic Wars. It consists of hefting a kettlebell—essentially a large cannonball with a handle—from the ground over your head as many times as you can, first with one hand, and then the other. Kettlebells are a Russian invention; they have been around for centuries and their use clearly favors the short and the stocky. So it is surprising to see someone as attenuated as Trush, who has the Law of the Lever weighted so heavily against him, heave these seventy-pound spheres around with such apparent ease.

Trush learned to shoot, first, from his father and, later, in the army. He also studied karate, aikido, and knife handling; in these, his rangy build works to his advantage because his long reach makes it nearly impossible to get at him. He is so talented at hand-to-hand fighting that he was hired to teach these skills to the military police. Trush's physicality is intense and often barely suppressed. He is a grabber, a hugger, and a roughhouser, but the hands initiating—and controlling—these games are thinly disguised weapons. His fists are knuckled mallets, and he can break bricks with them. As he runs through the motions of an immobilizing hold, or lines up an imaginary strike, one has the sense that his body hungers for opportunities to do these things in earnest. Referring to a former colleague who went bad and whom he tried for years to catch red-handed, Trush said, "He knows very well that I am capable of beheading him with my bare hands." This

tension—between the kind and playful neighbor, friend and husband, and the Alpha male wilderness cop ready to throw down at a
moment's notice—energizes almost every interaction. It is under
the latter circumstances that Trush seems most alive.

———

The deeper Trush and his men drove into the forest, the rougher
the road became. Once past Verkhny Pereval, their route took
them through the snowbound village of Yasenovie, a sister logging community of the same size and vintage as Sobolonye. Here,
they picked up a young deputy sheriff named Bush, but his presence on this mission was more formal than practical. Bush was a
cop, and tiger attacks were beyond his purview; however, if there
was a body, he was required to witness it. With Bush onboard, they
trundled on upriver.

It was already afternoon by the time they reached Sobolonye,
an impoverished village of unpainted log houses that at first
glance seemed barely inhabited. Gorborukov was behind the
wheel, and here he steered the truck off the main road, such as it
was, and plunged into the forest on a track wide enough for only a
single vehicle. Several inches of new snow had fallen earlier in the
week and, as they drove, Trush scanned the roadside for fresh
tracks. They were about fifty miles from the nearest paved road
and a couple of hard-won miles east of Sobolonye when they
crossed a wide and improbably located gravel highway. This road
had been conceived during Soviet times as an alternative to Primorye's only existing north–south throughway, which follows the
Ussuri River north to Khabarovsk (the same route used by the
Trans-Siberian Railway). Despite handling every kind of traffic,
including transcontinental freight trucks, the Ussuri road is poorly
maintained and only as wide as a residential street; it was also considered vulnerable to Chinese attack. This new highway, though
safer, wider, and ruler-straight, was never finished and so it is
essentially a highway to nowhere—in the middle of nowhere.
The only people who benefit from it now are loggers, poachers,
and smugglers—pretty much the only people around who can
afford a vehicle. But sometimes tigers use this highway, too.

There is an unintended courtesy in the winter forest that occurs around pathways of any kind. It takes a lot of energy to break a trail through the snow, especially when it's crusty or deep, so whoever goes first, whether animal, human, or machine, is performing a valuable service for those following behind. Because energy—i.e., food—is at a premium in the winter, labor-saving gifts of this kind are rarely refused. As long as the footpath, logging road, frozen river—or highway—is going more or less in the desired direction, other forest creatures will use it, too, regardless of who made it. In this way, paths have a funneling, riverlike effect on the tributary creatures around them, and they can make for some strange encounters.

The last three miles of the journey were on a logging track so tortuous and convoluted that even a veteran Russian backcountry driver is moved to shout, in a torrent of fricatives and rolling Rs, "Paris–Dakar! Camel Trophy!" The road contoured east through the rolling woods, crossing creeks on bridges made of log piles stacked at right angles to the road. Two miles short of a privately owned logging camp, Gorborukov took an unmarked turn and headed north. After a few minutes, he pulled up at a clearing, on the far side of which stood a cabin.

The cabin belonged to Vladimir Markov, a resident of Sobolonye, and a man best known for keeping bees. The crude structure stood by itself on the high side of a gentle south-facing slope, surrounded by a thick forest of birch, pine, and alder. It was a lonely spot but a lovely one and, under different circumstances, Trush might have seen its appeal. Now there was no time; it was three o'clock in the afternoon and the sun was already in the southwest, level with the treetops. Any warmth generated during this brief, bright day was quickly dissipating.

The first sign of trouble was the crows. Carrion crows will follow a tiger the same way seagulls follow a fishing boat: by sticking with a proven winner, they conserve energy and shift the odds of getting fed from If to When. When Trush and his men climbed down from the Kung, they heard the crows' raucous kvetching concentrated just west of the entrance road. Trush noted the way their dark bodies swirled and flickered above the trees and, even if he hadn't been warned ahead of time, this would have told him all he needed to know: something big was dead, or dying, and it was being guarded.

Parked in front of Markov's cabin was a heavy truck belonging to Markov's good friend and beekeeping partner, Danila Zaitsev, a reserved and industrious man in his early forties. Zaitsev was a skilled mechanic and his truck, another cast-off from the military, was one of the few vehicles still functioning in Sobolonye. With Zaitsev were Sasha Dvornik and Andrei Onofreychuk, both family men in their early thirties who often hunted and fished with Markov. It was evident from their haggard appearance that they had barely slept the night before.

Judging from the density of tracks, there had clearly been a lot of activity around the cabin. Several different species were represented and their trails overlaid each other so that, at first, it was hard to sort them out. Trush approached this tangled skein of information like a detective: somewhere in here was a beginning and an end, and somewhere, too, was a motive—perhaps several. Downhill from the cabin, closer to the entrance road, two tracks in particular caught his attention. One set traveled northward up the entrance road at a walking pace; the other traveled south from the cabin. They approached each other directly, as if the meeting had been intentional—like an appointment of some kind. The southbound tracks were noteworthy, not just because they were made by a tiger, but because there were large gaps—ten feet or more—between each set of impressions. At the point where they met, the northbound tracks disappeared, as if the person who made them had simply ceased to exist. Here the large paw prints veered off to the west, crossing the entrance road at right angles. Their regular spacing indicated a walking pace; they led into the forest, directly toward the crows.

Trush had a video camera with him and its unblinking eye recorded the scene in excruciating detail. Only in retrospect does it strike one how steady Trush's hand and voice are as he films the site, narrating as he goes: the rough cabin and the scrubby clearing in which it stands; the path of the attack and the point of impact, and then the long trail of horrific evidence. The camera doesn't waver as it pans across the pink and trampled snow, taking in the hind foot of a dog, a single glove, and then a bloodstained jacket cuff before halting at a patch of bare ground about a hundred yards into the forest. At this point the audio picks up a sudden, retching gasp. It is as if he has entered Grendel's den.

The temperature is thirty below zero and yet, here, the snow has been completely melted away. In the middle of this dark circle, presented like some kind of sacrificial offering, is a hand without an arm and a head without a face. Nearby is a long bone, a femur probably, that has been gnawed to a bloodless white. Beyond this, the trail continues deeper into the woods. Trush follows it, squinting through his camera while his squad and Markov's friends trail closely behind. The only sounds are the icy creak of Trush's boots and the distant barking of his dog. Seven men have been stunned to silence. Not a sob; not a curse.

Trush's hunting dog, a little Laika, is further down the trail, growing increasingly shrill and agitated. Her nose is tingling with blood scent and tiger musk, and she alone feels free to express her deepest fear: the tiger is there, somewhere up ahead. Trush's men have their rifles off their shoulders, and they cover him as he films. They arrive at another melted spot; this time, a large oval. Here, amid the twigs and leaf litter, is all that remains of Vladimir Ilyich Markov. It looks at first like a heap of laundry until one sees the boots, luminous stubs of broken bone protruding from the tops, the tattered shirt with an arm still fitted to one of the sleeves.

Trush had never seen a fellow human so thoroughly and gruesomely annihilated and, even as he filmed, his mind fled to the edges of the scene, taking refuge in peripheral details. He was struck by the poverty of this man—that he would be wearing thin rubber boots in such bitter weather. He reflected on the cartridge belt—loaded but for three shells—and wondered where the gun had gone. Meanwhile, Trush's dog, Gitta, is racing back and forth, hackles raised and barking in alarm. The tiger is somewhere close by—invisible to the men, but to the dog it is palpably, almost unbearably, present. The men, too, can sense a potency around them—something larger than their own fear, and they glance about, unsure where to look. They are so overwhelmed by the wreckage before them that it is hard to distinguish imminent danger from the present horror.

Save for the movements of the dog and the men, the forest has gone absolutely still; even the crows have withdrawn, waiting for this latest disturbance to pass. And so, it seems, has the tiger. Then, there is a sound: a brief, rushing exhale—the kind one would use to extinguish a candle. But there is something different about the volume of air being moved, and the force behind it—something bigger and deeper: this is not a human sound. At the same moment, perhaps ten yards ahead, the tip of a low fir branch spontaneously sheds its load of snow. The flakes powder down to the forest floor; the men freeze in mid-breath and, once again, all is still.

Since well before the Kung's engine noise first penetrated the forest, a conversation of sorts has been unfolding in this lonesome hollow. It is not in a language like Russian or Chinese, but it is a language nonetheless, and it is older than the forest. The crows speak it; the dog speaks it; the tiger speaks it, and so do the men—some more fluently than others. That single blast of breath contained a message lethal in its eloquence. But what does one do with such information so far from one's home ground? Gitta tightens the psychic leash connecting her to her master. Markov's friends, already shaken to the core, pull in closer, too. The tiger's latest communication serves not only to undo these men still further, but to deepen the invisible chasm between them—poachers to a man—and the armed officials on whom their liberty and safety now depend. Markov's friends are known to Trush because he has busted them before—for possessing illegal firearms and hunting without a license. Of the three of them, only Zaitsev's gun is legal, but it is too light to stop a tiger. As for the others, their weapons are now hidden in the forest, leaving them more helpless than Trush's dog.

Trush is unarmed, too. There had been some back-and-forth at the entrance road about who was going to follow that grisly trail, and comments were made implying that Trush and his men didn't have what it took. Fear is not a sin in the taiga, but cowardice is, and Trush returned the challenge with a crisp invitation: *"Poshli"*—"Let's go." One of Markov's friends—Sasha Dvornik, as Trush recalled—then suggested that Trush's team could handle it themselves. Besides, he said, they had no weapons. Trush called his bluff by urging him to fetch his unregistered gun from hiding. "This is no time to be confiscating guns," he said. "What's important now is to protect ourselves." Still, Dvornik hesitated, and this is when Trush offered him his rifle. It was a bold gesture on several levels: not only did it imply an expectation of trust and cooperation, but Trush's semiautomatic was a far better weapon than Dvornik's battered smoothbore. It also short-circuited the argument: now, there was no excuse, and no way that Dvornik—with six men watching—could honorably refuse. It was this same mix of shame, fear, and loyalty that compelled Zaitsev and Onofrecuk to go along, too. Besides, there was safety in numbers.

But it had been a long time since Dvornik was in the army, and Trush's weapon felt strangely heavy in his hands; Trush, meanwhile, was feeling the absence of its reassuring weight, and that was strange, too. He still had his pistol, but it was holstered and, in any case, it would have been virtually useless against a tiger. His faith rested with his squad mates because he had put himself in an extremely vulnerable position: even though he was leading the way, he did so at an electronic remove—in this drama but not of it, exploring this dreadful surreality through the camera's narrow, cyclopean lens. Because Zaitsev and Dvornik couldn't be counted on, and Deputy Bush had only a pistol, the Tigers were Trush's only reliable proxies. Those with guns had them at the ready, but the forest was dense and visibility was poor. Were the tiger to attack, they could end up shooting one another. So they held their fire, eyes darting back and forth to that single, bare branch, wondering where the next sign would come from.

Behind the camera, Trush remained strangely calm. "We clearly see the tiger's tracks going away from the remains," he continued in his understated official drone, while Gitta barked incessantly, stiff-legged and staring. ". . . the dog clearly indicates that the tiger went this way."

Up ahead, the tiger's tracks showed plainly in the snow,

brought into sharp relief by the shadows now pooling within them. The animal was maneuvering northward to higher ground, the place every cat prefers to be. "It looks like the tiger's not too far," Trush intoned to future viewers, "around forty yards." The snow wasn't deep and, under those conditions, a tiger could cover forty yards in about four seconds. This may have been why Trush chose that moment to shut off his camera, reclaim his gun, and step back into real time. But once there, he was going to have to make a difficult decision.

In his professional capacity as senior inspector for Inspection Tiger, Trush acted as a medium between the Law of the Jungle and the Law of the State; one is instinctive and often spontaneous while the other is contrived and always cumbersome. The two are, by their very natures, incompatible. When he was in the field, Trush usually had no means of contacting his superiors, or anyone else for that matter; his walkie-talkies had limited range (when they worked at all) so he and his squad mates were profoundly on their own. Because of this, Trush's job required a lot of judgment calls, and he was going to have to make one now: the tiger is a "Red Book" species—protected in Russia—so permission to kill had to come from Moscow. Trush did not yet have this permission, but it was Saturday, Moscow might as well have been the moon, and they had an opportunity to end this now.

Trush decided to track it. This had not been part of the plan; he had been sent to investigate an attack, not to hunt a tiger. Furthermore, his team was short a man, dusk was coming on, and Markov's friends were a liability; they were still in shock and so, for that matter, was Trush. But at that moment, he was poised— equidistant between the tiger and the harrowing evidence of what it had done. The two would never be so close again. Signaling Lazurenko to follow, Trush set off up the trail, knowing that every step would take him deeper into the tiger's comfort zone.

2

"You're from Russia?"
"Yes, from Russia."
"I've never been there at all."

Anton Chekhov, From Siberia

IF RUSSIA IS WHAT WE THINK IT IS, THEN TIGERS SHOULD NOT BE POSSIBLE there. After all, how could a creature so closely associated with stealth and grace and *heat* survive in a country so heavy-handed, damaged, and cold? The nearest jungle is two thousand miles away. For these and other reasons, neither Russia the Idea nor Russia the Place are useful ways of describing the home of the Siberian tiger, which is, itself, a misnomer. This subspecies is known locally—and formally—as the Amur tiger, and it lives, in fact, beyond Siberia. Sparsely inhabited, seldom visited, and poorly understood, the "far side" of Russia is not so much a frontier as a margin for error. The humans who share space with the Amur tiger—who fear it, revere it, tolerate it, and sometimes hunt it—will tell you their tiger lives in the Far East, in the taiga,* and this is true enough, but still, no coherent picture emerges. A biologist might say that this animal occupies a geographical range bounded

---

* The mixed (broad leaf and conifer) forests of Siberia are generally referred to as taiga. While the forests of Primorye differ in some very significant ways, they go by this name as well.

by China, North Korea, and the Sea of Japan. This may be so, but a foreigner will be hard-pressed to understand what that means, even after consulting a map.

The Russians have had trouble making sense of it, too. When the railroad and telegraph engineer Dmitry Romanov arrived on Primorye's south coast aboard the steamship *Amerika* in the summer of 1859, he was astonished by what he saw: "The area around these harbors is covered with lush sub-tropical forests, woven by lianes," he enthused in a St. Petersburg newspaper,

> where oaks have a diameter of one sagene [over six feet]. Some other examples of gigantic vegetation are marvelous. We have seen them before in tropical America. What a wonderful future this place can have with prehistoric forests and the most splendid harbors in the world! . . . It is appropriate that the best port here is called Vladivostok ["Power in the East"], because it will be home to our navy in the Pacific, and the beginning of Russian influence over a vast ocean territory.

The Chinese knew this country as the *shuhai,* or "forest sea." It may have been marvelous to contemplate from the deck of a ship, but on the ground, it took a savage toll on humans and animals alike. When you weren't battling arctic cold, or worrying about tigers, there were insects on a scale that is hard to imagine. Sir Henry Evan Murchison James, a member of the Royal Geographical Society and no stranger to jungles or arthropods, was astounded: "There are several kinds," he wrote in 1887,

> one striped yellow and black, like a giant wasp; and the rapidity with which they can pierce a mule's tough hide is inconceivable. In a few moments, before one could go to its assistance, I have seen a wretched beast streaming with blood. . . . When we went to bed or when marching in the early morning, and at meals we enveloped ourselves with smoke. . . . If there be a time when life is not worth living, I should say it was summer in the forests of Manchuria.

More than one poor soul has been bound to a tree here and con-
signed to a hideous death from insect bites, and even Yuri Trush
has used this method to make stubborn poachers more compliant.

———

Once considered part of Outer Manchuria, Primorye, or Primorskii Krai, is Russia's southeasternmost territory; it is the man-
made container for most of the Amur tiger's current range, and
about two million people live there. Protruding conspicuously
from Russia's vast bulk, Primorye is embedded in China's eastern
flank like a claw or a fang, and it remains a sore spot to this day.
The territory is an embodiment of the tension between proximity
and possession: the capital, Vladivostok, which is home to more
than half a million people, is just a two-day train journey from
Beijing. The trip to Moscow, on the other hand, is a week-long,
5,800-mile epic on the Trans-Siberian. No other major city lies so
far from its national capital; even Australia is closer.

It is hard to express how far over the horizon this region lies in
relation to Russia's political, cultural, and economic centers, but a
nickname can offer insight to a place just as it can to a person.
Many Siberians refer to western Russia as the *materik*—the Main-
land, which is similar to the way Alaskans think of the Lower 48.
But most of Siberia is thousands of miles closer to the capital than
Russia's Far East. In terms of sheer remoteness—both geographic
and cultural—the Maritime Territory is more like Hawai'i. As a
result, visitors will find themselves standing out conspicuously in
a geographic vortex where the gravitational pulls of Europe and
North America are weak, and familiar landmarks are virtually
nonexistent. Primorye doesn't get many visitors and, out here on
Eurasia's ragged eastern rim, you are more likely to find kinship
in your foreignness with a North Korean "guest" worker than
with a wayward German tourist.

Vladivostok, which is the home base of Inspection Tiger, lies
further south than the French Riviera, but this is hard to reconcile
with the fact that the bays here stay frozen until April. Tigers used
to roam the wedge-shaped hills above the harbor, and one of these

is still called Tiger Hill; down below is a Tigrine Street. In hard winters, their namesakes still prowl the outskirts of the city, hunting for dogs; in 1997, one had to be shot after repeatedly charging cars by the airport. In this and other ways, Primorye represents a threshold between civilization and the frontier. This territory—and the Far East in general—occupies its own strange sphere, somewhere between the First World and the Third. That the trains are clean and run on time is a point of honor and pride, but when they get to the station there may be no platform and the retractable steps might be frozen shut, forcing you to simply heave your luggage into the darkness and jump out after it.

Because so much of life here is governed by a kind of whimsical rigidity—a combination of leftover Soviet bureaucracy and free market chaos—even simple interactions with officialdom can leave you feeling as if you have wandered into an insane asylum. To this day, the Russian Far East is a place where neither political correctness nor eco-speak have penetrated, and patriotism is vigorous and impassioned. Vladivostok is about as far as one can be from the Eastern Front and still be in Russia, but huge monuments to the heroic fallen command the squares, along with an intermittently eternal flame. To get an idea how large the Second World War's legacy of sacrifice and heroism still looms in the popular mind, one need only stand on Svetlanskaya, one of the two principal shopping streets framing the harbor where the Pacific Fleet is berthed. Here, on an early-twenty-first-century Sunday, more than sixty years after the Red Army took Berlin, two grandsons of that generation—pink-cheeked family men out for lunch with their wives and young children—will invoke the legacy of that time with a ferocity few Westerners could muster. After reasserting Russia's indispensable role in the defeat of the Nazis, and brushing aside the contributions of the Allies, one of these young men will go on to say, "If you stand with us, we will protect you with all our Russian soul. But if you are against us [a finger is jabbing now], we will *fight* you with all our Russian soul. We will fight you to the end!"

The speaker looks at his mate, and their eyes lock in solidarity;

then they laugh, embrace, and knock their heads together so hard you can hear the crack of bone on bone.

In Primorye, the seasons collide with equal intensity: winter can bring blizzards and paralyzing cold, and summer will retaliate with typhoons and monsoon rains; three quarters of the region's rainfall occurs during the summer. This tendency toward extremes allows for unlikely juxtapositions and may explain why there is no satisfactory name for the region's peculiar ecosystem—one that happens to coincide with the northern limit of the tiger's pan-hemispheric range. It could be argued that this region is not a region at all but a crossroads: many of the aboriginal technologies that are now considered quintessentially North American—tipis, totem poles, bows and arrows, birch bark canoes, dog sleds, and kayak-style paddles—all passed through here first.

Primorye is also the meeting place of four distinct bioregions. Like their far-flung human counterparts, plants and animals from the Siberian taiga, the steppes of Mongolia, the subtropics of Korea and Manchuria, and from the boreal forests of the far north have all converged here, pushing the limits of their respective growing zones between coastline, alpine, floodplain, and forest. As a result, attempts by botanists to classify the region have produced marble-mouthed results: "Manchurian and Sakhalin-Hokkaido Provinces of the Eastern Asiatic Region" is one; "Transbaikalian Province of the Circumboreal Region" is another.

Here is an alternative suggestion: the Boreal Jungle.

It sounds like an oxymoron, but it acknowledges the blended nature of this remote and slender threshold realm in which creatures of the subarctic have been overlapping with those of the subtropics since before the last Ice Age. There is strong evidence suggesting that this region was a refugium, one of several areas around the Pacific Rim that remained ice-free during the last glaciation, and this may help explain the presence of an ecosystem that exists nowhere else. Here, timber wolves and reindeer share terrain with spoonbills and poisonous snakes, and twenty-five-pound Eurasian vultures will compete for carrion with saber-beaked jungle crows. Birch, spruce, oak, and fir can grow in the same valley as wild kiwis, giant lotus, and sixty-foot lilacs, while pine trees bearing edible nuts may be hung with wild grapes and magnolia vines. These, in turn, feed and shelter herds of wild boar and families of musk deer whose four-inch fangs give them the appearance of evolutionary outtakes. Nowhere else can a wolverine, brown bear, or moose drink from the same river as a leopard, in a watershed that also hosts cork trees, bamboo, and solitary yews that predate the Orthodox Church. In the midst of this, Himalayan black bears build haphazard platforms in wild cherry trees that seem too fragile for the task, opium poppies nod in the sun, and ginseng keeps its secret in dappled shade.

This region, which feels so like an island, could almost be described as one because it is nearly separated from the rest of Asia by two major rivers—the Ussuri and the Amur—and Lake Khanka, the largest lake in the Far East. The Amur, for which the local tigers are named, is northeast Asia's mother river; the Chinese call it Heilongjiang: the Black Dragon. Rising from two different sources in Mongolia, it flows for nearly three thousand miles before terminating in the Tartar Strait opposite Sakhalin Island. It is the third longest river in Asia, and the longest undammed river in the world. An ecosystem unto itself, it nurtures scores of bird species and more than 130 kinds of fish. Here, sturgeon—some the size of alligators—work the river bottom along with pearl-bearing freshwater oysters, and taimen, an enormous relative of the salmon that was once hunted with harpoons from birch bark canoes.

Primorye's bizarre assemblage of flora and fauna leaves one with the impression that Noah's ark had only recently made landfall, and that, rather than dispersing to their proper places around the globe, many of its passengers had simply decided to stay, including some we never knew existed. Within this waterbound envelope live unclassifiable species like the raccoon dog, as well as a bizarre tropical canid called a dhole that hunts in packs, and has been reputed to attack humans and tigers, along with more traditional prey. Here, too, can be found red-legged ibis, paradise flycatchers, and parrotlike reed sutoras, along with five species of eagle, nine species of bat, and more than forty kinds of fern. In the spring, improbable moths and butterflies like the Artemis Emperor, the Exclusive Underwing, and the as-yet unstudied Pseudopsychic hatch out to spangle and iridesce by the roadsides. In the dead of winter, giant ladybugs with reverse color schemes cruise the walls of village kitchens like animated wallpaper. This Boreal Jungle (for lack of a better term) is unique on earth, and it nurtures the greatest biodiversity of any place in Russia, the largest country in the world. It is over this surreal menagerie that the Amur tiger reigns supreme.

——

Of the six surviving subspecies of tiger, the Amur is the only one habituated to arctic conditions. In addition to having a larger skull than other subspecies, it carries more fat and a heavier coat, and these give it a rugged, primitive burliness that is missing from its sleeker tropical cousins. The thickly maned head can be as broad as a man's chest and shoulders, and winter paw prints are described using hats and pot lids for comparison. As the encyclopedic reference *Mammals of the Soviet Union* puts it, "The general appearance of the tiger is that of a huge physical force and quiet confidence, combined with a rather heavy grace." But one could just as easily say: this is what you get when you pair the agility and appetites of a cat with the mass of an industrial refrigerator.

To properly appreciate such an animal, it is most instructive to start at the beginning: picture the grotesquely muscled head of a pit bull and then imagine how it might look if the pit bull weighed a quarter of a ton. Add to this fangs the length of a finger backed up by rows of slicing teeth capable of cutting through the heaviest bone. Consider then the claws: a hybrid of meat hook and stiletto that can attain four inches along the outer curve, a length comparable to the talons on a velociraptor. Now, imagine the vehicle for all of this: nine feet or more from nose to tail, and three and a half feet high at the shoulder. Finally, emblazon this beast with a primordial calligraphy: black brushstrokes on a field of russet and cream, and wonder at our strange fortune to coexist with such a creature. (The tiger is, literally, tattooed: if you were to shave one bald, its stripes would still be visible, integral to its skin.) Able to swim for miles and kill an animal many times its size, the tiger also possesses the brute strength to drag an awkward, thousand-pound carcass through the forest for fifty or a hundred yards before consuming it.

A tiger may greet a mate or a cub with a gentle nuzzle, but it meets its prey paws-first. The tiger's forepaws differ from the hind ones in that they are larger with five claws arranged in an almost handlike spread. By contrast, the hind paws have only four claws. In addition to walking, running, and climbing, the forepaws can serve as twin maces, enabling a tiger to club its prey to death. And yet, they are also gentle and dextrous enough to catch a fly in the fold of a pad and release it, unharmed. Tigers tend to attack from the rear or the side, giving them the advantage of surprise, but they fight head-on, often rearing up on their hind legs. In this stance, with ears laid flat against a bull-necked head, a fighting tiger bears a startling resemblance to a fighting man, specifically a heavyweight boxer. Surprisingly delicate hind legs give way to slender hips and waist, which then swell dramatically into a deep chest hung with massively proportioned "arms" that flex much as ours do as they jab and parry.

Unlike wolf or bear claws, which are designed primarily for traction and digging, a cat's claw is needle-sharp at the end, and bladed along a portion of its inside length. With the exception of a snake's fang, it is about as close to a surgical tool as one can find in nature. When extended, the claws of the forepaw become slashing blades with the result that the victim is not so much sliced as flayed. But this is almost incidental to the forepaws' most important purpose, which is to plant a pair of virtually unshakable anchors in an animal's flesh. Once the forepaws are fully engaged, a tiger can literally ride its prey into the ground.

In the final nanoseconds of an airborne attack, a tiger's tail will become rigid, balancing and stabilizing the hindquarters almost like the tail fin on an airplane. Meanwhile, the tiger's forepaws, combined with its fangs, form a huge three-point grappling device, as if, for a moment, the claws had become extensions of the jaws. Working together in this way, they can cover an area of a square yard or more to manifest a gathering and gripping capability comparable to the mouth of a much larger creature—something more on the order of a saltwater crocodile or an allosaurus. The interplay of paws and jaws shifts according to the task at hand, and one way to envision their fluid and complementary roles is as a basketball team: the jaws are the center—the big star around which the action revolves; the forepaws are, of course, the forwards, driving and rebounding in the midst of the fray, while the smaller hind paws, which set up and then assist on the periphery of the attack, are the guards. The hind legs provide the power for the attack leap, or drive, but, once launched, they become levers and stabilizers, supporting the larger players. Once the prey is down, these same assault weapons can become the most delicate scalpels and clamps, able to disembowel an animal, organ by organ.

For all these reasons, there is no creature in the taiga that is off limits to the tiger; it alone can mete out death at will. Amur tigers have been known to eat everything from salmon and ducks to adult brown bears. There are few wolves in Primorye, not because the environment doesn't suit them, but because the tigers eat them, too. The Amur tiger, it could be said, takes a Stalinist approach to competition. It is also an extraordinarily versatile predator, able to survive in temperatures ranging from fifty below zero Fahrenheit to one hundred above, and to turn virtually any environment to its advantage. Though typically a forest dweller, Amur tigers may hunt on the beaches as well, using sea fog as a cover for stalking game, and driving animals into heavy surf before subduing them. One young male was observed subsisting exclusively on harbor seals, going so far as to stack their carcasses like logs for future use.

Unlike most cats, tigers are skilled, even avid, swimmers, and there are hunters and fishermen on the Bikin River who have had tigers crawl into their boats. Many encounters, including those observed by scientists and captured on video, seem lifted from myth or fiction. The occurrence, and subsequent recounting, of such incidents over dozens of millennia has embedded the tiger in our consciousness. The tiger has been a fellow traveler on our evolutionary journey and, in this sense, it is our peer. In Asia, there is

no recess of human memory in which there has not—somewhere—lurked a tiger. As a result, this animal looms over the collective imagination of native and newcomer alike.

———

Within every major ecosystem nature has produced, she has
evolved a singularly formidable predator to rule over it. In Primorye, the Amur tiger is the latest, most exquisitely lethal manifestation of this creative impulse. The indigenous peoples of
Primorye—the Udeghe, Nanai, and Orochi—have always understood and acknowledged the tiger's supremacy, and some clans
claimed the tiger as a direct ancestor as much to placate it as to
share its power. There appears to be no ritual of tiger killing here
(as there is for bears), but there are many stories of tigers taking
human wives—and husbands—and of tigers killing humans who
dared to challenge them. The tiger, as indigenous peoples know it,
is a consummate hunter and the undisputed lord of the taiga, possessing the ability to change shape or disappear at will. Shrines
were erected in the tiger's honor, and some of these remain;
hunters would lay their weapons down and beg forgiveness if they
crossed its path. The native population is now small and dilute,
having suffered from the same imported diseases and depreda-
tions that wreaked havoc on their North American counterparts.
Nonetheless, many veteran Russian hunters learned much of
what they know about Primorye's taiga from their Udeghe and
Nanai counterparts, just as the famous Russian explorer and
author Vladimir Arseniev did from Dersu Uzala, a Nanai hunter
and trapper who enjoys a potent legacy here to this day.

Vladimir Arseniev was the son of an illegitimate former serf
who did for Primorye what it took the combined efforts of Lewis
and Clark and James Fenimore Cooper to do for the American
West. Arseniev, who was born in St. Petersburg in 1872, volunteered for the czar's army at eighteen and became a career military officer, bandit fighter, and ethnographer. Between 1900,
when he was reassigned from Poland to the Far East, and his death
in 1930, he led nine major expeditions during which he explored
and mapped much of Primorye, in addition to the Commander

Islands and the Kamchatka Peninsula. A subtext of these missions was to assess these regions' vulnerability to Japanese attack. Throughout his life and travels, Arseniev took a keen interest in indigenous culture, and he kept careful records of the flora, fauna, and peoples he came across. In the process, he conceived a literary style that managed to blend hard science and high adventure with subtle characterization and disarming honesty.*

During his journeys, which lasted for months at a time, Arseniev encountered wild animals, Chinese bandits, typhoons, blizzards, hunger, and swarms of biting insects. He faced them all with a small retinue of Cossack soldiers and Siberian riflemen, guided by several different local hunters. It was the guides who kept him and his men alive and there was one in particular he grew to love—not as a father exactly, but as a wise and gentle protector. "Now I felt afraid of nothing," wrote Arseniev in his perennial classic, *Dersu the Trapper,* "neither tigers nor brigands, nor deep snow or floods. Dersu was with me."

Dersu Uzala was a solitary and elderly Nanai hunter whose family had been killed by smallpox and whose world was disintegrating before his steadily weakening eyes. Both Dersu and Arseniev understood that the primeval jungle through which they sojourned was in a state of rapid and irrevocable transformation. The Ussuri leg of the Trans-Siberian Railway had just gone

---

* Arseniev's account of his adventures with Dersu Uzala reflects a tendency among many Russian writers to use facts not as inflexible units of information, but as malleable elements that may be arranged, elaborated on, or added to as the author sees fit. Evidence of this can be found throughout the country's nonfiction and journalism. On a practical level, fact checking and the documentation of sources is pursued much less rigorously in Russia than in many Western countries. But there is a more serious problem and that is that the notions of "truth" and "fact" have been so aggressively stifled in Russia since czarist times that its effects have impacted the collective psyche of the country, including writers, who, if they told the truth, did so at considerable risk. As a result, many "factual" Russian narratives should probably be approached as memoirs: subjective interpretations of events that may not have occurred exactly as described. It is by no means unique to Russia, but the most egregious examples of this freewheeling approach to reportage are to be found in the State's representation of itself, a tendency that transcends regime and political philosophy.

through and with it came immigrants and industry on a scale that had never been seen in the region before. When Dersu's aim began to waver, Arseniev took him home to live with his wife and daughter in Khabarovsk, the capital of the neighboring territory. But life in a box did not suit Dersu: "The prohibition on shooting within the town was an unpleasant surprise for him," Arseniev wrote. Later, he was arrested for felling a tree in a local park. "He realized that in a town a man cannot live as he wishes, but as other people wish. Strangers surrounded him on every side and hampered him at every step." It wasn't long before Dersu returned to the forest, armed only with his increasingly unreliable rifle. Arseniev could not stop him, but he had a presentiment of dread.

Two weeks later, word got back to Arseniev that Dersu had been murdered in the snow while he slept, his pockets emptied, and his gun stolen. Arseniev traveled to the site and oversaw his burial there in the forest. A pair of tall Korean pines stood nearby, and Arseniev took note of these for future reference, but when he returned some years later to visit the grave of his old friend, it was as if they had never been. "My . . . landmarks had vanished. New roads had been made. There were quarry faces, dumps, embankments. . . . All around bore the signs of another life."

"Arseniev," wrote one biographer, "had the good sense not to live to be old." By the time he died at age fifty-seven, there was a warrant out for his arrest and the remote imperial colony he had come to know more intimately than any man before or since had become a police state. Stalin had come to power, and the shadow he cast reached all the way to the Pacific; Arseniev was accused of spying for the Japanese, and his personal archives were ransacked. He died before he could be arrested, due to complications from a cold he caught on his final expedition. His widow, however, was punished in his stead: she was arrested and interrogated twice; in 1937, at the height of the purges that came to be known as the Great Terror, she was executed, also on suspicion of aiding the Japanese. According to the historian Amir Khisamutdinov, the total elapsed time from the beginning of her trial to her execution was sixteen minutes. The Arsenievs' daughter, found guilty by association, spent the next fifteen years in prison camps, an ordeal from which she never fully recovered.

Somehow, the legacy of the trapper Dersu survived this scourge and the others that followed: there exists at least one photo of him and Arseniev together, and somewhere may survive a wax recording Arseniev made of Dersu's voice. There is also the book and, more recently, a film: Akira Kurosawa's *Dersu Uzala* (1975), which has itself become a classic. Between the Bikin River and a peak called Tiger Mountain is a village that bears his name. The tiger was the most potent being in Dersu's world, an object of fear and reverence; as a young man, he had been mauled by one. He called the tiger *amba,* a word that lives in the language to this day. It was believed in Dersu's time that if you killed a tiger without just cause, you in turn would be killed. Likewise, if a tiger were to kill and eat a human, it would be hunted by its own kind. Both acts were considered taboo and, once these invisible boundaries had been crossed, it was all but impossible to cross back. There was an understanding in the forest then—an order. Judging from the following events, this order still exists in some places and it is not forgiving.

But we are what we are, and we might remember
Not to hate any person, for all are vicious

ROBINSON JEFFERS,
"Original Sin"

YURI TRUSH AND VLADIMIR MARKOV WERE BORN WITHIN A YEAR OF
each other, both in European Russia, but they were drawn into
this exotic sylvan netherworld by very different paths. That they
would represent opposing points on the spectrum of possibility
was as much a reflection of personality as it was an adaptation to
opportunity. Trush, like Markov, was a relative latecomer to the
Far East. He was born in 1950, and raised in a village outside the
city of Nizhny Novgorod, about halfway between Moscow and
the Ural Mountains. His maternal grandfather was a decorated
major general who died in battle at the outset of the Second World
War. His father, Anatoly, a senior lieutenant, survived the siege of
Leningrad, which lasted two and a half years. Father and son
hunted in the pine forests surrounding his village, and Yuri saw
some things there that left deep impressions.

In the early 1960s, when Trush was about fourteen, he remembers going to the local tavern with his father. There were other
hunters there, friends of his father, and they were discussing boar
hunting. One man—half drunk—spoke loudly of the pregnant
sow he'd shot out of season. It is a generally accepted rule among
hunters that you don't shoot pregnant animals, and a silence fell
over the room. Then the voices rose again and overwhelmed the
bragging man, who was taken outside and beaten severely.

In his early twenties, Trush had another formative experience, this time on the steppes of western Kazakhstan. His job at a gold mine there had ended, and he was briefly unemployed. An able hunter, Trush turned to his gun for sustenance. He answered a call to join in a market hunt for saiga, a bizarre-looking antelope with translucent corkscrew horns and a trunklike snout that looks like a throwback to the Pleistocene. In the 1970s, saiga roamed the steppes of Central Asia in herds of thousands. The plan was to kill the animals en masse and sell the meat and skin to the European market and the horns to China where they are believed by many to boost male potency. This was a government-sanctioned operation, and it took place at night. About a dozen armed men in trucks headed out shortly after dusk; they had powerful lights with them, and when a herd was located they turned them on. The animals froze in their tracks, mesmerized, and the men opened fire at uncountable pairs of glowing eyes. Dozens of antelope were killed on the spot, but many more escaped, mortally wounded. "We would go back out in daylight to collect the injured ones, but we couldn't get them all," Trush recalled. "You weren't able to see it at night, but it was obvious during the day how much the animals suffered. It was a sea of blood." He stuck with it for a few weeks, and then quit in disgust. Animals, he feels, should have a sporting chance; the field should be level between hunter and prey. "I can still see the blood, the heat and their suffering," he said. "That's why I didn't last long there: it was too barbaric. And that's why I'm so ruthless with the hunters now who hunt at night with the help of jack lights. I don't consider that hunting; I think it is a massacre."

Trush's affinity for the land and its creatures stuck with him throughout the years he spent underground maintaining mine shaft elevators in Kazakhstan. During his off time he volunteered as a fishing inspector and this was where he discovered his true calling. "There would be situations with these poachers," he explained. "Sometimes fights would ensue; shots would be fired. Escape and chase were possible. I like those things; I like being in confrontational situations."

But they didn't pay the bills, so when Russia invaded

Afghanistan, Trush volunteered to go. When it began at the end of 1979, the Afghan War was seen by many Russian men as an opportunity not only to serve the cause of socialism, but to grasp the coattails of their fathers' glory in the Great Patriotic War (World War II). Though he already held the rank of lieutenant, Trush was refused because of his age. Instead, he spent fifteen more years in the mines where he earned a reputation for diligence and integrity that caught the attention of his bosses. In spite of his eligibility, Trush never joined the Communist Party; he had no illusions about the corruption rampant within it.

In 1994, while working as a foreman at a coal mine in Primorye, Trush was approached by an acquaintance who worked in environmental protection. A new agency was being formed, and he thought that Trush, with his athleticism, pugnacity, and interest in hunting, might be a good candidate. Trush was intrigued and, in March of that year, he found himself in Vladivostok, standing before a short, barrel-chested man with a predilection for pipes and military finery; the man's name was Vladimir Ivanovich Schetinin, and he was the deputy chairman of Primorye's Ministry of Environmental Protection. Schetinin was in the process of creating something unprecedented in the history of Russian wildlife conservation.

———

Tiger poaching is the most visible symptom of an environmental problem the size of the continental United States: Siberia's forests represent an arboreal subcontinent covering 2.3 million square miles; altogether, they account for a quarter of the world's total wood inventory and more than half of its coniferous forests. They are also one of the planet's biggest carbon sinks, helping to mitigate one of the chief causes of climate change. While tigers were being stolen from the forests, the forests were also being stolen from the tigers, and from the country. The combination of a desperate need for hard currency, lax forestry regulations, and vast markets that lay only a border crossing away set loose a monster in the woods, which is wreaking havoc to this day. In the Far East, legal and black market logging (along with every shade in between) continues to jeopardize the habitat of tigers, humans, and the game that supports them both.

The most valuable timber in the Far East grows in Primorye, and a person can be murdered here for showing too much interest in the means by which southbound railcars and freighters are loaded with the perfectly symmetrical cylinders of aspen, oak, larch, and poplar that the Asian market demands. Much of what China makes from this Russian wood finds its way into American big box stores. The reason chain store prices—e.g., $20 for a solid oak toilet seat—seem too good to be true is because they are. Stolen hubcaps are cheap for the same reason. In the Far East, paying protection money to the mafia and bribes to customs officials is cheaper than legitimate timber licenses and export duties. On a late night drive through the snowbound woods of the Bikin valley, it is not unusual to meet the black-market night shift—a Toyota van loaded with fallers and their saws, followed by a flatbed crane truck—heading in to work.

Because Russia's forests are so big and so vulnerable, some American scientists became concerned in the early 1990s when they realized that perestroika had opened the door to a run on Russia's natural resources. A handful of journalists reported on this and, when they looked more closely, they noticed the tigers, which came as a surprise to many Westerners, who had no clear idea where "Siberian" tigers actually lived, or even what color they were. At the same time, Vladimir Schetinin and other local biologists and hunting managers realized that, in addition to other forest crimes, the number of tigers being killed and smuggled out of Russia was accelerating at a frightening rate. Federal and local governments were in turmoil at the time and offered little support; in some cases, they actively contributed to the problem. Meanwhile, wardens charged with forest protection were surviving on miserable salaries, and many were turning to poaching themselves. According to Schetinin, the tide didn't really start to turn until the summer of 1993, when an American freelance writer named Suzanne Possehl published a detailed article in the

"Environment" section of *The New York Times*. "Her article was a very important trigger," said Schetinin. "I will be grateful to her until the end of my days."

This, and other prominent articles published around the same time, focused the attention of international conservation groups on Primorye, and had a galvanizing effect. It was at this point that the idea of highly trained teams dedicated to intercepting poachers and smugglers, and working with local people to minimize human-tiger conflicts, began to take shape and attract crucial funding from abroad. While Schetinin deserves much of the credit on the Russian side, the person who masterminded the structure and methodology behind Inspection Tiger was an American named Steve Galster. Galster is a fearless and legendary American criminal investigator who, even in person, appears larger than life: he is strikingly handsome and stands about six-feet-four. For the past twenty-five years, he has been analyzing, exposing, and disrupting the traffic in humans, arms, and wildlife across Asia, and he has designed a number of wildlife protection programs that are now well established around the continent. In 1993, before coming to Russia, Galster led a successful investigation into China's largest rhinoceros horn smuggling syndicate. In 1994, he founded the Global Survival Network, which evolved into WildAid and, later, Wildlife Alliance, which is currently focused on illegal wildlife interdiction programs in Southeast Asia.

What Galster brought to Russia was a formidable list of contacts, compelling presentation skills, and a clear understanding of the synergistic relationship between law enforcement training, weaponry, rapid deployment, and video documentation. Galster called this new agency Operation Amba, and Schetinin was cast as "Commander Amba," but Inspection Tiger was the name that stuck in Russia. Galster and Schetinin were an effective, if unlikely, pair; by the start of 1994, they had negotiated full inspector status for their teams, and attracted funding for trucks, cameras, radios, and uniforms from the U.K.'s Tiger Trust and the World Wildlife Fund. More followed and, by 1997, half a dozen fully equipped inspection teams were working across Primorye.

By sheer coincidence, another Russian-American tiger initiative was launched at almost exactly the same time: in 1989, before anyone envisioned a poaching crisis in the Russian Far East, a summit meeting of Russian and American big cat biologists took place around a campfire in Idaho. The Americans were doing cutting-edge research on mountain lions using radio collars to track their movements, and one of the Russians suggested they collaborate on a similar study of Amur tigers. In January 1990, two researchers from the Idaho-based Hornocker Wildlife Institute paid their first visit to the Sikhote-Alin Zapovednik, a 1,500-square-mile biosphere reserve on the Pacific slope of the Sikhote-Alin mountain range.

The Americans were deeply moved by what they saw and, two years later, in February 1992, at virtually the same moment that Amur tigers began dying in numbers not seen since the early twentieth century, the Wildlife Conservation Society's Siberian Tiger Project was launched. Dale Miquelle, a former moose researcher who had just come off a one-year tiger project in Nepal, was there at the outset and he has never left. In 1995, he was joined by John Goodrich and, together with their Russian colleagues, they have been tracking, trapping, and radio-collaring tigers in the Sikhote-Alin Zapovednik ever since. As a result, a much more complete picture of the behavior, habits, and long-term needs of the Amur tiger has emerged; chief among the latter is better protection: over the years, a number of the project's collared tigers have been killed by poachers, in spite of the fact that they reside in a protected area. The Sikhote-Alin Zapovednik is considered one of the Amur tiger's key breeding grounds and, because of this, one of the six Inspection Tiger teams was based there.

———

Vladimir Schetinin assigned Trush to lead the Bikin unit, whose territory encompassed the northwest corner of Primorye, including the confluence of the Bikin and Ussuri rivers. It was a good fit because Trush had already lived and hunted in the area for five years. He and his wife, Lyubov (Love), still make their home in Luchegorsk, a mining town of twenty thousand, and a "four-minute" stop on the Trans-Siberian Railway. The town's location seems counterintuitive—the train station is twenty minutes away, down a long dirt road—but this is typical. Most of Siberia and the Far East were settled by Central Committee: a map would be spread out in Moscow, or maybe Irkutsk; a location would be chosen, usually with a particular industry in mind, and a village, town, or city would be thrown up—in many cases by forced labor, or soldiers (which, in Russia, amounts to almost the same thing). Construction was generally hasty, with little thought for the long term, and the harsh utility of these settlements suggests a thinly veiled gulag. Main roads in and out are punctuated by checkpoints manned by armed guards. It is only when you get past the steel bulkheads that pass for apartment doors here that you are allowed to return to a world of color, warmth, and human scale.

One visiting scholar described the Soviet urban anti-aesthetic as "Terminal Modernism," and Yuri Trush's forty-year-old home-town, perched as it is on the rim of a vast open-pit coal mine, is a classic example. The town proper is a battered collection of urine-stained apartment blocks placed at irregular intervals along pot-holed, gravel-strewn streets. In some cases, these slab-sided, wire-draped five-story buildings are arranged around grassy commons littered with bits and pieces of playground equipment so badly damaged that they look as if they had weathered some kind of natural catastrophe. There are strangely few children and fewer dogs, but many cats in a state of what seems to be perma-nent heat. Trush's building is a short walk from the town square, which is overseen by the once obligatory statue of Lenin. This par-ticular Lenin—a two-tone plaster bust—faces the town's digital thermometer, which spends months in negative territory while the father of Russian communism looks on from beneath a lumi-nous skullcap of snow. From his vantage he can catch a glimpse of a rickety but gaily colored Ferris wheel that stands, motionless now, several blocks away. Over his left shoulder is the power plant.

Luchegorsk means "Light City"; it is home to the region's biggest coal-fired power-generating station, and its belching stacks are visible from fifty miles away. About ten hours up the Trans-Siberian from Vladivostok and four hours down from

Khabarovsk, Luchegorsk is a place where no one stops unless they have to, but this is true of most communities in the Far East. There are far bigger towns in Primorye where the first inquiry made of a stranger can easily be "So, what brings you to this asshole of the world?" Yuri Trush, however, is a bright spot on the landscape; he is well known around town and has a vigorous handshake, hug, or slap on the back for many of the people he encounters. But he had a different greeting for Vladimir Markov.

Trush had visited Markov's cabin once before he was killed. A year and a half earlier, in the summer of 1996, Trush and Alexander Gorborukov had been on a routine patrol when they found a dead badger cooling in a metal pot in a creek that flowed nearby. Markov was at home and Trush confronted him. Visibly nervous, he gave a lame story about how the badger had gotten into the pot. Killed by dogs, he'd said. Trush looked closely at Markov, then drew his knife and sliced open one of the badger's wounds; after probing for a moment with his fingers, he withdrew a shotgun pellet. Markov had no choice but to own up. Because he had neither a hunting permit nor a gun license, Trush was in a position to put him out of business then and there. Instead, he gave Markov a choice: give up his weapon, or get charged on multiple counts. Markov balked at this until Gorborukov gestured toward his hunting knife, which, at the time, required an additional license. "We can write you up for the knife, too," Trush said. "Or you can give us your gun and we'll leave it at that."

Markov told Trush he'd be back in a few minutes and disappeared into the forest. It is because of situations like this that poachers rarely leave evidence of their activities around their cabins. Illegal fish spears, which look exactly like the tridents used by Nanai and Udeghe fishermen a century ago, are broken down, the shafts stored in one spot and the iron tips somewhere else. Nets and traps may be buried or stashed in a hollow tree. Guns are trickier because they are so sensitive to climate. They are rarely kept indoors because sudden temperature changes cause the steel hardware to condense and rust. Typically, they are stored in a paper or canvas bag, which allows the weapon to breathe, and then hidden in some dry location outside. It was to just such a hiding place that Markov had gone. Trush, trained to fix events as firmly as possible in time and space, checked his watch.

Trush and Gorborukov had been through this before, and, with the clock running, they occupied their time by searching the premises. Technically speaking, the nearly windowless wooden box Markov occupied wasn't a cabin at all but a portable caravan— a sort of no-frills Gypsy wagon that is commonly found on remote worksites around Russia and its former satellites. This one had been taken off its wheels, and a rough, open shed had been built onto the east side. Both caravan and shed were covered with sheets of corrugated asbestos. No formal inventory was taken, but the shed was filled with a random assortment of things, most of which were related to beekeeping: metal tubs and tanks; beehive parts; a large, manually operated spinner for separating the honey from the comb; and a small sledge for hauling water, wood, and supplies.

Inside the caravan, on the rude table jammed between plank beds and a barrel stove, was a kerosene lamp and a jar filled with the saved butt ends of cigarettes, some of which were rolled from newspaper. Beyond this, Trush didn't find much beyond the typical signs of a man living very close to the bone. There was, however, one detail that struck Trush as somewhat out of character for the average poacher; it was the way Markov handled a cigarette: "He smoked," said Trush, "very suave and stylish—very chic." It was an odd conceit given the reality of his day-to-day existence, but it was in keeping with his nickname, which was Markiz—the Russian equivalent of "Duke." According to friends, Markov also fancied himself something of a gourmet, and several of them remarked on his ability to liven up the most basic meals with wild herbs and mushrooms. Without these, there wasn't much to choose from: in Markov's world, rice, tea, potatoes, and meat were the key ingredients for basic survival, though vodka, sugar, tobacco, and pine nuts would have been high on the list as well.

Along with more easily identifiable equipment, a typical tayozhnik's (forest dweller's) cabin will have a couple of steel trays, roughly the size of large baking pans, hanging under the eaves. Dotted with crude perforations like a giant cheese grater, these

trays are used for stripping pinecones. In addition to being prime
building material, the Korean pine produces nuts, usually in cycles
of three or four years. These nuts, which grow inside the cones,
look like oversized corn kernels in a durable brown shell. Once on
the ground, they can remain viable—and edible—for years. They
are a cruder, earthier cousin to European and North American
pine nuts: not as sweet and with a bit more turpentine. Nonetheless, a taste for them is easy to acquire, and they can be as addictive
as sunflower seeds. More than a century ago, Far Eastern settlers
called them "Siberian conversation" due to the central role they
played in frontier social gatherings where few other delicacies (or
pastimes) existed. They have also been called "the bread of the
forest" because they can be ground into flour; oil can be extracted
from them as well. Pine nuts are a staple for bear, deer, elk, and
boar, not to mention humans and countless smaller creatures.
They have even been found in the scat of tigers.

If there were such a thing as decadal time-lapse photography,
one would be able to observe a series of incongruous processions
trailing across the high country of Primorye: Korean pine forests
following the lay of the land; deer, boar, and bear following the
pinecones (which tend to roll downhill); the rootings of these
creatures, in turn, advancing the cause of germinating pine seeds.
Leopards, tigers, and wolves follow the deer and boar while crows
and vultures follow them. Humans and rodents bring up the rear.
All of these creatures play a role in disseminating the seeds still
further, thus helping to define and push the boundaries—not just
of the Korean pine's range, but that of each participating species.
It is not overstating the case to say that Korean pine nuts, as small
and innocuous as they are, represent the hub around which the
wheel of life here revolves. Whoever isn't eating the nuts themselves is eating the creatures who do. And yet, so well disguised are
they that a visitor could walk the length and breadth of Primorye
and never notice them. After all, who eats pinecones? This is both
wonderful and frightening to consider: that, in the absence of
something so small and so humble, an entire ecosystem—from
tigers to mice—could collapse.

Markov had become part of this age-old cycle of consumption

and dispersal; he was both its agent and dependent, accomplice and beneficiary. But on that humid August afternoon, he had other things on his mind. Trush and Gorborukov were watching for him and he returned nineteen minutes later, bearing a sawed-off shotgun. The gun was in poor condition and Markov had cut it down, not to make it more lethal, but simply to keep it functioning as the muzzle had been damaged. Whether this was his only firearm, Trush couldn't be certain, but Markov had fulfilled his obligation and Trush was satisfied. He held up his end of the deal and kept his citation book in his pocket. After telling Markov to stay out of trouble, he and Gorborukov continued on their way, but no one present that day had any illusions that this would be their last encounter. This was an age-old game they were engaged in, this hunting of hunters. Robin Hood started out as a poacher, too, and the current situation in Primorye bears striking similarities to that found in the forests of Western Europe five hundred years ago.

The combination of Russia's current hunting regulations and gun licensing policy has effectively re-created the medieval laws that forbade peasants to own weapons or to hunt. Then, as now, the complementary forces of logging and hunting had seriously impacted European forests and the game they supported. As a result, most intact woodlands doubled as game reserves and were off limits to everyone with the exception of noble hunting parties. An analogous situation has developed in parts of post-perestroika Russia where legal hunting has become a luxury accessible only to the rich. In a sincere effort to protect existing game populations, the number of hunting licenses has been drastically reduced in Primorye with one result being that the few remaining permits go, inevitably, to the wealthy and well connected. Unfortunately, the wealthy and well connected often approach the forest and its creatures with the same sense of entitlement their medieval counterparts did, only without the discipline, skill, or ceremony. There is a sense among many of Russia's nouveau riche that they are above the law, and many of them are: what has emerged since the collapse of the Soviet Union is a kind of ersatz aristocracy, one that enjoys its noblesse *sans* oblige. "For such men," says Trush, "it is a matter of pride to shoot at a tiger or a bear, regardless of whether the shot hits its mark. It is no difference to them whether they injure a tiger or kill it. There are many such hunters, and they shoot without thinking."

This flagrant disregard for nature and the law can take surprising forms: once, Trush intercepted a tank. It was a "civilian" model (no gun turret), lined inside with oriental carpets, and filled with corporate executives hunting like rajahs on a latter-day elephant. Needless to say, the vehicle was illegal. Its occupants weren't pleased to see Trush, or his video camera, and they tried to intimidate him. "I filmed all this," explained Trush, "and it was aired on a national program. When these men saw themselves on TV, they called me in for a dressing-down, and I agreed to go. They said, 'You are not afraid to meet with us?' And I said that I wasn't. They threatened me. They said, 'What are you doing? Don't you understand? This is not America or Germany; this is Russia: you might get "lost" in the forest.' Then they asked me for the videotape. I said to them, 'Guys, I'm only doing my job. The tape is in Vladivostok. Go and talk to my supervisors.' After that, they told me that I was incorrigible and that it would be easier to kill me than to convince me."

It was high praise—of a dangerous kind. Hiking through the forest one day, not far from Markov's cabin, Trush nodded toward a dead poplar that had blown down, roots and all, leaving a large cavity behind. "This is how you hide a body in the forest," he explained. "Put it in a hole like that and then cut the trunk off low, just above the roots. That way, you can lift the stump back up." Trush elevates his hound-dog brows, wags his head, and shrugs. "No one will ever know."

Trush has been threatened many times, and his attitude is: "A barking dog doesn't bite." He knows how things are done in Russia, and that if someone powerful wanted him killed there would be little he could do to prevent it (in the taiga, the same is said to be true of a tiger when it has set its sights on a victim). On his rounds in the Bikin valley, all of Trush's skills and weapons have served him well: he has been shot at and attacked with hatchets and knives. When illegal loggers have tried to run him off the road with their trucks, he has not hesitated to fire on the vehicle. He confesses rather sheepishly that, during raids, he tends to use up more ammunition than anyone else. However, his bullets are directed toward tires and radiators, or simply fired for effect. Trush is clearly proud of the fact that he has never shot a person, "although," he is quick to add, "I have many times been within my rights to." But this is what makes Trush such an unusual presence in this brutal milieu: he is a man who relishes the role of the authoritarian heavy, and he has carefully honed himself into a dangerous weapon that he is more than ready to unleash. And yet this capability is tempered by deep veins of mercy and compassion; life is hard in the taiga for man and beast alike, and Trush understands this. When he finds bear cubs orphaned by poachers (eight at last count), he nurses them in his apartment. Somehow, he is able—even in the heat of the moment—to keep both sides of the story in mind, and both sides of himself under control.

"I could have started criminal proceedings and he would have gone to jail," said Trush of a poacher who shot at him and whom he subdued and handcuffed while he was trying to reload. "But I took pity on this young guy and decided not to ruin his life. We wrote a report on him citing hunting violations and we confiscated his gun, but I felt sorry for his parents; I saw the conditions they lived in. That boy went into the forest in order to put some food on the table, and that fact played a significant role in my decision."

Trush is well aware that, for many of Russia's disenfranchised citizens, the acts of owning a gun and using it to procure food represent a last vestige of independence and self-respect. However, even if they were able to get their hands on a hunting license, most tayozhniks' firearms would fail a modern inspection, and new rifles are prohibitively expensive by Russian standards. To make matters worse, the process of getting licensed to own a gun is onerous and time-consuming: not only are medical and psychological tests required, but the applicant must pay for them. This doesn't include the cost of transportation to the appropriate offices, which might be a day's travel from the applicant's village, and which may not be open anyway. The total bill for tests, licenses, gun, and ammunition can easily approach $1,000, a sum many inhabitants of the Bikin valley may not see in a year. In parts of Primorye, the current system has created a "poach or starve" situation, and it's not hard to see why many would rather risk a fine or the confiscation of a cheap gun.

There is a deep irony in Trush's work, and it lies in the fact that he lives in Russia, a country where many people will tell you that it's impossible to live without breaking the law. In the taiga, the combination of poverty, unemployment, and highly dangerous people and animals exacerbates a situation that is, at best, untenable. Trush represents a lonely act of faith in a largely faithless system. His mission—to impose order on a world in which desperate beings compete and collide to their mutual destruction—is as difficult as it is necessary, and the situation has improved little in the past decade. Despite their integrity and dedication, Trush and his comrades are modestly paid and rarely thanked for their work, and yet, courageously, quixotically, they persevere.

While Trush's sympathy and understanding are admirable, there are times when he seems almost too forgiving. As if he didn't have enough trouble, there have been two occasions on which Trush has nearly been killed by inexperienced police officers who were supposed to be assisting him. While on a raid in 2005, Trush and three other men were traveling over a rough road in Trush's Toyota pickup, and sitting in the front passenger seat was a young policeman with an AK-47 resting on the seat between his legs. In spite of his recent military and police training, the young man had his finger on the trigger while idly thumbing the switch that shifted the gun from single shot to automatic. With the gun on automatic, he squeezed the sensitive trigger and the rifle began firing, filling the cramped cab with smoke, fire, and a deafening roar. The soldier panicked for a moment, tightening his grip instead of releasing it, and his gun blew hole after hole in the cab roof, just inches above their heads. AK-47s have a tendency to pull upward when firing, and they eject spent shells to the right; the combination of these forces caused the barrel to swing toward Trush, whose shouts were drowned out by the blazing gun. While driving with one hand, he had to fend off the weapon with the other until the policeman finally came to his senses.

Trush, understandably, was furious; he was also deafened in his right ear, a condition from which he has never fully recovered. But his response to this nearly disastrous screwup is telling. Trush was within his rights to beat this idiot within an inch of his life, and to end his career then and there. Instead, Trush, who has two grown children of his own, covered for the young man. In most police departments, officers are required to account for their bullets, and this officer had a lot of accounting to do—nearly half a clip's worth. But through some army contacts, Trush made arrangements for the procurement of replacement bullets and, after a memorable tongue-lashing, the young man's penance was limited to repairing Trush's roof. In a similar accident at a stakeout in the forest, another junior officer inadvertently shot up the dirt around Trush's feet. Trush gave that boy another chance, too.

"In situations like this, my rule is from the Bible," Trush explains: " 'First, there was the word and then a deed.' It is always better to warn a person first; if he does not understand that warning, take action. That's the principle that I follow. Not for everyone, though."

Trush is a practicing Christian in a largely secular society and, in this sense, patience, compassion, and forgiveness could be seen as revolutionary acts against a system that has, for generations, demonstrated a minimum of these qualities. While Trush will make allowances for youth, inexperience, and desperation, there are some things he will not forgive. Along with young, careless policemen, Trush must also deal with the old and cynical ones. In Primorye, as in many parts of Russia, policemen have poor reputations and are generally perceived as corrupt and dangerous bullies. Well armed, with the freedom and the means to go where they please, police are implicated in many poaching incidents. They can be extremely dangerous when caught in compromising positions, especially in remote areas. Nonetheless, one winter day, when a group of four police officers refused to get out of their car after he'd stopped them on a back road, Trush pulled out a canister of Mace and sprayed it into the car's air intake. The heater was on so the Mace quickly filled the passenger compartment. Recalling the incident, Trush smiles broadly and spreads his arms like wings, exclaiming, "And the doors flew open!" It is because of situations like this that the Tigers never work alone.

Given the remoteness of his beat, and the ease with which the taiga can absorb a body, Trush has reason to be much more cautious than he is. But Trush has a contagious confidence, and some of this is due to his beagle-sized Laika, Gitta. The two are inseparable. Gitta has saved Trush's life at least twice, and he has returned the favor an equal number of times. She is his eyes, ears, and sixth sense in the forest. It seems both comical and poignant that such a small dog could mean so much to such a large man, and yet the intensity and clairvoyance of their bond is profound—one best understood by K-9 corps officers, waterfowlers, and the blind. Gitta keeps Trush's heart strong in the forest, but it is Lubov Trush who simply keeps his heart. They have been married for forty years. Fully a foot shorter than Trush, she is his emotional backbone, and it is a steely one. Herself a former kayak champion, Lubov is tightly bundled, kind and industrious. Goodwill and good food seem to emanate from her. Yuri may run you hard in the bush, but a visitor can still grow fat at Lubov's table.

At home in their fifth-floor apartment, Trush seems too large for the space, and the simple furniture appears insufficient to hold him, as if it had been designed for a smaller scale of human. In this calm and cozy sanctuary, where Lubov holds sway, there are few signs of her husband's working life. But there are some hints: the kettlebells in the corner, shiny with use; the tiger-striped blanket on the guest bed; the improvised punching bag filled with wheat germ hanging in the hallway. Stashed in closets and drawers are more obvious clues: a pair of Udeghe-style hunting skis; a tiger's claw; a Dragunov "Tiger" sniper's rifle; a mangled bullet, its crevices still packed with matter from a tiger Trush shot in the icy spring of 1996.

4

What the hammer? What the chain?
In what furnace was thy brain?

WILLIAM BLAKE, "The Tyger"

THE BADGER AND SHOTGUN INCIDENT WAS THE ONLY TIME TRUSH SAW
Markov alive, and he had underestimated him. Then, he had figured Markov for one more unemployed subsistence hunter who
wasn't above taking a lynx or a badger if the opportunity presented itself. When Trush finds himself, as he often does, in that
murky place between the letter of the law and the fact of a man's
circumstances, he is reminded that the line between right and
wrong can be a crooked one. But how, in the forest there, with that
sorry badger in a pot, could Trush have imagined what would happen to Markov, a known poacher with illegal weapons who was fed
up with being poor? And how, for that matter, could he have
known what would happen to Lev Khomenko?

Lev ("Lion") Khomenko was a thirty-six-year-old hunter and
herbalist from the village of Lesopil'noye, near the confluence of
the Ussuri and Bikin rivers. He had a degree in hunting management and was a staff hunter for Alufchanski, the State Forest
Management Company, which oversaw the region's commercial
meat and fur industry. But the 1990s were the toughest years
many Russians could remember, and the winter of '96 found
Khomenko unemployed with four children to feed. He and his
family lived a marginal existence on the edge of the taiga; their
house was old and made of logs, and it leaned precariously to one

side. There were cracks in the walls big enough to put a hand through. Trush had been making his rounds one day when he came upon Khomenko hunting in the forest; while doing a routine document check, he discovered that Khomenko's gun was registered not in his own name but in his father's. Trush was within his rights to confiscate the weapon, but he had sympathy for the man's obvious poverty and was impressed that all his other papers were in order, so he let him go.

Not long afterward, Khomenko hitched a ride up the Bikin in a logging truck. He wore fleece-lined boots that were much better suited to town use and, over these, he wore a green forester's uniform. He was hunting, as many in the taiga do, with a double-barreled shotgun. In the backwoods of Primorye, these relatively light firearms tend to be old—sometimes very old—and of dubious quality; their killing range is usually under a hundred yards, and they are accurate only to around seventy yards, which is almost laughable by the standards of modern hunting weapons. Khomenko's gun was loaded with a single large ball in the right barrel, and with lead shot in the left; this way he would be prepared for any kind of game, be it big or small. Khomenko was traveling alone; there was about ten inches of snow on the ground, and it was forty degrees below zero.

Save for one's own breaths and footfalls, the forest at this temperature is as silent and still as outer space and, to the barefaced Khomenko, it may have felt almost as cold. Nothing moved. The white trunks of birch trees rose almost seamlessly from the snow. The grays and browns of oak and poplar and smaller shrubs provided contrast and reference points, but they also offered places to hide. Around midday, Khomenko ran across the trail of a tiger; the tracks were recent and he decided to follow them. There was a logging camp nearby, and when the watchman there saw Khomenko coming, he came out to greet him. The two men talked for a while and, when Khomenko expressed interest in the tiger tracks, the watchman said he had heard some kind of a fight in the woods the previous night. He thought the tiger might have had a run-in with a huge wild boar that he had been seeing around the camp. Ussurian boars can grow to enormous size, some weighing in excess of five hundred pounds; they usually travel in herds, but this one was strangely solitary. It was so big that the watchman had given it a nickname: GAZ-66, after a large, virtually unstoppable military truck that is often used in forest work. Its tusks were massive, and the watchman figured the tiger had met its match. Khomenko was intrigued and, despite the watchman's admonitions against going alone after a possibly wounded tiger, he seemed determined to do so.

Khomenko was an experienced hunter—a professional—and, as such, his interest was understandable. Fresh tiger tracks aren't something you see every day, and many have spent their entire lives in the taiga without ever setting eyes on a live tiger. Maybe Khomenko was curious; maybe he was very hungry, or maybe he thought he had just won the lottery. Tigers go by several different names here, and one of them is Toyota—because, during the 1990s, that is what you could buy with one. The risk, of course, is great. The animal is deadly, and hunting one is a federal offense, but that is the case with many black market commodities, and it is safe to say Khomenko was desperate. One look at his rhombus of a house was proof enough.

When Khomenko failed to return that evening, the watchman grew concerned. The following morning, he and some loggers climbed onto a bulldozer—there was no way they were going in there on foot—and went looking for him. They found Khomenko about half a mile down the trail, lying on his back in a peculiar position and veiled in a light dusting of snow. They left him where he lay and called the police, who arrived the next day. For those who know the language, the whole story was written in the snow, and this was how it read:

Within a few hundred yards of the logging camp, Khomenko had come upon the site of the battle reported by the watchman, only there was no sign of the rogue boar. The only tracks were those of tigers. Most likely, they had been fighting over territory. Khomenko had studied the scene, found the two sets of exit tracks, and followed the bloody ones. Once again, he didn't have far to go. There is no way to know precisely what happened next—if the tiger revealed its position somehow, or if Khomenko spotted it first. In any case, Lev Khomenko saw or sensed the tiger in time to take off his gloves and lay them neatly on the snow. With his hands free for shooting, he turned toward the tiger's hiding place, stepping from side to side as if searching for a clean sightline. By the time he brought his rifle to his shoulder, the tiger was already charging. One can only imagine the rush of chemistry coursing through those superheated bodies, the pounding in Khomenko's chest as those molten, spectral eyes closed on him at dream speed.

Apparently, Khomenko maintained his composure because he emptied the barrels individually rather than together. Both shots hit their mark but had absolutely no effect; the tiger came on in a blur of twelve-foot leaps and swatted Khomenko in the face with its paw, knocking him to the ground. Then the tiger picked him up in its jaws. Khomenko was carrying a canvas rucksack, and it was clear from the shredded axe handle sticking out of it that this was how the tiger lifted him. The tiger then proceeded to shake Khomenko like a rag doll—so violently that it broke his wrist and both of his legs. Then the tiger put him down and went away.

Khomenko was probably unconscious for a time, but he came to and, with his remaining usable hand, he drew his knife. Then he began to crawl back the way he had come. He was found a few feet from his neatly laid gloves, frozen to death, his legs jutting off at odd angles. The temperature that day was minus forty-five. When Khomenko's body was lifted gently onto the back of the loggers' bulldozer, it was as rigid as a mannequin.

Only afterward, when the exit tracks were followed, did it become clear the tiger had never left the site. Despite the presence of heavy machinery and half a dozen men, it had remained nearby, watching, just as it had the day before. As one taiga hunter said, "The tiger will see you a hundred times before you see him once."

One of the most striking details of this case is that Khomenko had only two visible wounds on his body: a single claw mark on his face and some lacerations on his broken hand. The tiger had no interest in Khomenko as food, and probably had never intended even to scratch him. It turned out later that this tiger had a defective claw that did not retract with the others. This was probably the claw that wounded Khomenko's face, and it was also by this faulty claw that Yuri Trush would identify this tiger's prints, track it down, and shoot it from the top of a farm tractor. Far more difficult for Trush, though, would be walking up to that crooked house filled with all those anxious faces, and knocking on the door. "I was overwhelmed," said Trush. "My eyes filled with tears. At that moment, when I saw their circumstances, I felt sorry for the man, not for the tiger."

It was the timing that had been especially cruel: on January 26, Trush had stopped Khomenko and seriously considered disarming him. On the 29th, Khomenko met the tiger.

———

Now, nearly two years later, Markov was dead and, once again, lives would be saved or lost depending on how Trush read his hunches. While he, Lazurenko, and Gorborukov studied the melted, trampled snow, trying to take the measure of both man and tiger, it was left to Deputy Bush and Markov's grieving friends to gather Markov's remains onto the blanket that Zaitsev had been carrying for that purpose. All of these men were hunters; they had seen animal kills and had butchered animals themselves. But Markov was a man—a close friend—and now it was as if he had exploded, shattered into pieces by this brutal, frigid life. The task of gathering, of re-membering, was almost too much to bear so the men worked slowly, numb and mechanical. "Try to get all the bones," mumbled Onofrecuk, more to himself than anyone else. "Let's try to get as many as we can for the grave."

There is a costly wisdom in this, the stoic execution of deeds that must be done. It is a survival skill that is closely linked to Fate, and Fate has always been a potent force in Russia, where, for generations, citizens have had little control over their own destinies. Fate can be a bitch, but, as Zaitsev, Dvornik, and Onofrecuk had discovered, it can also be a tiger. By then, it was clear to everyone present that this wasn't forest business as usual; there was more going on here than bad luck or carelessness. What had Markov done to bring this upon himself? Markov's friends, the same ones who hid his shotgun before Inspection Tiger arrived, had a pretty good idea.

Sorting through the heap of blood-stiffened clothing, Deputy

Bush pulled out a knife sheath—empty—and then a small military first-aid kit, the only pieces of equipment that weren't torn off or left behind. "Where's the knife?" asked Bush.

"Somewhere in the woods," answered Onofrecuk, quickly. "In the snow."

Bush was young, but he was no fool; in all likelihood, the knife and gun were together—wherever they were. The deputy let it go, and opened the first-aid kit. There were no bandages or medicines inside, only cigarettes. When the gathering was done, Gorborukov and Deputy Bush escorted Markov's friends back to the cabin with Markov's remains, but Trush and Lazurenko stayed behind. Together, they followed the tiger's exit trail through ankle-deep powder. The trail was hot—that is, as fresh as it could possibly be without actually laying eyes on the animal. Snow has a muffling effect on all sounds, but in the case of a tiger, especially one making an effort to avoid detection, this effect is absolute. Meanwhile, Trush and Lazurenko announced themselves with every step; despite their best efforts, they might as well have been on radar. Their disadvantage was striking; it was as if the tiger had removed itself from the same plane of physical consequence to which they remained bound. This was not an animal they followed, but a contradiction, a silence that was at once incarnate and invisible. Track and scent were the only signs it couldn't disguise. Trush had stalked tigers before, and he had also been stalked by them, so he understood what was going on: the tiger was controlling the situation now, bending the future to its will.

Trush was badly shaken by what he had seen and this, combined with the steadily failing light and the absence of a shooting order, caused him to hesitate. It was clear to him now that this tiger was not the same kind of animal that had killed Khomenko. Considering the audacity of Khomenko's transgressions—tracking the tiger down and then trying to kill it—that animal had showed admirable restraint. Russians call man-eating tigers cannibals, but Khomenko's tiger—an old male—was not one of those; he had already been injured twice (first by the rival tiger and then by Khomenko's bullets), and he was simply immobilizing the latest threat. When Trush encountered that tiger again, six weeks later in the village of Verkhny Pereval, he had drawn attention to himself by killing a young horse and hauling it over a six-foot fence. Self-defense and livestock killing both fall under the category of normal tiger behavior, but something else was going on here, east of Sobolonye; Markov's tiger was in another realm altogether.

Trush and Lazurenko continued to follow and study the tracks for a cautious quarter mile. Every fourth print, they noticed, was dotted with blood, the hot droplets boring holes in the snow on their way to the frozen ground below. It was the forepaw, right side. Some of the holes were ringed with a halo of yellowish green, a sign of infection. Even so, all of the paws seemed to be making equally deep impressions, so the injury didn't appear to be crippling. The tiger was proceeding carefully and steadily, but the men were not certain where it actually was; for all they knew, it could have doubled back and been tracking *them*. Trush could feel it now, by the hairs on his own skin, that he was being drawn into a strange and terrible conflict. He was duty-bound to go there—he knew this—but he was also beginning to understand why Markov's friends were so frightened, and it was not because they were cowards. Because of this, and because he didn't want to risk an ambush, Trush called off the hunt and headed back to the cabin. It was a decision that, though sound in the moment, would come back to haunt him.

———

As Trush, Lazurenko, and Gorborukov worked their way back to Markov's cabin and up the tiger's entrance trail, they found evidence of the animal's method and, in some ways, this was more unnerving than what they had just seen. By an improvised well-head made from a beehive, they discovered the heavy aluminum water dipper Markov used for drinking; it was all but unrecognizable. It had been chewed so savagely that it looked as if it had been used for target practice and then run over by a truck. Next to it was an enameled steel saucepan that had also been badly scratched and dented. They located Markov's axe, its handle gnawed to splinters. His latrine, his beehives—everything that might have his scent on it—had been thoroughly explored and much of it destroyed. His washstand had been knocked off the cabin's outer wall, and there was a swipe of tiger blood by the door. Tiger tracks were everywhere, circling the cabin, interrupted only by packed depressions in the snow where the animal stopped to wait and watch before circling the cabin yet again. In one spot, by the wellhead, the tiger had lain on a patch of snow long enough to partially thaw it out. When it finally moved on, a furry shadow of itself remained behind, frozen in place. The tiger had clearly been on the premises for a while, perhaps days—long enough to defecate at least twice, both times within a few feet of the cabin. It was as if the tiger had staked a claim to the premises and all they contained.

———

Animal attacks are relatively common in the taiga, but they probably would be anywhere you had two species of bear, two species of big cat, and humans all vying in earnest for similar prey. In Amgu, a dicey, off-grid village on the coast, an alarming percentage of the male population carries evidence of mauling; even Trush has been attacked by a bear. However, such encounters are usually spontaneous, impulsive responses to immediate threats, competition, or surprise. Everything Trush was seeing now suggested something else. With each piece of evidence, new colors were being added to the spectrum of his understanding.

Tigers are ambush hunters, and this—the practice of stealth coupled with the element of surprise—is what has enabled this solitary predator to kill fast-moving, often dangerous game for eons, through major variations in climate and landscape. But this tiger, on this occasion, made no attempt whatsoever to conceal itself. Not finding what it sought at the wellhead or around the cabin, the tiger lay down in the open by the entrance road and waited—again. Seen together, all of these signs, and all of these behaviors, implied an alarming confidence and clarity of purpose. As Trush and his team pieced the evidence together, they came to understand that this tiger was not hunting for animals, or even for humans; he was hunting for Markov.

And menacingly the mighty vastness envelops me,
reflected with terrible force in my depths.

NIKOLAI GOGOL,
Dead Souls

VLADIMIR MARKOV HAD A HISTORY WITH TIGERS, AND IT TOOK THE
form not of a linear continuum but of a steadily tightening spiral.
The first loose turns appeared to be accidents of history, but many
Russians would call them twists of fate. Were one to try to identify
the single most important influence on Markov's destiny—besides
Markov himself—it would probably be a toss-up between Mao
Zedong and perestroika. Had there been no Cultural Revolution,
and no pitched battle for control of China's Communist Party, it is
unlikely that Markov ever would have ventured past the Urals.
Had perestroika not occurred, Markov and many others would not
have found themselves desperate enough to do virtually anything—including hunt tigers—for money.

Vladimir Markov was born on February 14, 1951, at the
extreme opposite end of Russia, on the shattered margin of a shell-
shocked empire in which his parents were not so much citizens as
survivors. They lived in Kaliningrad, the diminutive province
wedged between Poland and Lithuania on the Baltic Sea that was
formerly a German territory. Most of the capital city, Königsberg,
and its strategic port were still in ruins after being heavily bombed
by the British during the summer of 1944 and then shelled relentlessly by the Soviets during the winter and spring of 1945. After
the war, Königsberg was renamed Kaliningrad. It became the base

for the Soviet Baltic Fleet and, like Vladivostok, its Pacific counter-
part, the city was declared off limits to outsiders.

This occurred at the same time that George Orwell's *1984* was
introducing Western readers to a terrifying new reality, one that
resembled the nascent Kaliningrad more closely than Orwell
could have imagined. As Kaliningrad crawled to its feet out of the
rubble and ash of Königsberg, it did so in the Stalinist image of
urban development and social control. Replacing medieval towers,
parapets, and gargoyles were bleak and poorly built concrete
apartment blocks enlivened only by statues and murals of Lenin's
goateed visage that oversaw one's every move and bannered slogans that intruded on one's private thoughts.

Lenin may have envisioned it, but Stalin mastered it: the ability to disorient and disconnect individuals and large populations,
not just from their physical surroundings and core communities
but, ultimately, from themselves. Kaliningrad was a case in point.
After being flattened, purged, and renamed, both city and
province were repopulated with ethnic Russians. Markov's parents
were part of this mass geopolitical revision and, in their case, it
wasn't a random assignment. Ilya Markov was a ship's mechanic
who, though seriously injured during the war, was needed for service in the Baltic Fleet. Markov's mother had worked to support
the war effort, too, and one can only imagine the Orwellian fever
dream she now found herself in: raising a family under Stalin,
often single-handed, in the ruins of a stolen medieval city that
had been transformed into a military zone and then sealed off
from the outside world.

The Great Patriotic War had scarcely concluded before the
USSR began rebuilding and retooling for the Cold War. While
Soviet engineers and scientists perfected the now ubiquitous
AK-47 and tested the country's first nuclear weapons, the general
population reeled from the catastrophic synergy generated by six
years of war and the seemingly endless nightmare of Stalin's psy-
chotic reign. During the two decades prior to Markov's birth, the
Soviet Union lost approximately 35 million citizens—more than
one fifth of its population—to manufactured famines, political
repression, genocide, and war. Millions more were imprisoned,

exiled, or forced to relocate, en masse, across vast distances. With the possible exception of China under Mao Zedong, it is hard to imagine how the fabric of a country could have been more thoroughly shredded from within and without.

Almost as soon as Stalin died, in 1953, the untenable nature of the Soviet empire began to reveal itself to the outside world, and it wasn't long before the fraternal solidarity that had existed between the Soviets and the Chinese since 1949 began to break down as well. The stresses began to tell in the late 1950s, after Mao accused Stalin's more moderate successor, Nikita Khrushchev, of betraying Marx's vision. China, then in the throes of Mao's Great Leap Forward, was mimicking some of Lenin's and Stalin's most disastrous policies and programs with one result being that the country suffered the worst famine in its history—perhaps in all of history. Between 1958 and 1962, China strove to create an illusion of industrial progress by producing ton upon ton of useless low-grade steel, but it did so at the expense of basic food production. Not only did the massive project draw countless workers away from the fields, it claimed their tools as well: in a futile effort to reach unattainable production quotas, even shovels and plowshares were melted down. Hoping to save face and conceal the true costs of this Great Leap Forward, China continued to export grain (to Russia, among other countries) with the result that tens of millions of peasants starved to death.

In an effort to deflect the blame for this catastrophe, Mao chastised Khrushchev for recalling China's Soviet advisors and for calling in the substantial debts China had incurred during the Korean War. In fact, China's Communist Party was in the midst of a vicious power struggle, which Mao would win, but at enormous national cost. Many in the Kremlin, still recovering from thirty years of Stalin, saw a frighteningly familiar scenario developing with Mao's own cult of personality, and this was one of several reasons the Soviets sought to distance themselves from their communist "little brother." As relations deteriorated, the tension manifested itself along contested sections of their shared border, which, at the time, was 4,650 miles long. The scabs Mao chose to pick at were more than a century old, but they served his purpose well.

The wounds Mao sought to reopen had been inflicted during the nineteenth century when the future superpowers were grinding against each other like so many tectonic plates. The world as we know it was forming then, along fault lines of race, culture, and geography. By mid-century, though, China was in trouble: embroiled in the Opium Wars with France and England, it was further hobbled by a protracted internal rebellion that had left Manchuria effectively defenseless. Imperial Russia had already taken advantage of this window of weakness on its Pacific frontier by annexing all disputed lands north of the Amur River in 1858. Two years later, Czar Alexander II went a step further and coerced the Chinese into signing the Treaty of Peking, thereby adding another slice of Outer Manchuria—what is now Primorye and southern Khabarovsk Territory—to the Russian empire. In the mid-1960s, it seemed as if Mao might try to get them back.

While Chairman Mao was engineering his Great Leap Forward and vying for control of China's Communist Party, he was also publicly criticizing the Treaty of Peking, even going so far as to demand reparations from Russia. By 1968 Sino-Soviet relations had sunk to a historic low, and one of the by-products was a new front in the Cold War. It yawned open in a surprising place: a small island in the middle of the Ussuri River, twenty miles due west of Yuri Trush's hometown. The Russians call it Damansky Island and the Chinese call it Zhen Bao (Treasure Island); either way, this seasonally flooded smear of field and forest exhibits no obvious strategic value. Nonetheless, its ambiguous location met Mao's criteria for a contentious and unifying reminder of past humiliations at the hands of a long-dead imperialist.

By the winter of 1968, the island and adjacent riverbank had become the site of increasingly violent skirmishes—brawls, really—between Chinese and Soviet border guards. "Each Siberian would be confronted by a cluster of Chinese servicemen armed with boat hooks, pickets and sticks with spiked heads," wrote Lieutenant General (Ret.) Vitaly Bubenin, who was declared a Hero of the Soviet Union for his bravery during the climax of these confrontations. "We didn't have body armor back then. My men were wearing thick winter sheepskin jackets. The fights occurred on a daily basis and . . . we realized that we wouldn't last long using our bare hands. We got ourselves some bear spears and maces with metal heads similar to those used by epic warriors. . . . The weapons become hugely popular with all the border guards stationed around the area."

Seen from a distance as they played out across the moonlit snow and through the leafless willows, these running battles would have borne a striking resemblance to the first confrontations between Cossacks and Manchus three hundred years earlier. Mao, it is now generally believed, was capitalizing on these historic rivalries in an effort to whip up some politically useful nationalistic fervor. However, he had chosen to do this with the world's leading nuclear power: it was brinkmanship of a bold and frightening kind. On March 2, 1969, two weeks after Vladimir Markov reached draft age, the border guards' strict no-shooting order was violated in the form of a carefully orchestrated ambush by the Chinese. In the ensuing gun battle, the first of its kind on a Russian border since the Second World War, thirty-one Russians were gunned down. Within days, thousands of Russian and Chinese troops, backed by artillery, were massed along the frozen Ussuri.

On March 15, three days before the United States began its four-year bombing campaign against Cambodia, there was a major battle at Damansky/Zhen Bao in which hundreds of Russian and Chinese soldiers died. Both nations, sobered by the potential for a full-blown war, withdrew to their respective sides. Mao ordered extensive tunnel networks to be dug on the Ussuri's left bank, allegedly in preparation for a nuclear attack by Russia. Moscow, too, prepared for the worst, calling for a major troop buildup along the Ussuri and Amur rivers. Five thousand miles away, in Kaliningrad, Vladimir Markov received his draft notice. By the end of 1969, twenty-nine divisions of the Soviet army (nearly half a million soldiers) were massed along the border, and Private Markov was among them. For a seaman's son from Baltic Russia, it would have been hard to imagine a more remote posting, or a less auspicious one.

———

Soviet Russia's secrecy and paranoia are legendary to the point of caricature, but they were also real: information of all kinds was so strictly controlled that ordinary Russians were uninformed, or intentionally misinformed, about politically sensitive areas. The Far East contained many such zones, including important mines, gulags, and military bases. Because Primorye and southern Khabarovsk Territory were effectively sandwiched between China and the Pacific coast (which was deemed vulnerable to Japanese and American infiltration), security was particularly tight there. As a result, Markov was going from one forbidden zone to another; this was a place that he and many of his fellow draftees may not have even known existed. Despite nearly two decades of relative openness, this is apparently still the case, if for different reasons. When a literate young Muscovite, bound for a prestigious American music school, was asked about Primorye in July of 2008, he said he hadn't heard of it. "Maybe it's near Iran," he guessed. To the more straightforward question, "Are there tigers in Russia?" he answered, "I think only in the circus." For many Russian urbanites, "Russia" stops at the Urals, if not sooner. Beyond that is Siberia—a bad joke, and after that, well, who really cares?

In the minds of most Russians, the Far East lies over the edge of the known world and is, itself, a form of oblivion. For any European Russian, whether ordinary worker or privileged member of the nomenklatura,* a one-way ticket like Markov's was tantamount to banishment. His was the same route undertaken by hundreds of thousands of exiles dating back to Czarist times. Some of the country's most notorious prisons and labor camps were located there, including the dreaded and, for many years, unmentionable Sakhalin Island, a frigid and lonely sub-planet from which many never returned.

Regardless of what he knew beforehand, Markov's nonstop

---

* Nomenklatura, literally "list of names," refers to the ruling elite of communist society who held key positions in all spheres of Soviet endeavor. The privileges they enjoyed and the proportion of the population they represented bore striking resemblances to those of the nobility under the czar.

train ride from the thickly settled shadowlands of the Iron Curtain to the vast and empty wilderness hugging Asia's Pacific coast would have been radical and disorienting, not to mention interminable. The journey from Kaliningrad to Khabarovsk, the regional capital of the Far East, takes one a quarter of the way around the world. To get there in 1969 would have meant two to three weeks on the Trans-Siberian, the tracks unspooling into the future with agonizing slowness like a real-time progression of Eurasian conquest and collapse. Khabarovsk is situated at a strategic bend in the Amur River, less than ten miles from its confluence with the Ussuri and the Chinese frontier. One hundred and fifty miles to the south, just over the Primorye border, lies the Bikin valley and the site of Sobolonye, a village that did not exist when Markov first arrived in the region.

The magnitude of such a move for a provincial like Markov cannot be underestimated. Beyond the language, nothing would have been the same, and many of his new acquaintances would have been outcasts of one kind or another. There was no tradition of serfdom in the Far East and, historically, the region has been a haven for a multiethnic rabble of bandits, deserters, poachers, fur trappers, and persecuted Old Believers (a conservative branch of Orthodox Christians), all of whom favored voluntary banishment over a wide range of unappealing alternatives. Add to this the exile population—both Russian and Chinese, and the Cossack soldiers sent by the czar to settle and guard this new frontier—and the results become uniquely volatile, more crucible than melting pot.

Today, the Bikin valley is seen by many outsiders as a place as dangerous for its human inhabitants as it is for its animals. It is dotted with small, isolated villages, many of which operate off the grid and outside the law. To a pair of foreign journalists, a friend of Markov's once exclaimed, "You came here alone? Aren't you afraid? Usually, outsiders only come in big delegations."

Evidence suggests that Markov found this environment more liberating than frightening and, in Soviet Russia, liberty was a rare thing. In any case, Markov adapted and, ultimately, adopted this frontier as his home, and it may have been thanks to the army.

According to friends and neighbors, Markov was trained in reconnaissance, and these skills—wilderness survival, orienteering, stealth, and the handling of arms—would serve him well in ways he never anticipated. Denis Burukhin, a young trapper from Sobolonye who knew Markov as Uncle Vova (a diminutive form of Vladimir), would later recall how Markov taught him to navigate the dense and trackless forest along the Bikin.

During his military service, Markov also became a paratrooper, maybe because he was strong and well coordinated, and maybe because—at five and a half feet tall (the same height as Stalin)—he had something to prove. If fate had taken one more twist, Markov and Trush could have been jumping out of planes together. Both men were in the army in 1969 and Trush was a paratrooper, too. Because he was eleven months older, he had already been assigned to a battalion in Turkmenistan, but after the Damansky clashes in the spring of 1969, his battalion was mobilized to Primorye. Only at the last minute were they recalled.

In the end, Markov never had to test his skills in battle, despite the fact that both Russia and China remained on a war footing for years after the Damansky incident.* The stakes were high enough that the Chinese and Russian premiers, Zhou Enlai and Alexei Kosygin, saw fit to meet personally in order to resolve the festering border issue. Although the meeting was considered successful, Moscow continued its Far Eastern troop buildup into the early 1970s.† By the time Markov was discharged from the army in 1971, his father was dead; ten years later, he lost his sister. Markov never returned to Kaliningrad (perhaps it was simply too far) and, according to his wife, Tamara Borisova, none of his surviving family ever visited Sobolonye. Had they taken the opportunity to do so, they probably wouldn't have recognized the die-hard tayozhnik as their own.

---

* According to R. Craig Nation, the Far Eastern theater of operations during this period [1970s and '80s] came to "absorb no less than one-third of Soviet military assets."

† Damansky/Zhen Bao was formally ceded to China by Boris Yeltsin in 1991.

6

The tiger answered, "Your son has been boasting. If he
is the stronger, let him kill me; if I am the stronger,
I will kill him. Tell him my command!"

"The Brave Gilyak and the Grateful Tiger,"
COLLECTED BY L. Y. STERNBERG, C. 1900

IT HAD BEEN ANDREI ONOFRECUK, A SHORT MAN WITH NICOTINE-
varnished fingernails and a stove-in nose, who had first discovered
Markov on Thursday, one day prior to Inspection Tiger's arrival.
Onofrecuk was a regular at the cabin, and the two men had agreed
to meet there to do some ice fishing. But Onofrecuk had gotten
drunk and was late—by about a day. After hitching a ride to the
turnoff, he had gone the last half mile on foot, arriving close to
noon. The first thing he noticed was blood by the entrance road. "I
didn't quite understand at first what was what," he recalled.
"Maybe Markov shot some animal and didn't clean up after himself. I was surprised. Usually, he is really careful about that kind of
thing. The hunt is not legal after all, and you know there might be
rangers coming. So then I started walking, thinking: what the hell
is going on? Then I saw his hat. It was as if I'd been clubbed over
the head. I stopped thinking clearly. I had a bad feeling, but I still
couldn't understand what was happening. Then I saw the tiger
tracks.

"So, I'm thinking: maybe he's just hurt. Maybe I could help
him. I walked some more, past pieces of his clothes. I saw the dog's
paw sticking out of the snow. I went a bit further, but the tiger
didn't let me any closer. I couldn't see Markiz—neither him nor

her. [In Russian, tigers are often referred to in the feminine, like ships.] But I heard her growling. I couldn't figure out which direction it was coming from, but I knew then that she'd got him. Right there, that fucking carrion eater's got her meat-head down, growling over him. So I stood for a little while, and then I slowly turned around. I was thinking, the main thing was not to start running because then she would run after me—eat me."

Onofrecuk was unarmed. He made his way back to the cabin and started a fire in the cold stove. He was in shock. "My head became empty," he recalled. "Like a vacuum. You know, it was hard to understand—he was my friend, after all. So many years out there together."

He sat in Markov's cabin, drinking tea and smoking cigarettes, one after the other, for a long time. It took him three tries before he could summon the nerve to leave the cabin to go for help. Onofrecuk was ten years younger than Markov and saw him as something of a mentor. While he was fond of reading, he was not ambitious and he lacked the skill and patience required for bee-keeping or fur trapping. He was, primarily, a meat hunter and fisherman—often under the supervision of Markov—and he lived day to day. They shared the cabin and fought like brothers, but they always made up. Markov had been his best friend.

Nonetheless, that night, it fell to their mutual friend, Danila Zaitsev, to tell Tamara Borisova what had happened to her husband in the forest. Markov had not been home in nearly a month and Borisova was eager to see him. "The scariest thing was telling his wife," recalled Onofrecuk. "I was afraid to go to her house by myself, so I asked Zaitsev to come with me. But I couldn't go in. I stayed on the road. 'Go,' I told him. 'Tell her.' Because the image of him there—it was like I'd just seen him."

Danila Zaitsev—skewed nose, furrowed brow, penetrating eye—is a tough and steady man, and he went in to face Borisova alone. He tried to be as gentle as he could, but who knows how to say such things? "I wanted to choose the words carefully," Zaitsev explained. "I told her that a tiger had attacked him and, at first, she didn't understand. She thought he had survived."

So Zaitsev tried again while Onofrecuk stood listening on the dark and frozen road. He knew when Zaitsev told her by the screaming.

Borisova seemed to go out of her mind then: she was a maelstrom, grieving mad. She insisted on seeing her husband, demanding him in ways that were hard for his friends to deny. Wisely, they refused to allow it. They had sequestered Markov's remains at the home of an old man named Kuzmich, a carpenter who lived alone at the edge of the village. Onofrecuk and Zaitsev gathered some planks of Korean pine for a coffin, and Kuzmich built it—full size. But Markov could not be buried right away because Borisova had ordered a new suit for him. That there was virtually nothing to put in it was beside the point. Borisova's world was tilting badly and she needed some order; she *needed* her husband to be buried in a suit. Her friends obliged her, but the round-trip to Luchegorsk, the nearest shopping town, would take a day. In the meantime, Markov's friends went to the village cemetery to prepare the grave.

The cemetery is laid out on a forested knoll about half a mile south of the village, where it is overseen by a massive, dead Korean pine. The cemetery is small, not only because Sobolonye is so new, but because the people hired to work for the company and thereby allowed to live in the village were generally too young to die. Nonetheless, some of them have and so there is a high proportion of small children and young people represented there—some by Orthodox crosses of crudely welded steel, others by crosses of brightly painted wood, a few by formal gravestones. If the family can afford it, an enameled photograph of the deceased will be mounted on the grave. Today, the graveyard is the only place one can view a likeness of Vladimir Markov.

Compact and solidly built, Markov had high cheekbones, melancholy-looking eyes, and an athlete's chin. Both Onofrecuk and his wife, Irina, noted a certain "Gypsy" quality about him. Tamara Borisova put it a bit differently, saying, "He was a Russian, but there was something Armenian or Georgian about his face." Its effect was not wasted on her: Markov was handsome, with olive skin; dark, wavy hair; and blue-green eyes. Short as he was, he was still exceptionally strong: before Sobolonye's disco burned down,

Markov used to help out there, and Borisova recalls him carrying 100-liter beer kegs (about 25 gallons) with ease (full, these weigh about 250 pounds).

After the army, Markov had gone to a technical school for logging and, from there, to work in the woods in southern Primorye, not far from a town named for the explorer Arseniev. Around 1980, when Markov was in his late twenties, he moved up to Sobolonye, which offered both better prospects and an opportunity to put some distance between himself and a failed marriage. Sobolonye had been carved out of the forest a few years earlier by the Middle Bikin National Forest Enterprise, a state-owned logging company that had been set up to log the old-growth poplar, oak, and pine throughout the Bikin valley. Primorye contains some of the biggest and most varied timber anywhere east of the Urals and, at the time, the middle and upper Bikin were largely unexploited.

Sobolonye is the last settlement at the end of a road that, when not buried in snow, can go from choking dust to sucking mud in the space of an hour. At its peak, the village was home to about 450 people who lived in small log houses built in haphazard tiers on a hillside above the river. The place has the feel of a North American mining town circa 1925, only with fewer straight lines. There are no sidewalks or paved streets, and no plumbing; the houses are heated with wood, and water is drawn from common wells. Telephones—of any kind—are a rarity. Electricity, which was viewed as a symbol of modernity by the Soviets and a means of keeping pace with the West, is provided by a diesel generator on the edge of town. Where the village ends the taiga begins, stretching away for miles in all directions.

For a certain kind of person, Sobolonye offered a life that was hard to improve on: decent housing, predictable employment, ready access to a river full of fish, and, for those who knew what to look for, a forest full of nuts, berries, mushrooms, medicinal roots, and wild game. In the summer, you could even grow watermelons. The logging company was as generous as the forest, providing a school, clinic, library, general store, recreation center, and even a hairdresser. Sobolonye, at the time Markov arrived, was a place of optimism and fresh starts, and the young people who settled there felt lucky. From their vantage, communism worked: here, it truly seemed that Man, Nature, and Industry could coexist for the common good. Most of these young men and women had arrived from other parts of the Far East, including Khabarovsk Territory and Sakhalin Island. Some had done time in the far north. They were a rugged, salty bunch, and many of the women worked, hunted, drank, and occasionally fought alongside the men. Markov and Borisova had met in the forest when she was working as a log trimmer and he was sorting logs. She was divorced, too, and she couldn't believe her good fortune. "At first, when I was with him," she recalled, "I felt as if I were in heaven. I would ask myself, 'Could I be so lucky?' He helped me with everything."

They had a son together in 1982, raising the number of children under their roof to four. Her new husband's affection for young children impressed Borisova deeply. "He was so unconditionally kind, it was almost painful," she explained. "If someone's child got ill, he would heat lynx fat and take it to him, even if it was the last drop. He would give you the shirt off his back."

Like many people who live in small communities, Markov seemed to have a wide variety of jobs and skills. He was a competent welder, and even fabricated a Soviet Hammer and Sickle for the local school. In addition to this and forest work, he pulled shifts at the village generator station with Danila Zaitsev, and moonlighted at the disco in the rec hall. Markov had been trained as a log sorter, truck driver, and heavy equipment operator, but these are common skills in the logging industry. What set Markov apart was his personality: he was funny and charismatic, and people liked being around him. He could always wring the humor out of mundane situations, and there are a lot of those in a place like Sobolonye.

Irina and Andrei Onofrecuk told the following story one winter afternoon over a cup of gut-wrenching tea: "One time," Andrei began, "Markiz spent the night here in our house. Our youngest son, Ivan, was very little—couldn't walk yet—and Irina brought him into the room where Markiz was sleeping . . ."

"I put Ivan down in the chair," continued Irina, "close to the bed, and Markiz's hand is hanging like this [palm up]. I gave Ivan a bit of food and said, 'Be careful, it's hot.' Well, he took a bite, and then he put the rest into Markiz's hand."

The food was hot enough that it woke him up. Without missing a beat, Markov emerged, joking, from a sound sleep. Playing on "Ivan," as in Ivan the Terrible, he exclaimed, "Oh! Father Czar himself is feeding me."

"Ivan is grown up now," Andrei explained, "but to this day he has a nickname—the Czar. It was Markiz's blessing."

Some of Markov's jokes were set-pieces and when he told them he would affect a Caucasus accent and the gender confusion that often goes with it, both of which are funny to many Russians in the same way that Southern accents combined with poor grammar are funny to many Americans. Stalin was from the Caucasus, so for Russians of a certain age this accent has a certain chilling significance.* Mocking it is one way for survivors of that era to siphon off some of the residual toxins. Included in Markov's repertoire were queries to a fictitious call-in show on Armenian Radio. Armenian Radio is an imaginary station that emerged in the Russian consciousness during the 1950s and is known throughout the former Soviet Union. Broadcasting out of the southern Caucasus, it offers free advice on topics ranging from sex to socialist doctrine. The ground rules are simple and reflect the reality of many Russians: "Ask us whatever you want, we will answer whatever we want."

One example goes like this:

> This is Armenian Radio. Our listeners asked us:
> "Is it all right to have sex in Red Square?"
> We're answering:
> "Yes. But only if you want lots of advice."

---

* After studying the files of Stalin's political prisoners, historian Roy Medvedev concluded that 200,000 people were imprisoned for telling jokes.

The Soviet regime was a popular target:

> This is Armenian Radio. Our listeners asked us:
> "Why is our government not in a hurry to land our men on the moon?"
> We're answering:
> "What if they refuse to return?"

Markov was well disposed toward this brand of humor and, in his own small "listening area," he functioned as a kind of pirate station, a one-man Sobolonye Radio.

It was due, in part, to his humor and good nature that Markov attracted the attention of the boss of the logging company, a man known to his hundreds of employees as Boris Ivanovich.* Given his combination of talents, Markov would have been good company on long trips through rough country, and this was why Boris Ivanovich hired him as his personal driver, making Markov one of very few people ever to chauffeur a limousine through tiger country. Under the circumstances, Boris had made an odd choice of vehicles: a Volga sedan. Volgas are considered luxury cars and, during Soviet times, they were usually associated with diplomats and high-ranking Party officials. Needless to say, they are a much more plausible sight on the broad boulevards of Moscow and St. Petersburg than in the backwoods of Primorye. It conjures an image that is both poignant and faintly bizarre: Markiz, the short and cheery jokester, dressed in a white shirt and trousers, conveying his well-connected communist boss in high style through the mud, dust, and snow of the Bikin valley. Given the available options, it is hard to imagine a safer occupation. It would have been hard to believe that Markov would earn the tragic distinction of being the only chauffeur in Russia—perhaps anywhere—ever to be eaten by a tiger.

---

* When addressing or referring to elders and other respected persons in Russia, it is customary to use the patronymic without the last name, e.g., "Boris Ivanovich"—literally, "Boris son of Ivan."

Markov was also registered as a professional hunter with Alufchanski, just as Lev Khomenko had been. Markov, like most hunters and trappers in the region, focused on sable, a large member of the weasel family that is to Russian fur trappers what the beaver was to their North American counterparts (Sobolonye means, literally, "Sable Place"). Alufchanski purchased furs and wild meat from local hunters and trappers at centrally established rates, thereby creating a stable and secure national market that made it possible to earn an honest living from the forest. Until very recently, the fur industry was a mainstay of the Far Eastern economy and a key supplier to the world market. Like early accounts from the United States and Canada, most folktales, histories, travelogues, and biographies from Primorye address the fur trade in one way or another. Its central role offers a graphic illustration of Primorye's quasi-colonial status as resource-rich and industry-poor: to this day, pelts gathered here are shipped 1,500 miles west to Irkutsk, Siberia, for processing, just as they were three hundred years ago. Irkutsk is located near Lake Baikal, which once marked the western boundary of the Amur tiger's range. Until about a century ago, the provincial coat of arms featured a tiger bearing a sable in its jaws.

———

In addition to being a robust singer and life of the party, Markov liked to read, and Tamara Borisova remembers a number of his favorites, including Arseniev's *Dersu the Trapper*, but there was one in particular that he couldn't seem to get enough of. Based on a true story, the book was called *The Headless Horseman: A Strange Tale of Texas*. It was first published in 1866 by the bestselling Irish-American author Captain Mayne Reid, a journalist and adventurer who also fought in the Mexican-American War. Reid's works have been largely forgotten by English readers, but they remained popular in Russia through the Brezhnev era. Theodore Roosevelt and Vladimir Arseniev were both fans, and so was Vladimir Nabokov, who, as a boy, particularly liked *The Headless Horseman*, going so far as to translate part of it into twelve-syllable alexandrine verses. Reid's prose is thick, florid, and long-winded by today's standards and, in Russian, his books run to five and six hundred pages. They combine Victorian romance with red-blooded action and have titles like *No Quarter!* and *Tracked to Death.* Another was called *The Tiger-Hunter.* Borisova couldn't explain why *The Headless Horseman* captured her husband's imagination, but she recalls him reading it at least three times. "Soon, you will know it by heart," she told him.

The 1980s were good years for Markov: the work was steady and he led what some might call a balanced life. His wife adored him. But when he was off hunting and trapping in the taiga, she worried. Sometimes, he would be gone for weeks at a time. "He would come home and tell me he had seen tiger tracks," Borisova recalled in her kitchen, next to a monolithic Russian stove made of crumbling concrete. "I would say, 'You have to be more careful out there,' and he would say, 'Why should I be afraid of her? She should be afraid of me!'"

7

Confucius was passing by Mount Tai when he saw a
distraught woman weeping by a grave. Resting his
hands on the wooden bar at the front of his carriage, he
listened to her wailing. Then, he sent a student to speak
the following words: "A great misfortune must have
befallen you, that you cry so bitterly." She answered,
"Indeed it is so. My husband and his father have both
been killed by tigers, and now my son, too, has fallen
prey to them." Confucius asked, "Why do you remain
here?" She answered, "No callous government rules
here." Confucius said, "Remember that, my students.
Callous government is more ravenous than tigers."

"The Book of Rites"

BY THE MID-1980S, THE SOVIET UNION HAD BEGUN TO UNRAVEL AS THE
gross inefficiencies of central planning began manifesting themselves in painfully obvious ways. However, the country was far too
unstable and encumbered by its own history to allow a gradual
transition toward a market economy, or the democracy such a
transition was supposed to bring about. Mikhail Gorbachev's
attempt to open the Soviet Union resembled Pandora's attempt to
open her box: there was simply no way to do it gradually. Once
that lid was cracked, it blew off altogether. In Russia's case, the
walls fell down, too. As the Communist Bloc disintegrated,
decades, generations—entire lifetimes—of frustration, discon-
tent, stifled rage, and raw ambition came boiling out, never to be

contained again. The vast majority of Russians were completely unprepared for the ensuing free-for-all.

But Armenian Radio kept up with the times:

Our listeners asked us:
"What is chaos?"
We're answering:
"We do not comment on economic policy."

"What is 'Russian business'?"
We're answering:
"To steal a crate of vodka, sell it, and drink the money away."

Many Russians blame Boris Yeltsin for "breaking everything," but he had plenty of eager assistants. In an eerie parallel to the Bolshevik Revolution seventy years earlier, a wholesale looting of the country took place as the pendulum swung to the opposite extreme. Entire industries were commandeered and privatized, and vast territories were transformed into virtual fiefdoms. While there was a halfhearted attempt to include the public by issuing shares in these new private companies, most Russians had no idea what they were and sold them immediately, often for a pittance. On Yeltsin's watch, the ignorance of many, combined with the cleverness of a few, allowed for the biggest, fastest, and most egregiously unjust reallocation of wealth and resources in the history of the world. It was klepto-capitalism on a monumental scale, but it wasn't the first time. The Bolsheviks had done something similar under Lenin.

The scale of theft following the October Revolution of 1917 was equally grand for its time, but the motives and methods were even more ruthless. During the heady and violent period following the Revolution, there was a mass pillaging of privately held lands and property. Anyone who had employees or a surplus—of anything—was branded an "enemy of the people." Thievery, vandalism, and murder were performed by the imported thugs who did much of Lenin's heavy lifting, encouraged by self-serving

Party slogans like "Rob the Robbers!"* Lenin may have preached Marx, but his methods were decidedly Machiavellian: *"It is precisely now and only now,"* he wrote, in a top secret memorandum to the Politburo during a severe famine in 1922,

> when in the starving regions people are eating human flesh, and hundreds if not thousands of corpses are littering the roads, that we can (and therefore must) carry out the confiscation of church valuables with the utmost savagery and merciless energy . . . so as to secure for ourselves a fund of several hundred million gold rubles. . . . We must teach these [clergy] a lesson right now, so that they will not dare even to think of any resistance for several decades.

Under both Lenin and Yeltsin, it was a small elite with close ties to the Kremlin who controlled these acquisitions and identified the beneficiaries. In part because of the abuses of power perpetrated during Soviet times, there is an enormous cynicism among contemporary Russian leadership that resounds like an echo from communism's earliest days. Today, it manifests as capitalism in its most primitive and rapacious form. In the chaos following the privatization cum fire sale of the Soviet Union's most valuable assets, one ambitious and well-connected young man named Roman Abramovich effectively acquired the vast Far Eastern autonomous region of Chukotka, along with its staggeringly lucrative oilfields. By the time he was thirty, Abramovich had become one of the richest men in the world, which he remains to this day (he resigned as governor in 2008). But he is only one example. In 2008, nineteen of the world's one hundred richest people were Russians. This statistic is all the more remarkable when you consider that most major fortunes are either inherited or built systematically, over the course of a lifetime. Russia's oli-

---

* In November 1918, at the height of the looting, six members of Arseniev's family, including his father, were murdered for their property by local peasants.

garchs, on the other hand, became multibillionaires virtually overnight, many while still in their thirties.

———

Throughout the early 1990s, state-owned companies collapsed and shriveled, one after another, like deflating balloons, and among them was the company that was Sobolonye's sole reason for being. An elderly huntress and former tree faller who now goes by the name of Baba Liuda summed up her community's rise and fall: "We came in 1979, and everything was new and beautiful; the roads were good; the loggers were taking trees out day and night. Life was good to us. Then, perestroika came and everything was 'reorganized.' Who needs Sobolonye now? Nobody does."

The Middle Bikin National Forest Enterprise died a slower death than most, first pulling out of Sobolonye around 1992, and then out of its sister village, Yasenovie. By 1994, the operation had retreated to Verkhny Pereval, where it shut down altogether, leaving the residents of Sobolonye with two stark choices: they could abandon their homes and social network on the off chance they would find something better elsewhere (an unlikely prospect in mid-1990s Russia). Or they could stay and live off the land in defiance of a system of laws that seems strategically designed to punish the poor.

At this point, Markov was in his early forties; he had spent more than half his adult life in Sobolonye and he had made some good friends there. He had also made some serious commitments. Because of this, and because the forest offered him and his neighbors a measure of security that nothing else in Russia could match, he decided to stay, along with about 250 others. What emerged over the next fifteen years was a kind of feral community, left largely to its own devices. In this sense, Sobolonye offers a foretaste of a postindustrial world.

By 1997, the village of Sobolonye, then only twenty-five years old, was already falling into ruin. Though still inhabited, it had the feel of a ghost town, a place where the boom had busted and the life drained out, leaving the survivors to struggle on in a desolate, man-made limbo. By then, the rec center had burned down, along with a number of houses, including Markov's. The family moved to another house, but very little had survived the fire. As if in response to the prevailing spirit of decay, the two-story brick building that housed the diesel generator began crumbling in on itself. And yet the generator continued to rumble away inside, like a stubborn heart in the dying body of the village. Danila Zaitsev and a few others, including Markov, took shifts, sleeping next to it in a decrepit trailer, nursing it along.

Sobolonye has, like Chernobyl, become a kind of accidental monument to a Russian catastrophe, only nobody outside the Bikin valley has ever heard of it. Though it was hailed as a positive development in the West, few Westerners fully grasp the toll perestroika took and continues to take on the country. Among Russians, it has since earned the ignominious nickname "Katastroika." Proof of this abounds in Sobolonye, a place where civilization as most of us understand it has effectively collapsed. The status quo of dysfunction here was summed up by the local postman, who traveled his hairy, backcountry route in a government van decorated with tassels, fringe, and an inverted American flag. After stopping in at Sobolonye's administrative offices one winter day in 2007, he returned to his vehicle shaking his head. "There's no government here," he said. "It's anarchy!"

To get an idea of day-to-day village life, one need look no further than Grigori Peshkov, the local gas merchant, a man who supplements his meager income by wading through thigh-deep snow in subzero temperatures to search for pinecones. The Chinese, whose voracious appetite for natural resources is keenly felt in this part of Russia, prize the wood of the Korean pine, and they consider the nuts a delicacy. Peshkov can get 30 rubles (about one dollar) for every pound of cones he finds buried beneath the snow. If he takes the time to remove the individual nuts, he might—if he's lucky—make 100 rubles per pound. One could argue that this is an activity better suited to a pig or a squirrel, and one would be right, but, as a young Nanai woman from a neighboring village observed, "People don't live in Sobolonye, they survive."

Sometimes, they don't even manage to do that.

Under these circumstances, Markov's humor became a precious commodity and, for many who knew him, he was a rare bright spot in an otherwise bleak situation. Incidental humor of the kind Markov specialized in tends to defy translation, having less to do with a punch line than it does with what one might call situational alchemy. It is one of the keys to surviving in Russia, where random insults and deprivations seem to occur more often than other places, and where the sum of these can break a person. Once, on a long bus trip through Primorye, a young man named Gena gestured to the bottle of vodka he had brought along and proclaimed, "It's not vodka; it's a time machine!" Humor plays a similar role: not only does it speed the journey, it softens the thousand small blows of daily Russian life. On a regular basis, Markov was able to defy the gravity of a given moment and transform yet another broken thing or stalled project into a brief interlude of absurdist escape. "Somehow his tongue worked like that," recalled his young neighbor, Denis Burukhin. "No matter what the subject was, he always found the joke in it."

Indeed, there was little else; the supply chain providing most basic goods had broken down so completely that remote villages like Sobolonye were turned into virtual islands. Making matters worse was the inflation rate, which, by 1993, was approaching 1,000 percent, rendering the ruble virtually worthless. In subsequent years, it settled down somewhat, but only in relative terms; throughout the mid-1990s, Russians were seeing annual price increases of 200 and 300 percent. Then, in 1997, the Russian ruble went into free fall, much as the deutsche mark had done prior to World War II. A ruble, which, a decade earlier, could have bought a pack of cigarettes, five ice cream cones, or a cafeteria lunch for two, was now worth about one one-hundredth of a U.S. cent and could not cover the price of a nail. On January 1, 1998, a month after Markov's death, Russia's currency was "revised" with the introduction of the so-called new ruble. While this radical measure stabilized the currency and brought the exchange rate back onto a recognizable scale, it wiped out whatever remained of most people's savings. When one considers that this was the seventh time in a century such a revision had been made, it is easy to understand why so many Russians seem cynical and world-weary, and why they place so much faith in the potato crop.

For the residents of Sobolonye and their sister village, Yasenovie, these changes made little difference. Assuming you had something to put it in, finding gas could still be a days-long project; finding the money to pay for it could take even longer. Currency remained a part of their economy, but it was not the principal medium through which basic needs were met. That distinction fell to the forest—the off-grid benefactor of last resort that Markov's friend Sasha Dvornik and many of its other dependents refer to as Taiga Matushka: Mother Taiga.

When Russians wax eloquent about their homeland, they will often invoke Mother Russia, but Mother Russia is not the nation, and She is certainly not the leadership; She is the Land. The deep Russian bond to the earth—specifically, the soil—transcends all other affiliations with the exception, perhaps, of family. Likewise, the forest and its creatures—plant and animal alike—have a significance that most of us in the West lost touch with generations ago. It is a connection—a dependence, really—that exists in stark contrast to the State's willful, capricious, and alarmingly comprehensive destruction of the environment. Come May 15 or so, the vast majority of Russians—regardless of where they live or what they do—stop and interact with the land more intensely, and with more devotion and genuine understanding than most Westerners, who may perceive themselves as environmentally aware, could ever hope to. May is potato planting time in Russia, and just about everybody participates. It's a tradition, it's a ritual, and it's how you make it through the winter in a country where winter seems to last forever and salaries are inadequate, when they are paid at all. Armenian Radio has addressed this issue, too:

> Our listeners asked us:
> "Is it possible to make ends meet on salary alone?"
> We're answering:
> "We don't know, we never tried."

———

Before the Revolution, the czar was often referred to as the "Little Father" (the "Big Father," of course, being God). This notion of a supreme (human) being who unifies, protects, and guides the country is a theme that dates back to Ivan the Terrible, the first "Czar of all Russia," a savage and canny expansionist who set the tone for the next five centuries of Russian rule. Today, the tradition is alive and well: Vladimir Putin has been described as a "Good Czar" and a "Strong Man for Russia," just as "Iron Joe" Stalin was in the 1930s. This is considered a good thing, especially if you believe your country—as many Russians do—to be a glorious but underappreciated stepchild of the First World surrounded by enemies. It is one of the principal reasons Putin enjoys such wide popularity, even in the neglected hinterlands of Primorye, and why Stalin is still admired by millions of Russians. The Russian State, in other words, is masculine and paternalistic. But the State, in addition to being secretive, xenophobic, and heavily armed, is also fallible, shortsighted, and prone to betrayal. In fact, over the past century, broken faith has become something of a national characteristic. It is no coincidence that, in Russia, the divorce rate is one of the highest in the world, and single mothers (both literal and practical) are nearly as common as children. Fathers get drunk, have affairs, take off, die young, or simply give up—for all kinds of reasons. When this happens, and there is no extended family to rely on, there are only a couple of options left, besides an orphanage: struggle on with the mother, or brave a risky existence on the street. The taiga offers a combination of the two.

After the logging company closed down and the State abandoned them, the working people of the Bikin valley fell into the tough but bountiful arms of Mother Taiga, but they did so in a way that was technically illegal and often dangerous. More often than not, homemade vodka and homemade bullets went hand in hand. A corollary to this brand of betrayal and abandonment is an intensified, overdetermined relationship between mothers and their children, particularly between mothers and only (surviving) sons (Joseph Stalin being but one example). The same held true for Mother Taiga and her desperate boys.

———

By 1997, Sobolonye had become a profoundly unhealthy place to be: morale in the village plummeted and alcoholism, already a kind of cultural norm, became rampant. Things began to break and burn, and people began to die—in all kinds of ways. Today, three of the huntress Baba Liuda's five children lie in the village graveyard. "I can't call it life anymore," she said. "It's just an existence."

Under these circumstances, time, as most of us know it, begins to blur into irrelevance. Replacing it in Sobolonye was a far more approximate chronology that could be called subsistence time: when you're broke and disconnected and living in the woods, the steady pronouncements of clocks and calendars no longer carry the same weight. Maybe, if you're lucky, the arrival of a meager pension check will give some structure to the month, but if some or all of this money is invested in vodka, it will only serve to blur time further. As a result, subsistence time includes periods of suspended animation combined with seasonal opportunities determined by the natural cycles of fish, game, bees, and pinecones. These, in turn, may be punctuated by potato planting and the occasional stint on a logging or road building crew. It's a kind of ancient schedule that is all but unrecognizable to many of us, despite the fact that millions of people live this way all over the world.

Markov did his best to dodge the depression and inertia that stalked so many of his neighbors, and one way he did this was by spending more and more time in the taiga. "He was a good man," recalled his neighbor Irina Peshkova. "He knew everything in the forest—everything. He could find any root. He even saved some bear cubs once."

"He was always running around doing something," said Denis Burukhin. "One cannot afford to be lazy in the forest: you need firewood; you need water. You have to be checking your traps and your nets, hunting for meat—you have to be hustling all the time."

Perhaps recognizing the need for some kind of objective order and discipline, Markov kept an alarm clock in his cabin. But the longer one spends in the elemental and self-directed world of the taiga, the harder it can be to put up with the demands of a domestic routine. By the time Trush ran into him and confiscated his gun, Markov's preference had clearly shifted away from village life. During a brief visit home, a Nanai hunter named Vasily Dunkai summed up the tayozhnik's dilemma: "The taiga is my home," he said. "When I come back to my house, I feel like a guest. That's how most hunters feel. I've been home for a week now, and I am sick and tired of it."

Vasily Solkin, a fifty-year-old filmmaker, magazine editor, and leopard specialist, is also an experienced hunter and a friend of Dunkai's. Like him, he has spent months on his own in the taiga. Originally trained as a war journalist and propagandist with the Pacific Fleet, Solkin resigned from the Party in the late 1980s and became a dissident folksinger. He is a restless whip of a man with long hair and a full beard who comes to work at the Far Eastern Institute of Geography, outside Vladivostok, wearing jeans, vest, and cowboy boots. Solkin's unique combination of education and experience has enabled him to articulate the tayozhnik mind-set better than most, and he was sympathetic to Markov's situation. "The most terrifying and important test for a human being is to be in absolute isolation," he explained. "A human being is a very social creature, and ninety percent of what he does is done only because other people are watching. Alone, with no witnesses, he starts to learn about himself—who is he really? Sometimes, this brings staggering discoveries. Because nobody's watching, you can easily become an animal: it is not necessary to shave, or to wash, or to keep your winter quarters clean—you can live in shit and no one will see. You can shoot tigers, or choose not to shoot. You can run in fear and nobody will know. You have to have something— some force, which allows and helps you to survive without witnesses. Markov had it.

"Once you have passed the solitude test," continued Solkin, "you have absolute confidence in yourself, and there is nothing that can break you afterward. Any changes, including changes in the political system, are not going to affect you as much because you know that *you can do it yourself.* Karl Marx said that 'Freedom is a recognized necessity.'* I learned this in university, but I didn't understand what it meant until I'd spent some time in the taiga. If you understand it, you will survive in the taiga. If you think that freedom is anarchy, you will not survive.

"It becomes like a drug," he said, "you have to have it. So, it's a strange feeling when you come back [to civilization] because, in the taiga, the most important things are your bullets. But as soon as you get to the main road and see the bus coming, you understand that those bullets don't mean anything in this other life. All of a sudden, you need money—strange paper, which you couldn't even use to start a fire, and your bullets aren't going to help you. This transition can be very difficult."

On a shelf in Solkin's office are several cat skulls, including one belonging to a tiger. It is only when you study it closely that you see the bullet holes, and it is clear from their placement that the tiger was shot head-on at close range. "Poachers can be brave, too," said Solkin.

———

Outside of Primorye's nature preserves, the Bikin valley is one of the wildest places left in the territory and Markov had come to know it well. In previous years, he had hunted and kept bees further upriver in Ulma, a tiny settlement accessible only by boat or snowmobile. Between his local explorations and seasonal migrations, Markov had gained a comprehensive knowledge of the region and its loosely scattered inhabitants. His charm worked to his advantage here, too: he befriended a reclusive hunter named Ivan Dunkai (Vasily Dunkai's father) who gave him permission to hunt in his territory. This is when Markov's gyre began to tighten.

In the taiga, to this day, there are small but well-developed industries and markets for many kinds of forest products ranging

* This quote, often attributed to Marx, is Engels's paraphrasing of Hegel: "The truth of Necessity, therefore, is Freedom."

from honey and nuts to mushrooms and medicinal roots. In Primorye, the collection of ginseng, laminaria (a species of edible kelp), and trepang (sea cucumber) were, along with fur trapping and gold mining, among the region's founding industries and still remain profitable. Until the 1970s, opium poppies were cultivated openly in some villages and they are still grown, though, as with more recent marijuana plantations, greater efforts are now made to conceal them.

Before Markov acquired his portable barracks, his friend Danila Zaitsev had used it as a remote plant for processing fir needle oil, a multipurpose folk remedy rumored to be effective on everything from coughs to rheumatism. After perestroika, the niche market for fir oil collapsed, and the project was abandoned. With Zaitsev's help, Markov moved the caravan into the sunny clearing where it now stood, ringed by tiger tracks. In addition to being his new hunting base, he and Zaitsev ran a honey operation from there, consisting of about forty hives. On the side, they brewed *medovukha,* a honey-based drink comparable to mead. Apparently, Markov had a gift. "He liked bees," recalled his son, Alexei, who shares his father's stature, eyes, and cheekbones, "and they liked him. He would go to the hives without his shirt. He wasn't afraid." So at ease was Markov that the bees would cluster about his half-naked body, stinging him only occasionally.

It was from these hunting grounds that Markov started poaching game in earnest. His guns, of course, were unregistered, his bullets homemade. He was desperately poor. When he managed to bag a deer or a boar, he would often barter the meat for essentials like sugar, tobacco, gunpowder, and tea. (This, incidentally, is exactly how Dersu Uzala was making his living when Arseniev first encountered him in 1906.) It was the taiga, and the creatures it contains, that kept him and his family alive. But by 1997, this hand-to-mouth existence was taking its toll. A heavy smoker, Markov was approaching fifty in a country where the average life expectancy for men was only fifty-eight. For his demographic, it was even lower than that. When Yuri Trush encountered him the previous year, he recalled being struck by the unhealthiness he saw in Markov's eyes: they were badly bloodshot and had a yellow cast to them. Trush couldn't tell if this was the result of a recent drinking binge, or something more serious, but Markov had other problems as well: ever since taking a bad fall on his hunting skis several years earlier, he had acquired a permanent limp. No longer able to cover the ground or carry the weight he once could, something had to change, but without money—a lot of it by Sobolonye standards—there was no way to leverage himself out of his situation.

Many people reach a point where they realize that the shape their life has taken does not square with the ambitions they once had for it. In Russia, there are entire generations for whom this is the case. Since 1989, though, a whole new frontier of opportunity has opened up, much of it on the black market. Oil, timber, humans, and tigers all have their niche here, and the line between politicians and mafia, and between legitimate business and crime, has blurred almost beyond recognition. This is the Wild East, and business is booming. You can see the affluence enjoyed by these "New Russians" parading down Aleutskaya and Svetlanskaya streets along Vladivostok's Golden Horn: leggy women in spike-heeled boots, barely visible beneath sumptuous, ankle-length coats of sable and mink, their carefully made-up faces hidden in voluminous cowls; the men in sharp European suits, speeding by in fleets of right-hand-drive Toyota Land Cruisers fresh off the boat from Japan.

Markov didn't witness this explosion of wealth firsthand, but he certainly heard about it and saw it on television, and he already knew what it felt like to drive a fine car. There are a lot of people in Primorye who cook with wood and draw water from community wells who wonder how they might get a piece of this new and glamorous pie. Some of them believe the answer lies in making what, in urban terms, might be called a big score. In the forest, there is really only one thing that qualifies, and that is a tiger. After a game warden named Yevgeny Voropaev was ordered to shoot an aggressive tiger on the outskirts of Vladivostok, he was approached by a Russian gang member. "He made an offer to me," Voropaev said. "Fifty thousand American dollars for the whole tiger—meat and skin and all."

He let that number sink in.

"Fifty thousand dollars if I got it to the border."

Markov had heard these stories, too, and, while they may have been part fact and part urban myth, it was well known that the Chinese had strange appetites, and some of them had lots of money. They also had ready access to the Bikin, which flows directly to the Chinese frontier. For someone as broke and isolated as Markov, even a fraction of this kind of money would represent a spectacular payoff, but it was a payoff that would come with a unique set of complications and liabilities—kind of like selling a briefcaseful of stolen cocaine.

8

How with this rage shall beauty hold a plea?

SHAKESPEARE,
Sonnet 65

IT IS GENERALLY UNDERSTOOD THAT THE ANIMAL WE RECOGNIZE AS A tiger has been with us at least since the Pleistocene Epoch (1.8 million to 10,000 years BCE). The oldest definitively identified tiger fossils date to roughly two million years ago and were found in China, which is where many scientists believe the species first evolved and then disseminated itself across Asia. The tiger's historic range was vast, spanning 100 degrees of longitude and 70 degrees of latitude, and including virtually all of Asia with deep inroads into Siberia and the Middle East. Five hundred years ago, large predators that were almost certainly tigers were reported in the Volga and Dnieper river valleys, just a few days' travel from Kiev, Ukraine.

Fossil evidence of tigers has also been found further north and east, in Japan and on the Russian side of the Bering Strait, and it raises the question: why didn't this skillful and adaptable predator simply keep going? The mixed broadleaf and conifer forests of the Ussuri valley share a lot in common with historic European and American forests; it is unnerving to imagine a tiger at home in such a landscape because it implies that tigers could have infiltrated Europe and the New World. Given time and opportunity, tigers could—in theory—have emerged from Asia to rule every forest from the Bosphorus Strait to the English Channel, and from the Yukon to the Amazon. But for some reason, they didn't. Why they failed to colonize the Americas is a mystery: something about that northern land bridge—Too cold? Not enough cover to stage an ambush?—barred their way. Perhaps it was the cave lions that stopped them.

Life in the higher latitudes has always been precarious and, by some estimates, the Russian Far East has never supported more than a thousand tigers. Due to the extreme climate and its impact on prey density, large mammals, in general, are more sparsely distributed in the taiga than in the tropics. As a result, Amur tigers must occupy far larger territories than other subspecies in order to meet their needs for prey. In Primorye, these territories can be so large that, after trying to follow several tigers on their winter rounds, a pioneering tiger researcher named Lev Kaplanov speculated in the early 1940s that Amur tigers were simply wanderers. "The entire winter life of a solitary tiger takes place as a sequence of long journeys," wrote Kaplanov, the Amur tiger's most famous early advocate. "The tiger is a born nomad."

The tiger was first classified as a distinct species of cat in 1758. The subspecies known variously as the Korean, Manchurian, Siberian, Ussuri, Woolly, or Amur tiger was first designated *Felis tigris altaica* in 1844. Since then, the taxonomic scent tree has been marked and marked again, to the point that this subspecies has been *re*classified seven times. The last man to stake his claim was Nikolai Baikov, a lifetime member of the Society for Study of the Manchurian Territory, and of the Russian Academy of Sciences. In his monograph "The Manchurian Tiger," Baikov begins by paying homage to the explorer Vladimir Arseniev and to the novelist Mayne Reid (*The Headless Horseman*, etc.). He then proceeds to go out on a limb that both of those brave romantics would have appreciated: in Baikov's opinion, the creature he reclassified as *Felis tigris mandshurica* was no ordinary tiger but a living fossil—a throwback to the Pliocene worthy of designation as a distinct species. "Its massive body and powerful skeletal system are reminiscent of something ancient and obsolete," wrote Baikov in 1925. "The Far East representative of the giant cat is . . . extremely close, both in its anatomical structure, and in its way of

life, to the fossil cave tiger, *Machairodus,* a contemporary of the
cave bear and the wooly mammoth."

Baikov supported his claim with detailed drawings comparing
the skulls of these two animals, which, based on his rendering, do
bear a strong resemblance. *Machairodus* was a genus of large
saber-toothed cat, which lived between two and fifteen million
years ago and overlapped with our protohuman ancestors. Specimens have been found all over the world. This thrilling if mis-
guided notion of a feline missing link surviving in the mountain
fastness of Manchuria caused a stir among museums and zoos of
the period and helped drive the market for live specimens. Baikov
did his best to promote this view, and, to some extent, his efforts
are still bearing fruit (and sowing confusion) to this day.

Even now, it is taken as a given that the Amur tiger is the
biggest cat of them all and, based on samplings of numerous tiger
skulls from all over Asia, the measurements bear this out. Viewed
on a graph, the Amur skulls show up as outliers, occupying a territory all their own. Seen in this context, it is easier to understand
the impulse to classify them as a separate species. The fact that
they seem to thrive in conditions that would kill most other tigers
is another reason, and it is here that size and climate have con-
spired to give the impression of an Ice Age throwback. Much has
been made of the Amur tiger's massive size by Baikov and others,
and extraordinary dimensions have been claimed: lengths up to
sixteen feet and weights up to nine hundred pounds have been
quoted in reputable publications. It reveals more about us than it
does about these animals that we wish them to be larger than life,
but anyone who has been close to an Amur tiger will tell you that
these creatures need no embellishment; they are big enough as is.
The snarling specimen in the American Museum of Natural History's Hall of Biodiversity is nearly the same size as the polar bear
in the adjacent Hall of Ocean Life.

One reason Amur tigers grew so big in the popular mind is
that, when Baikov and his contemporaries were describing them,
there were many more to choose from, and among this larger population there certainly would have been some huge individuals.
But there is also a lot of extra footage to be found in a tiger's tail,

which can comprise a third of the total length, and a further 10 percent (or more) can be gained by staking out a fresh, wet hide. In 1834, the *Bengal Sporting Magazine* described this technique in a how-to article that, had it been written today, could have been titled: "Turn Your Ten-Footer into a Twelve-Footer!" Such practices, combined with the trophy-hunting mind-set, the exotic locale, and a dearth of reliable recording equipment, created fertile ground for mythmaking. But when all is said and done, the record breakers, like so many of the best stories, always seem to come secondhand.

In spite of this, sincere attempts were made to fix these cats in real space. Ford Barclay, writing in *The Big Game of Asia and North America* (1915), the last in a deluxe four-volume compendium of hunting information from around the world, estimated the length of a tiger shot in the Vladivostok area to be thirteen feet, five inches, nose to tail. Barclay also interviewed the famous British taxidermist and author Rowland Ward, who assured him that a skin sold in London, also from that area, "must have belonged to an animal that measured 14 feet." That is roughly the length of a compact car. If this is accurate, it would make the Amur tiger the longest (if not the heaviest) carnivorous land mammal that ever lived. Ward, a conscientious and detail-oriented man, wrote *The Sportsman's Handbook to Practical Collecting and Preserving Trophies*, which went through a dozen editions between 1880 and 1925, the peak years of big game hunting. Ward saw and stuffed scores of tigers throughout his long career, and his size estimate should be judged accordingly. However, if such behemoths once roamed the boreal jungles of the Far East, they do so no longer. Baikov and Barclay, both hunters themselves, were making their audacious claims when tiger hunting was a cresting wave, about to break forever.

———

Tigers, it must be said, have taken a ferocious toll on humans as well. In India, some legendary man-eaters killed and ate scores of people before being hunted down. A number of these cases have been documented by the famous tiger hunter and conservationist Jim Corbett. It would be impossible to accurately tally the tiger's collective impact on humans through history, but one scholar estimated that tigers have killed approximately a million Asians over the last four hundred years. The majority of these deaths occurred in India, but heavy losses were suffered across East Asia.

Throughout Korea, Manchuria, and southeast China, tigers were considered both sacred and a scourge. Until around 1930, tigers continued to pose such a risk that, in North Korea, the bulk of offerings made to some Buddhist shrines were prayers for protection from these animals. Nonetheless, tigers were held in high esteem in part because it was believed that they, too, made offerings to heaven. In the tigers' case, these gifts took the form of the severed heads of their prey, a determination made, presumably, by the beheaded state of many tiger kills. Ordinary people were reluctant to retaliate against a predatory tiger for fear it would take offense, not to mention revenge, and so their day-to-day lives were shaped—and sometimes tyrannized—by efforts to at once avoid and propitiate these marauding gods.

According to Dale Miquelle, the American tiger researcher, the relatively low incidence of tiger attacks in Russia as compared to Korea at the turn of the last century, or in the Sundarbans today, is due to learning: "When the majority of people have no means of defense (i.e., firearms) tigers figure that out and include them on the list of potential prey," he explained. "However, where you have a heavily armed populace (e.g., Russia) tigers also figure that out and 'take people off the list.' The implication is that you have to teach tigers that people are dangerous. I think this holds for most large carnivores."

This logic holds up in many places, but in Primorye, the Udeghe and Nanai experience apparently defies it. Despite the fact that they made their home in a landscape regularly patrolled by tigers, there is no record—anecdotal or otherwise—of tiger attacks on a scale with their Chinese and Korean neighbors. Further south, along the China coast, tiger attacks and man-eating were common, and this combination of hazard and reverence made for some strange cultural collisions. In 1899, a tiger hunting missionary named Harry Caldwell relocated to Fujian province from the mountains of east Tennessee. Caldwell, a Methodist, soon realized that tigers were not only present and plentiful but that they were eating his converts. And yet, much to his dismay, his parishioners seemed to venerate these beasts almost as if they were sacred cows. Armed with a carbine and the 117th Psalm, Caldwell began shooting every tiger he saw, only to find that the large striped cats he and his coolies brought out of the hills were greeted with skepticism. Elders in his village claimed they lacked certain tigerish attributes, but the subtext seemed to be that if this foreign devil had been able to kill them then they couldn't possibly be real tigers. "Father's first two kills were immediately discredited on this score," wrote his son, John, in his memoir, *China Coast Family.* "The sages announced to the assembled crowds that these were not tigers at all, but some other evil animal masquerading in tigers' guise.

"According to the wisdom of the sages, the Chinese character [Wang: 王] meaning 'Lord' or 'Emperor' must be found in the markings of the forehead of a tiger if it be a tiger of whom the devils and demons are afraid. Another of Father's early kills, a magnificent male of which he was very proud, [was also] disqualified. . . . They announced that the animal could never have been born of tiger parents, but had come out of some strange metamorphosis from an animal or fish living in the sea."

Up north, Manchu peasants endowed the tiger with similarly elusive and ineffable qualities, as did the Udeghe and Nanai, who would sometimes go so far as to abandon a village site if tigers were active in the area (which may help explain the rarity of attacks). But in Korea, when the Buddha, luck, and shamans all failed, there was still one place left to turn, and that was to the Tiger Hunters Guild. Long before the Russians started hunting tigers in the Far East, members of the Tiger Hunters Guild had made a name for themselves as the boldest hunter-warriors in Northeast Asia, and their feats of daring are legendary. The so-called guild, a military organization that came into being during the late Joseon Dynasty (1392–1897), included both hunters and professional soldiers. In addition to their other feats, they are credited with repelling attacks by French and American forces in 1866 and 1871, respectively. The Koreans were much admired by the Western hunters who encountered them, in large part because they were still using matchlock rifles and pistols. Based on designs dating from the fourteenth century, these medieval Chinese weapons depended on a fuse to light the gunpowder, which allowed for only a single shot at suicidally close range. As one historian put it, "Those who missed . . . rarely lived to regret it."

When they weren't defending their king, members of the guild pursued man-eaters and other troublesome tigers and leopards. Their devotion to the practice was almost cultlike, one of their prime objectives being to acquire a cat's potency and courage through the act of killing and consuming it (though, when they could, they sold body parts to the Chinese as well). Yuri Yankovsky, a famous Russian tiger hunter, reportedly witnessed one of these rituals sometime around 1930: "Before long we came upon a startling scene. A Korean wearing the conical blue felt hat of the Tiger Hunters' Guild was leaning against a tree, holding in his hand an old-fashioned matchlock. . . . [Another] was kneeling on the ground, drinking blood from a bowl which he held against the throat of a dead tiger."*

This notion of self-enhancement by consumption cut both ways, however, and it was believed that a tiger could also make itself stronger by devouring both body and soul of a human being. Once consumed, the victim's soul would become a kind of captive guide, aiding the tiger in its search for more human victims. As fanciful as such reasoning may sound, there is no question that the strength and knowledge gained from eating humans will inform and influence a man-eater's subsequent behavior.

* Apparently, this is a timeless impulse: in the U.S. National Archives is a photograph of Marine Sergeant M. L. Larkins presenting the heart of an Indochinese tiger he has just killed to his commanding officer, Lieutenant Colonel W. C. Drumwright, May 25, 1970.

———

Relatively speaking, the tigers' appetite for us pales before our appetite for them. Humans have hunted tigers by various means for millennia, but not long ago there was a strange and heated moment in our venerable relationship with these animals that has been echoed repeatedly in our relations with other species. It bears some resemblance to what wolves do when they get into a sheep pen: they slaughter simply because they can and, in the case of humans, until a profit can no longer be turned. For the sea otter, this moment occurred between 1790 and 1830; for the American bison, it happened between 1850 and 1880; for the Atlantic cod, it lasted for centuries, ending only in 1990. These mass slaughters have their analogue in the financial markets to which they are often tied, and they end the same way every time. The Canadian poet Eric Miller summed up the mind-set driving these binges better than just about anyone:

> *A cornucopia!*
> *Bliss of killing without ever seeming to subtract*
> *   from the tasty sum of infinity!*

But infinity is a man-made construct that has no relevance in the natural world. In nature, everything is finite, especially carnivores. The order *Carnivora* (meat-eating mammals) represents approximately 10 percent of all mammal species, but only 2 percent of the total mammalian biomass. Apex predators like big cats represent a tiny fraction of this already small percentage and, between 1860 and 1960, big game hunters made it smaller still. In December of 1911, the freshly crowned King George V went on an elephant-borne *shikar* to Nepal, during which he and his retinue killed thirty-nine tigers in ten days. But they were amateurs compared to Colonel Geoffrey Nightingale, who, prior to his sudden death while attempting to spear a panther from horseback, shot more than three hundred tigers in India's former Hyderabad state. The Maharaja of Udaipur claimed to have shot "at least" a thousand tigers by 1959. In a letter to the biologist George Schaller, the

Maharaja of Surguja wrote: "My total bag of Tigers is 1150 (one thousand one hundred fifty only)."

————

When Russians like the Yankovskys went hunting for tigers at the turn of the last century, they would plan to be away for weeks at a time, covering ten to twenty miles a day through mountainous country. In Russia, at least as far back as the late nineteenth century, four men have been considered the minimum for a tiger hunting expedition. The same went for tiger *catching*, a seemingly lunatic enterprise, which fell out of favor only in the early 1990s. Tiger catchers, equipped with little more than hunting dogs, tree branches, and rope, would track down and capture live Amur tigers, usually for zoos and circuses. For obvious reasons, they preferred to go after cubs, but full-grown tigers have also been caught this way. Needless to say, these men were largely self-taught, and the learning curve would have been unforgiving in the extreme. Their courage inspired one tiger biologist to write, "No, the *bogatyri* [mythic Russian heroes] have not died out in Russia."

One of the last and most famous of the tiger catchers was Vladimir Kruglov, who learned the trade from an Old Believer named Averian Cherepanov. Cherepanov's method capitalized on one of the tiger's greatest weaknesses: its low endurance at speed. A tiger can walk for days, but it can only run for short distances. For this reason, tiger catching was always done in the winter, preferably in deep snow, which shortened the chase dramatically. Once the dogs scented a tiger, they would be set loose to chase it until, too tired to run further, the animal would turn and fight. With the dogs holding the tiger at bay, the men would approach with long, forked tree branches and—somehow—pin the animal down. Then, in a quick and carefully choreographed operation, they would immobilize the tiger's paws and head, hog-tie it, and stuff it in a sack. This, of course, is easier said than done. Nonetheless, in 1978, Kruglov used the stick and rope method to—literally—bag a tigress weighing more than three hundred pounds. He is one of the only human beings in the history of the species to grab wild tigers by the ears repeatedly and live to tell about it. "I

have never let anyone else handle the ears," he explained to Dale Miquelle in 2001. "You know, the ears are her steering wheel. You can turn off her teeth with the ears."

Kruglov died in a freak accident in 2005. After surviving more than forty live tiger captures, not to mention the gauntlet of other hazards that take Russian men before their time, Kruglov was killed at the age of sixty-four when a tree fell on him. His legacy lives on in the form of the thirteen-thousand-acre Utyos Rehabilitation Center for Wild Animals in southern Khabarovsk Territory, which he founded in 1996, and which is now managed by his son and daughter. Few foreigners have attempted to bag live game in the Far East—for good reason—but a British explorer and sinophile named Arthur de Carle Sowerby recounted the following live capture in his five-volume opus, *The Naturalist in Manchuria* (1922): "When I got it it was in a paroxysm of rage, snapping furiously, biting itself and everything that came within reach of its sharp teeth," he wrote without a trace of irony. "I have always found this the case with moles."

———

In 1925, Nikolai Baikov calculated that roughly a hundred tigers were being taken out of greater Manchuria annually (including Primorye and the Korean Peninsula)—virtually all of them bound for the Chinese market. "There were cases in [mating season]," he wrote, "when a courageous hunter would meet a group of five or six tigers, and kill them one by one, where he stood."

Between trophy hunters, tiger catchers, gun traps, pit traps, snares, and bait laced with strychnine and bite-sensitive bombs, these animals were being besieged from all sides. Even as Baikov's monograph was going to press, his "Manchurian Tiger" was in imminent danger of joining the woolly mammoth and the cave bear in the past tense. Midway through the 1930s, a handful of men saw this coming, and began to wonder just what it was they stood to lose.

One of them was Lev Kaplanov. Born in Moscow in 1910, he was a generation younger than Arseniev, but cut from similar

cloth. In a letter to a close friend, Kaplanov wrote that, as a boy in European Russia, he had dreamed of hunting a tiger one day, but when he found his calling in the Far East, he realized that blood-less pursuit, though less exciting, would be of greater benefit to tigers and to science. This was an unusual way to be thinking in the 1930s, when tiger research consisted solely of what might best be described as "gunbarrel zoology." With the exception of the pioneering wildlife photographer (and former tiger hunter) Frederick Champion, Kaplanov was the first person ever to write an account of tracking tigers with no intention of killing them once he found them. This was, in its way, a truly radical act—all the more so because it occurred in a remote corner of a traumatized country with restricted access to the outside world. While the notion of conservation and national parks was not new, the idea of focusing specifically on a nongame species, and a dangerous one at that, was unheard of. But Kaplanov could not have done it without the counsel and support of Konstantin Abramov, the founding director of Primorye's largest biosphere reserve, the Sikhote-Alin Zapovednik ("forbidden zone"), and Yuri Salmin, a gifted zoologist and zapovednik cofounder.

There is a famous quote: "You can't understand Russia with your mind," and the zapovednik is a case in point. In spite of the contemptuous attitude the Soviets had toward nature, they also allowed for some of the most stringent conservation practices in the world. A zapovednik is a wildlife refuge into which no one but guards and scientists are allowed—period. The only exceptions are guests—typically fellow scientists—with written permission from the zapovednik's director. There are scores of these reserves scattered across Russia, ranging in size from more than sixteen thousand square miles down to a dozen square miles. The Sikhote-Alin Zapovednik was established in 1935 to promote the restoration of the sable population, which had nearly been wiped out in the Kremlin's eagerness to capitalize on the formerly booming U.S. fur market. Since then, the role of this and other zapovedniks has expanded to include the preservation of noncommercial animals and plants.

This holistic approach to conservation has coexisted in the Russian scientific consciousness alongside more utilitarian views of nature since it was first imported from the West in the 1860s. At its root is a deceptively simple idea: don't just preserve the species, preserve the entire system in which the species occurs, and do so by sealing it off from human interference and allowing nature to do its work. It is, essentially, a federal policy of enforced *non*-management directly contradicting the communist notion that nature is an outmoded machine in need of a total overhaul. Paradoxically, the idea not only survived but, in some cases, flourished under the Soviets: by the late 1970s, nearly 80 percent of the zapovednik sites originally recommended by the Russian Geographical Society's permanent conservation commission in 1917 had been protected (though many have been reduced in size over the years).

In Kaplanov's day, the Sikhote-Alin Zapovednik covered about seven thousand square miles* of pristine temperate forest—the heart of Primorye. That there were tigers in there at all became evident only when guards and scientists noticed their tracks while trying to assess more commercially relevant populations of sable and deer. It was here that Abramov, Salmin, and Kaplanov conceived and conducted the first systematic tiger census ever undertaken anywhere. Kaplanov, a skilled hunter and the youngest and strongest of the three, did the legwork. During the winters of 1939 and 1940, he logged close to a thousand miles crisscrossing the Sikhote-Alin range as he tracked tigers through blizzards and paralyzing cold, sleeping rough, and feeding himself from tiger kills. His findings were alarming: along with two forest guards who helped him with tracking, estimates, and interviews with hunters across Primorye, Kaplanov concluded that no more than thirty Amur tigers remained in Russian Manchuria. In the Bikin valley, he found no tigers at all. With barely a dozen breeding females left in Russia, the subspecies now known as *Panthera*

---

* As of 1997, the zapovednik has a much reduced area of about 1,500 square miles.

tigris altaica was a handful of bullets and a few hard winters away from extinction.

Despite the fact that local opinion and state ideology were weighted heavily against tigers at the time, these men understood that tigers were an integral part of the taiga picture, regardless of whether Marxists saw a role for them in the transformation of society. Given the mood of the time, this was an almost treasonous line of thinking, and it is what makes this collaborative effort so remarkable: as dangerous as it was to be a tiger, it had become just as dangerous to be a Russian.

———

Following the Revolution of 1917, the former "Far East Republic" was the last place in Russia to fall to the Bolsheviks, and it did so only after a vicious civil war that dragged on until 1923. Initially, the conflict involved a veritable bazaar of nations, including Czech, Ukrainian, Korean, Cossack, Canadian, Chinese, Japanese, French, Italian, British, and American troops, along with assorted foreign advisors. However, as the embattled region grew more and more to resemble a vast and dangerous open-air asylum, most of the foreigners abandoned the cause. By 1920, three armies—the Bolshevik Reds, the anti-Bolshevik Whites, and the Japanese—had been left to fight it out on their own. Next to the Russians, the infamously brutal Japanese looked like models of restraint. In the spring of 1920, after a particularly gratuitous massacre in which the Bolsheviks slaughtered thousands of White Russians and hundreds of Japanese, and burned their homes to the ground, the Whites managed to capture the Bolshevik commander of military operations in the Far East. After stuffing him into a mail sack, his captors took him to a station on the Trans-Siberian where they delivered him into the hands of a sympathetic Cossack named Bochkarev. Bochkarev commandeered a locomotive and burned his captive alive in the engine's firebox, along with two high-ranking associates (the latter, also delivered in mail sacks, were shot first).

Even after the Bolsheviks took control of the region, there was no peace, only a series of increasingly savage repressions by the victors. Some of Russia's most notorious gulags, including the Kolyma gold fields, were located in the Far East and throughout the 1920s and 1930s their populations swelled steadily, as did their cemeteries. Already battered by what Alec Nove, an expert on the Soviet economy, described as "the most precipitous peacetime decline in living standards known in recorded history," Russian citizens in the late 1930s were now being arrested and executed on a quota system. It was an absolutely terrifying time: Russia was Wonderland, Stalin was the Queen of Hearts, and anyone could be Alice.

By 1937, the purges were peaking nationwide, and no one was safe: peasants, teachers, scientists, indigenous people, Old Believers, Koreans, Chinese, Finns, Lithuanians, Party members—it didn't seem to matter as long as the quota was met. The invented charge in Primorye was, typically, spying for Japan, but it could be almost anything. Torture was routine. At the height of the purges, roughly a thousand people were being murdered every day. In 1939, Russia went to war (on several fronts), and this obviated the need for purging—just send them to the front. By one estimate, 90 percent of draft-age Nanai and Udeghe males died in military service. The rest were forced onto collective farms, and millions more Russians of all ethnicities were banished to the gulag.

Under Stalin, science was a prisoner, too—bound and gagged by a particularly rigid brand of Marxist ideology, which declared, in short, that in order for Mankind to realize His destiny as a super-human, super-rational master of all, Mother Nature must be forced to bow and, in the process, be radically transformed. By the mid-1930s, most advocates of environmental protection had been silenced one way or another, and their ideas replaced by slogans like "We cannot expect charity from nature. We must tear it from her." In 1926, Vladimir Zazubrin, the first head of the Union of Siberian Writers, delivered a lecture in which he proclaimed,

Let the fragile green breast of Siberia be dressed in the cement armour of cities, armed with the stone muzzles of factory chimneys, and girded with iron belts of railroads. Let the

taiga be burned and felled, let the steppes be trampled. . . . Only
in cement and iron can the fraternal union of all peoples, the
iron brotherhood of all mankind, be forged.*

Some hard-line Marxists sincerely believed that plants and
animals unable to prove their usefulness to mankind should simply be exterminated. In the face of such hostile dogma, the tiger
didn't stand a chance. Falling squarely into the category of
"harmful fauna," it had become a kind of fur-bearing Enemy of
the State. Those stripes might as well have been bull's-eyes. There
was no formal edict or bounty, but anyone was free to shoot tigers
on sight (they were highly prized by army and navy officers stationed in Primorye), and there was a ready market across the border. Given this, and given the death toll among people who so
much as looked sideways at the regime, it is incredible that anyone
dared advocate for tigers at all. Nonetheless, Lev Kaplanov's land-
mark study, "The Tiger in the Sikhote-Alin," was completed in
1941, and in it he recommended an immediate five-year morato-
rium on tiger hunting.† That same year, Kaplanov's colleague Yuri
Salmin would go a step further: in a national magazine, he made
an urgent plea for a total ban on tiger hunting in the Russian Far
East. This was the first time in recorded history that anyone, anywhere, had made a public call for restraint with regard to the
killing of these animals.

World War II, and the fact that it removed so many armed and
able-bodied men from the forest, was a critical factor in turning
the tide for the Amur tiger, but it took a heavy toll on the tiger's
champions. Only Abramov survived; a longtime apparatchik, he
was able to mediate the deadly tensions between progressive sci-

---

* Zazubrin was arrested and shot sometime in 1937–1938. Fifty years later, in 1988, the
Kremlin's chief ideologist, Vadim A. Medvedev, finally conceded that " 'universal values' such as avoiding war and ecological catastrophe must outweigh the idea of a struggle between the classes."

† The study was not published until 1948 when it was included in his groundbreaking
book, *Tigr, izyubr, los* ("Tiger, Red Deer, Moose").

ence and Party membership. Yuri Salmin, however, was sent to the front, and he never returned. In 1943, at the age of thirty-three, Lev Kaplanov was murdered by poachers in southern Primorye where he had recently been promoted to director of the small but important Lazovski Zapovednik. His body wasn't found for two weeks and, because it lay deep in the forest, it had to be carried out by hand. In order to do this, a litter was fashioned from cherry boughs; it was May so the trees were in flower, and the men who carried him recalled the blossoms on the branches around his body. Since then, Kaplanov has become a kind of local martyr to the cause of the Amur tiger.

There was an investigation into Kaplanov's death, but there were also complications, made worse by a puzzling lack of interest on the part of the investigator who had come all the way from Moscow. As a result, people who are still alive and intimate with the case's details feel quite sure that the wrong man went to jail and that Kaplanov's murderer, who was well known around the town of Lazo, lived out his days a free man. Wisely, perhaps, he relocated to a small river town about twelve miles away. Looming over the floodplain there is an exposed ridge studded with eruptions of stone that form the enormous and unmistakable lower jaw of a tiger. The fang alone is more than a hundred feet high.

Today, "The Tiger in the Sikhote-Alin" remains a milestone in the field of tiger research, and was a first step in the pivotal transformation of the Amur tiger—and the species as a whole—from trophy-vermin to celebrated icon. In 1947, Russia became the first country in the world to recognize the tiger as a protected species. However, active protection was sporadic at best, and poaching and live capture continued. In spite of this, the Amur tiger population has rebounded to a sustainable level over the past sixty years, a recovery unmatched by any other subspecies of tiger. Even with the upsurge in poaching over the past fifteen years, the Amur tiger has, for now, been able to hold its own.

There have been some hidden costs. Since the Amur tiger's population crash, these animals no longer seem to grow as large as they once did. It wouldn't be the first time this kind of anthropogenic selection has occurred: the moose of eastern North America went through a similar process of "trophy engineering" at roughly the same time. Sport hunters wanted bull moose with big antlers, and local guides were eager to accommodate them. Thus, the moose with the biggest racks were systematically removed from the gene pool while the smaller-antlered bulls were left to pass on their more modest genes, year after year. Scientists have speculated that something similar may have happened to the Amur tiger, with one result being that postwar specimens no longer seem to be much larger than their Bengal counterparts. In Primorye today one would be hard pressed to find an Amur tiger weighing more than five hundred pounds, but that is still a huge cat by any era's measure. The tiger that killed Vladimir Markov was never weighed, but when he recalled it later, Trush's number two, Sasha Lazurenko, said, "As long as I've worked here, I've never seen a tiger as big as that one."

9

Men carry their superiority inside; animals outside.

Russian Proverb

FOLLOWING THE DISCOVERY OF MARKOV'S REMAINS, INSPECTION TIGER conducted a series of interviews with the last people to see him alive. There were about a half dozen all told and, despite the fact that they lived a considerable distance from one another—some with no road access whatsoever—each of them claimed to have seen Markov within hours of his death. Not surprisingly, all of them were men: ethnic Russian loggers and native hunters, and one of them—the key witness, as it were—was Ivan Dunkai.

Dunkai was a Nanai elder from the native village of Krasny Yar ("Red Bank"), which lies fifteen miles downstream from Sobolonye. Situated on the left bank of the Bikin, it had no road access until a bridge was built in the 1990s. About six hundred Udeghe and Nanai residents live in the village, along with a handful of ethnic Russian* spouses, officials, and other transplants. Arseniev and Dersu are reported to have passed through the area in 1908 and, were they to return there today, they wouldn't be surprised by what they found. Dugout canoes and slender, piroguelike *omorochkas* line the riverbank, livestock roam the tidy dirt streets, and virtually every structure, fence, and walkway is made of

---

* "Ethnic Russian" refers to the country's Slavic majority, which accounts for about 80 percent of the population and tends to be concentrated in western, or "European," Russia.

wood. Firewood is delivered in the form of a tree trunk, from which logs are sawed off and split as needed. Save for the predominance of Asiatic faces, Krasny Yar could be mistaken for the shtetl in *Fiddler on the Roof.* The only obvious differences between then and now are the electric lights, a handful of cars and snowmobiles, and several fanciful houses designed by a Ukrainian artist, one of which looks like a snarling tiger.

Ivan Dunkai, it is fair to say, was a latter-day Dersu Uzala—a last link to a time when the native inhabitants of this region saw the tiger as the true lord of the forest. Dunkai died in 2006. In life he was a twinkly-eyed, elfin man who evoked a gentleness and wisdom that seemed from another age. He was a gifted woodsman of the old school, known and respected throughout the middle Bikin. He had a nickname that translates to "In the World of the Animals." For Ivan Dunkai, the taiga was the source of all things, in which the tiger occupied a place of honor. In 2004, when Dunkai was about seventy-five years old, he was interviewed by a British documentary filmmaker named Sasha Snow. "The tiger is a sly but merciful creature," Dunkai explained to Snow. "You know that he is there, but you cannot see him. He hides so well that one starts thinking he is invisible, like a god. Russians say, 'Trust in God, but keep your eyes open.' We [Nanai] rely on ourselves, but pray for Tiger to help us. We worship his strength."

As a senior hunter in Krasny Yar, Dunkai oversaw a large hunting territory, which overlapped with an area known as the Panchelaza. The name is a holdover from the days of Chinese possession, and it refers to a tract of choice game habitat about one hundred miles square. Almost box-shaped, the Panchelaza is framed by three rivers—the Amba to the east, the Takhalo to the west, and the Bikin to the south. According to an Udeghe scholar named Alexander Konchuga, one of only two men to author books in the Udeghe language, the names of these rivers translate, respectively, to Devil, Fire, and Joy. The first two are tributaries of the latter. Well before Markov arrived, this beautiful and dangerous sanctuary had been identified, at least in name, as a kind of empyrean frontier, a threshold between Heaven and Hell. The concept of Amba—the same word Dersu uses to indicate "tiger"—— refers both to the animal and to a malevolent spirit—a devil—and not simply because the tiger can be dangerous as hell.

The spirit worlds of the Nanai, the Udeghe, and their northern neighbors, the Orochi, are hierarchal (like those of most cultures), and the Amba inhabits one of the lower, earthier tiers. Should one have the misfortune to attract an Amba's attention, it will tend to manifest itself at the interpersonal level, as opposed to the communal or the cosmic. Often, it will take the form of a tiger. So closely are these two beings associated that, in Primorye today, "Amba" serves as a synonym for tiger, even among those who have no awareness of its other meaning.* For some reason, probably because of its intactness, the area surrounding the Panchelaza supports an unusually high density of tigers. It was within this waterbound enclave, just west of the Amba River, that Markov had placed his hunting barracks with Ivan Dunkai's blessing.

At the time, Dunkai was living in a cabin of his own about four miles to the southeast, at the boggy, braided confluence of the Amba and the Bikin. After his second wife died, Dunkai left his home in Krasny Yar and gave himself over to the taiga almost full time, much as Dersu had done after losing his family to smallpox. Because his hunting territory was far more than one man needed (one local Russian waggishly compared it to France), Dunkai shared it with his sons, one of whom——Mikhail——had a cabin right on the Amba, northeast of Markov. Neither Mikhail nor his brother, Vasily, who hunted further east, seemed to have a problem with Markov's presence in their father's hunting territory. As they saw it, Markov was just another tayozhnik trying to make a living; by their estimation, he was *normalny*——a regular guy, nothing out of the ordinary.

The details of their arrangement——if there were any beyond a

---

* "Amba" is a Tungus word from a language family that includes the Manchu, the Udeghe, and the Nanai, among others. Its original meaning is similar to "Great." The Manchus (as in "Manchuria") invaded Beijing in 1644 and ruled China under the Qing Dynasty until 1911. In some cases, they used "Amba" to denote the titular rank of a leader.

request and a nod—were known only to Dunkai and Markov. They were both easygoing, personable men who knew and loved the taiga and were engaged in similar pursuits. They were also good friends: when Markov was first getting to know the Panchelaza, Dunkai had allowed Markov to stay with him for weeks at a time. Theirs was a close but casual friendship: if one needed a cup of tea, the loan of some supplies, or a place to stay for a while, the other would oblige. Like most forest encounters, their meetings were spontaneous affairs: there was no need to call ahead, nor was there the means to. For Ivan Dunkai, Markov was a familiar presence in the forest the same way the local tigers were: occasionally, he would run into him; more often, he would just take note of the tracks and factor them into the grand schematic in his head. "You can read the taiga as a book," he explained. "The twig is bent—why? What animal has passed here? The twig is broken—this means that a person has passed. It is interesting! If an animal stops paying attention to you, maybe it sees another animal. So, you should find out what causes this attention. That is how we were taught, and that is how I teach my sons."

On a sunny winter afternoon at the Far Eastern Institute of Geography, outside Vladivostok, a tiger biologist named Dmitri Pikunov told a story about Ivan Dunkai that could have been taken from the pages of *Dersu the Trapper*. Pikunov is a ruddy, robust man in his early seventies with piercing blue eyes and a dwindling silver crew cut, and he has spent decades studying and writing about tigers in the Bikin valley. It was he who first chronicled the Markov incident in 1998, in a local nature magazine called *Zov Taigi* ("Call of the Taiga"). Like Dunkai, Pikunov is a throwback to the old school and, like most early tiger advocates, he came to conservation through hunting. An expert marksman, he earned the rank of Master of Sports in skeet shooting and was invited to join Russia's national shooting team, which he did. "I am incredibly good with guns," he says, seeing no need for false modesty.

However, Pikunov's father, a highly regarded metallurgist in a tank factory, had other plans and urged his son to follow him into the industry. Had Pikunov done so it would have all but guaranteed him a secure and privileged life, but he found shooting and the hunt so compelling that he applied to the Irkutsk Institute's hunting management program instead. Tuition was free in those days, so the competition was fierce, but Pikunov excelled. Once out of school, he was hired to manage the Pacific Fleet's five-thousand-member hunting association in Primorye. From there, he was invited to join the Far East Division of the Environmental Protection Department as a researcher. "I was spending six months a year in the taiga then," explained Pikunov in a battered office with a commanding view of the ice-covered Amur Bay. "Even when I was on vacation, I would get a rifle, sign a contract to hunt for boar or deer, and sell the meat."

In an effort to express the depth of his obsession, Pikunov cited a Russian proverb usually reserved for wolves: "No matter how much you feed him, he keeps looking at the forest." Nonetheless, it would be ten years before Pikunov laid eyes on a tiger. When he finally did it was on a riverbank, by flashlight. "His eyes were fiery—greenish white," Pikunov recalled. "He was huge, but not aggressive at all. He just stood there, his eyes on fire the whole time."

One of Pikunov's responsibilities was to gather census data on game animals, a task most easily accomplished in winter when the tracks are easy to follow and count. Of course, tigers and leopards were following these tracks, too, and this is how Pikunov discovered what would become a lifelong fascination. Starting in 1977, he began tracking tigers cross-country over extended periods in order to determine how many kills they were making—crucial information for agencies trying to manage habitat, game species, and hunters. "Whenever I do field work, I always have a gun on me," Pikunov explained. "It makes me feel more secure, psychologically. But I have a subconscious feeling that if I have not hurt a tiger, he will not be aggressive toward me." Once, Pikunov tracked a single tiger continuously for six weeks, literally sleeping in its tracks, just as Kaplanov had done forty years earlier. "Even when I was on tiger tracks all the time," he explained, "and scavenging meat from their kills, none of those tigers demonstrated aggressive behavior toward me."

Today, even after a serious heart attack, Pikunov still has surprisingly powerful hands—and opinions to match. Among his colleagues, he elicits no neutral feelings, but his chin-first demeanor softens when he recalls the man he knew as "Vanya" Dunkai. Pikunov speaks of him with the same respect and affection Arseniev did of Dersu, and for many of the same reasons. Over the course of thirty years, the two men spent many months together in the taiga, tracking big game, and Pikunov paid close attention. To this day, tayozhniks typically go into the winter forest with very basic equipment consisting of felt-soled, wool-lined boots, woolen pants, jacket, and mittens. Incidentals are carried in a floppy canvas rucksack; if they know they'll be packing something heavy, like meat, they might mount it on a bentwood maple pack frame, Udeghe-style. Instead of snowshoes, winter travelers here use short, broad traditional skis called *okhotniki* ("hunters"). Many tayozhniks (including Markov) make these themselves.

In the winter of 1974, Dunkai and Pikunov were in the Bikin valley, tracking bears, when a blizzard came up. There had been little snow on the ground when they had set off that morning so they had left their skis back in camp. By the time the blizzard hit, they were a long way from home and ill-equipped for severe weather. Visibility is already limited in the forest and when driving snow and wind are added, it is easy to become disoriented. With the snow deepening by the minute, both men understood that they needed to get out of there fast. While Pikunov was preparing to simply race back along their rapidly filling tracks, Dunkai stopped and pulled a hatchet from his rucksack. Finding a tree about as thick as his leg, he chopped it down, cut the trunk to ski length and then split it into slender boards. "The snow was up to our waists," recalled Pikunov. "There was no way out of there without skis, and Vanya made them without any proper tools; all he had was a knife and an axe. He was a master of all trades."

In addition to having what Russians call "golden hands," Dunkai had an extraordinary rapport with his surroundings. In many ways, his daily routine bore a strong resemblance to the tiger's: both are built around a routinized practice of observing, deciphering, and mental cataloguing, often over well-trodden routes. Just as we might be familiar with certain cats and dogs in our neighborhood, Dunkai knew his neighbors, too, including the tigers. And they knew him. Despite spending more than seventy years in the taiga, much of it on foot or in a tent, Dunkai never had serious difficulties with a tiger. But "difficulties" is a relative term: over the years, he did lose a number of dogs. Dogs seem to trigger the tiger's wolf-killing instincts, and they also seem to relish the taste. Many is the Far Eastern hunter, farmer, or dacha owner who has risen in the morning to find nothing but a broken chain where his dog had been. When one former dog owner was asked what these attacks sounded like, he answered acidly, "It's more of a silence." But this is the price of doing business in the tiger's domain; it is a form of tribute, and it has ancient precedents.

Ivan Dunkai understood this: he knew that dog killing is in a tiger's nature, and he also knew that, in time, he would be compensated. Udeghe and Nanai hunters in particular made efforts to propitiate the tiger, first and foremost by staying out of his way, but also by leaving him a cut of the spoils. On occasion, these favors would be returned. Local people, Russian and native alike, told stories of how tigers would leave meat for "Uncle Vanya"— sometimes an entire carcass. An occurrence like this might easily be ascribed to chance by an outsider, or simply dismissed as a folktale, but when seen from a traditional tayozhnik's point of view it is only logical because, in his way, he has done the same for the tiger. For Dunkai, such an arrangement made perfect sense; after all, he was a person for whom skis literally grew on trees and could be summoned forth at will. When the creatures around you are keeping you alive, it necessarily changes the relationship; survival—both physical and psychic—demands it. "The tiger will help me," Dunkai once said, "because I've asked him."

There is, in a healthy forest, an almost tidal ebb and flow of resources and reciprocation. As with the unintended etiquette of winter trail breaking, this passive sharing of food is an integral part of coexistence in the wild. In this sense, the hunting "culture" of predators and scavengers bears a strong resemblance to Karl Marx's communist ideal: "From each according to his ability, to each according to his needs." Thus, what the bulldozer is to communal trail breaking, the tiger is to the food chain: among animals in the taiga, there is no more efficient or bountiful provider. By regularly bringing down large prey like elk, moose, boar, and deer, the tiger feeds countless smaller animals, birds, and insects, not to mention the soil. Every such event sends another pulse of lifeblood through the body of the forest. These random but rhythmic infusions nourish humans, too, and not just wolfish hunter-biologists like Dmitri Pikunov. Udeghe and Nanai hunters occasionally scavenge from tiger kills, and so do their Russian neighbors.

———

In 1969, George Schaller, the author of *The Deer and the Tiger,* a seminal study of predator-prey relations, took a series of walks through Tanzania's Serengeti National Park with an anthropologist named Gordon Lowther. While most students of early man seek to understand our ancestors through a combination of the fossil record and comparison with modern primates, a handful, including Schaller and Lowther, speculated that, by observing the behavior of other cooperative predators like lions, hyenas, and wild dogs, they might gain insights into how we evolved as communal hunter-gatherers. Initially, the two men were focused on hunting techniques, communications, and food sharing and so hadn't anticipated what ended up being a key discovery: after following one male lion for three weeks straight, they noted that "it killed nothing but ate seven times, either by scavenging or by joining other lions on their kill." Their attention shifted then to scavenging behavior, leading them to wonder whether our ancestors could have survived on leftovers alone.

Schaller and Lowther kept on walking, but this time, instead of viewing the vast herds of zebra, wildebeest, and gazelle as meat on the hoof that one must personally subdue, they imagined it as a movable feast, on the crumbs of which a band of small, unarmed early hominids might feed opportunistically—not by hunting but by gathering. They made some illuminating discoveries. It happened to be calving season so, first, they concentrated on calves and fawns. In the space of two hours, they spotted eighty pounds' worth of meat in the form of easily caught young animals and abandoned carcasses. The next time they went out they focused on scavenging only from existing kills, an activity that, unlike calf and fawn hunting, could be pursued year-round. Over the course of a week, during which they walked for twenty hours (with the aid of a car to move between locations), they turned up nearly a thousand pounds of edible animal parts (alive and dead). Taking into account that a) there were only two of them, instead of an extended family or clan group, and b) this experiment was conducted in an area where the game closely resembled prehistoric concentrations of migratory animals, Schaller and Lowther concluded "that under similar conditions a carnivorous hominid group could have survived by a combination of scavenging and killing sick [and young] animals."

This approach might seem obvious now, but in the late 1960s when these journeys took place, it was revolutionary. Because most anthropologists and archaeologists working then were male, and because hunting is considered to be our ancestors' primal drama—specifically, a man's drama—a disproportionate amount of time, ink, and wishful thinking has been devoted to the subject.* Enthusiasm for what came to be known as the Hunting Hypothesis took a quantum leap in the 1960s and 1970s when Robert Ardrey, a playwright and screenwriter with a background in anthropology, published a series of influential books culminating in a bestseller called *The Hunting Hypothesis* (1976). In them, Ardrey popularized this volatile idea that had been circulating among social scientists for nearly a century: that of man-as-killer-ape. Ardrey, influenced in part by his own traumatic experiences reporting on the Mau Mau Uprising in Kenya, summed it up this way: "If among all the members of our primate family the human being is unique, even in our noblest aspirations, it is because we alone

---

* With a few exceptions like the Inuit, and the whalers of Lamalera in Indonesia, fresh meat has typically been more of a supplement than a staple in the hominid diet.

through untold millions of years were continuously dependent on killing to survive."

Because of the environment we evolved in, and the stresses we faced, reasoned Ardrey, the act of hunting—killing—was central to our survival and has made us who we are today. In his view, virtually all our defining characteristics—from tools and language, to the division of labor between genders and our appetite for war— find their roots in this primal activity. The Hunting Hypothesis (also known as Killer Ape theory) was widely accepted at the time, not least because all of its proponents had lived through a period of unprecedented violence in the form of the Second World War; Vietnam, too, loomed large in the Western academic consciousness. As a result, many scholars were grappling with fundamental questions about human nature and wondering how men in particular had evolved into such ferocious hunter-killers. It wasn't only anthropologists who were trying to plumb these depths: in the early 1950s, at the same time Ardrey was conceptualizing his first book on the topic, Robinson Jeffers, one of only six American poets to make the cover of *Time* magazine, limned it this way:

> *Never blame the man: his hard-pressed*
> *Ancestors formed him: the other anthropoid apes were safe*
> *In the great southern rain-forest and hardly changed*
> *In a million years: but the race of man was made*
> *By shock and agony...*
>   *...a wound was made in the brain*
> *When life became too hard, and has never healed.*
> *It is there that they learned trembling religion and blood-*
>   *sacrifice,*
> *It is there that they learned to butcher beasts and to slaughter*
>   *men,*
> *And hate the world*

———

Jeffers's original "wound," whatever its cause, was probably not inflicted by big cats during the Paleolithic period. As tempting as it may be to imagine spear-wielding Stone Age hunters squaring off against saber-toothed tigers, both parties were most likely too smart, too specialized, and too pragmatic by then to bother with each other. That said, predation has been a recurring theme throughout our shared time on this planet, and the need to manage this threat, along with hunger, thirst, climate, competition, and the perils of overland travel, has impelled us toward our current state. Members of the evolutionary subtribe *Hominina*, from whom we directly descend, have been differentiated from chimpanzees for approximately six million years. There is no doubt that cats have been eating us and them—at least occasionally—since our collective beginnings.

Compared to such mythic encounters, scavenging, i.e., meat gathering, is far less evocative, but it was gathering, carnal and otherwise, that surely kept our ancestors alive. Describing the return of a successful hunting party in the Kalahari Desert, the ethnographer Lorna Marshall summed up the gatherer's age-old dilemma: "We heard the sound of voices in the encampment, rising in volume and pitch like the hum of excited bees. Some people ran toward the hunters . . . some danced up and down, children squealed and ran about . . . I venture to say no women have been greeted this way when they returned with vegetables."

And yet, as counterintuitive as it may seem, the practice of gathering may offer deeper insight into our relationships with big cats than hunting ever could. In the course of their scavenging experiments, Schaller and Lowther observed a phenomenon that would have had far greater implications for early humans than chance discoveries of abandoned meat: "All of the seven lion groups that we encountered while we were on foot fled when we were at distances of 80 to 300 meters."* If a pride of lions—*lions*—will flee at the sight of two unarmed human beings, what would they do if approached by a party of five or ten or twenty who were shouting, waving sticks, and throwing stones? Conceivably, such a group, emboldened by experience and empowered by growing brains and advancing technology, could have eaten their

---

* Schaller later speculated that this may have been due to the lions' prior experience of being hunted by Masai tribesmen.

way across the Serengeti for hundreds of millennia without lifting a spear. Taking this a step further, imagine the self-concept of such creatures: barely five feet tall with neither claws nor fangs and a clear understanding of their potential as prey who were, nonetheless, able to intimidate and steal from the deadliest creatures in their world more or less at will. Early humans, pre-fire, may well have been Paleolithic Wizards of Oz—masters of illusion and psyops who eventually, amazingly, willed their "impersonations" of superiority into fact. If only during daylight hours.

Elizabeth Marshall Thomas, the author of *The Tribe of Tiger* and *The Old Way*, is one of a privileged few who have been able to test this theory in situ. Thomas had the good fortune to spend extended periods of time among the Kalahari Bushmen before Boer and Tswana farmers subjugated and settled them. In 1950, when the Marshall family expedition arrived, the central Kalahari ecosystem was intact. Bushmen were the only humans around, and they had been living much as the Marshalls found them for millennia. For the !Kung Bushmen of the central Kalahari, it could be said that the Paleolithic period did not truly end until about 1965. Thomas was nineteen when she and her family first arrived there and, while her ballerina mother, Lorna Marshall, fashioned herself into a world-class ethnographer, and her eighteen-year-old brother, John, began work on what was to become a classic documentary film, she observed and wrote.

The Bushmen they lived beside and traveled with were small people, lightly clothed and armed, whose lives were structured around a series of dependable waterholes. Their diet was surprisingly varied, running the gamut from melons to meat, and one of their staples was the mongongo nut, which, like the Korean pine nut, was both plentiful and durable. Hunting was done most often with poisoned arrows, but, because this poison (one of the deadliest on earth) takes time to act, each hunt necessitated two rounds of tracking—the first to find the game, and the second to find the game again, once it had been shot. The process could take days, and sometimes a hunting party would arrive at their kill only to find that lions had gotten to it first. What struck Thomas was how these hunters dealt with such daunting competition: rather than abandoning the animal, or shooting arrows at the lions, the hunters would approach them calmly, telling them that this animal wasn't theirs and that they needed to go away. If the lions resisted these firm but collegial requests, a couple of clods of dirt might be tossed in their general direction. That was all it took for these hunters, who were in some cases greatly outnumbered by lions, to reclaim their prey. The absence of drama might be a letdown for the modern reader, but it sheds a bright and different light on our historic relations with legendary predators.

What is important to keep in mind here is that everyone involved had known one another, effectively, "forever." The lions had been raised—for millennia—with an awareness of Bushmen, and the Bushmen had been brought up with an understanding of lions. Each was part of the other's larger community and whatever imbalances may have existed were calibrated long before the Pyramids were even imagined. In other words, there was a culture in place—what Thomas describes as "a web of socially transmitted behaviours"—and all participating parties had been habituated to their particular roles. For the Bushmen, one of these was a birdlike caution: they always watched their back; they didn't wander around at night, the desert predator's preferred time of operation; and they kept a fire going throughout the night. Constant vigilance—that is, awareness of the possibility of becoming prey—was a way of life. In this way, the Bushmen treated the desert much as we treat a dangerous road: metaphorically (and metaphysically) speaking, they knew when it was safe to cross. "The lions around here don't harm people," a senior hunter named ≠Toma explained to Thomas. "Where lions aren't hunted, they aren't dangerous. As for us, we live in peace with them."

If one were to substitute "tigers" for "lions," these words could have been spoken by Dersu Uzala, Ivan Dunkai, or, for that matter, Dmitri Pikunov and any resident of Sobolonye.

The Bushmen's détente with the Kalahari lions, as ancient as it may have been, was still tenuous in the moment, and close encounters would often crackle with a primal electricity. "Beyond our fire were their shining eyes," wrote Thomas on one occasion, "which were so high above the ground that we thought at first we were seeing donkeys." The !Kung word for lion—*n!i*—was used as carefully as a god's and was seldom uttered in the daytime (why summon the beast when it is safely asleep?). Some individuals appeared to have supernatural relationships with these animals, and it was generally believed that werelions stalked the desert floor: some could leap enormous distances or cause an eclipse by covering the sun with a paw. The Bushmen, like the indigenous peoples of Primorye, lived *among* their gods. During an encounter with a lion, a Bushman would refer to it respectfully as "Big Lion," or "Old Lion," just as the Udeghe (and Manchus) referred to the tiger as "Old Man," or "Old Tiger." In Chinese, "old tiger" translates to *laohu* (虎), which is still the Chinese name for tiger.

That these beliefs and relationships are ancient and time-tested is without doubt, and the Paleolithic cave paintings at Chauvet-Pont-d'Arc in the Ardèche valley of southern France illustrate this vividly. These images, which were made in charcoal and ocher more than thirty thousand years ago, are twice as old as their more famous counterparts at Lascaux. They are noteworthy, not just for their startling accuracy but for their emphasis on big cats: Chauvet contains seventy-three confirmed images of lions, more than all the other known European caves combined. Cave lions were bigger than any living cat and yet what is clear from these works is that the artists who rendered them spent a lot of time observing these creatures in an uninhibited state, apparently from very close range. The attention to detail—down to the patterning of whisker spots and the depiction of subtle but specific leonine behaviors—translates to the present day. And yet, alongside these strictly literal representations one can see a lion with hooves instead of paws, and a possibly shamanic proto-Minotaur, or werebison. Seen together, these lavishly illuminated walls resemble the pages of a protean narrative form in which *Beowulf, The Book of Kells,* and *National Geographic* were elided into a cascading, fire-powered zootrope. While it is only natural to be impressed by such modern-seeming feats of artistic skill and interpretive nuance, one could argue that it is also condescending. After all, these artist/hunter/storyteller/shamans were *Homo sapiens,* too: our direct ancestors, equipped with the same brains and the same bodies. Only the knowledge base and circumstances differed.

These so-called cavemen, who lived much as the so-called Bushmen did in the 1950s, also shared the same motives and opportunities for observation and, no doubt, many of the same emotions (some Bushman groups made wall art as well). Thirty millennia is not that long on the Paleolithic scale of time, and there is no reason to suppose—other things being equal—that our relations with big cats would have changed much. Based on the accumulated evidence, it is not a stretch to suggest that the Chauvet cave artists, the Kalahari Bushmen, and the indigenous peoples of Primorye all perceived their enormous feline neighbors in similar ways: as fearsome, fascinating, supernaturally potent beings who charged their lives with meaning, and sometimes provided meat. Predation appeared to be a secondary concern.

But in the Bikin valley, in 1997, this primordial understanding had been disrupted, and the risk of attack had become paramount. This situation was so out of phase with the norm for this region that it led Trush's teammate, Sasha Lazurenko, to pose the following question over Markov's remains: "Why," he wondered aloud, "is the tiger so angry at him?"

10

Everything resembles the truth, everything can happen
to a man.

Nikolai Gogol, *Dead Souls*

THE FIRST ANSWER TO LAZURENKO'S QUESTION ARRIVED ABRUPTLY
from six feet away: "Who the hell knows? Why are you asking?"

It was Markov's good friend Andrei Onofreychuk, and there
was an edge in his voice. It would have been natural to chalk up
such a brusque reply to frayed nerves and exhaustion, but a suspi-
cious person might hear more in it. For one, it seemed almost too
quick—more deflection than information. Given that it came
from the same person who had found and hidden Markov's illegal
gun, it appeared that Lazurenko had touched a nerve of some
kind. He didn't pursue it, but the general feeling among Trush's
team on Saturday the 6th was that Markov's friends had closed
ranks. At the site of the attack, visible to all, remained the clear
impression of Markov's rifle in the snow, but no one seemed to
know where it was. Neither Danila Zaitsev nor Sasha Dvornik was
formally interviewed at the time, but Onofreychuk was—by
Trush. Onofreychuk's statement, though brief, was coherent and
consistent within its limited scope, describing his discovery of the
attack the previous morning, his aural encounter with the tiger,
his paralysis in Markov's cabin followed by his terrified foot journey to a nearby logging base where he sought help.

The logging base lay two miles southeast of Markov's cabin
through the forest. It bore a strong resemblance to a Gypsy

encampment, being little more than a collection of portable wooden caravans like Markov's, only with the wheels still attached. An early-twentieth-century American logger would have recognized it immediately and would have considered it primitive even then—what that generation called a "haywire outfit." The owner, Pyotr Zhorkin, was a bluff and opinionated drinker who wouldn't survive his fifties. His pay schedule was whimsical, and in this and other ways his business style exemplified post-perestroika private enterprise. Half a dozen men were based at the camp, where they worked twelve-hour shifts, twenty days on and five days off. Though they were paid literally millions of rubles, their wages barely covered groceries. Markov's young friend Denis Burukhin had tried working there but quit after a month, realizing he could do better on his own living off the forest. Logging for Zhorkin made the 1980s look like the good old days.

The men there were all refugees from the national logging company; they were familiar with tigers and they knew Onofreychuk, but they had never seen him look the way he did when he showed up in camp shortly after noon on Friday, December 5. He was pale—still in shock. "I felt like I was dreaming," he said as he went through the motions of getting help. But he was also strangely secretive. The men were eating lunch in the cook wagon when Onofreychuk arrived: "He came and called me outside," recalled a powerful, barrel-chested faller named Sergei Luzgan whose otherwise perfect nose veers off at a startling angle. "He was acting kind of odd: he said, 'Don't mention this to anyone.' Well, if someone's been killed by a tiger, what's there to hide? It's not a normal reaction, and I said, 'What the fuck do you mean "Don't mention it to anyone"? A man is *dead*, for fuck's sake. He's not a dog—you can't just throw dirt on him and forget about it. The police will have to be called. There's no way around it.'"

Realizing there was no hope of keeping it quiet, Onofreychuk relented. Luzgan found Zhorkin and, after absorbing his visitor's barely credible story, the three of them, along with another logger named Evgeny Sakirko, piled into Zhorkin's little Niva four-by-four and drove back to Markov's cabin. Sakirko was a faller like Luzgan, and his face shone with a hot, alcoholic rubescence behind a nose that had been crushed and stitched back together like a gunnysack. Because of the logging camp's remoteness and the presence of both tigers and game, there were rifles on hand and the men brought a couple along. Markov's weapon— wherever it was—was of no use because, at that point, all the ammunition for it was still strapped to his body.

When the men arrived at the cabin they announced themselves to the tiger with gunshots and shouts. One man found a pipe and started banging on it. Their entrance bore an uncanny resemblance to the hunters' theme in *Peter and the Wolf:* somehow, Prokofiev correctly intuited the sonic melding of aggression and fear. Like this, the four men made their way into the forest, starting at the trampled patch of blood-spattered snow and following the broad, shallow drag trail that led away from it. Far more impressive to the men, though, were the symmetrical paw prints that lined each side: the tiger, whatever its gender, was of a size that it could walk easily while dragging a grown man between its legs. This time, the tiger offered no indication of its whereabouts. Painfully familiar with gunfire and understanding that the odds were not in its favor, it did not hold its ground but retreated silently from that first dark circle where it had been feeding and resting now for nearly two days. Still, the tiger watched, and the men had no sense of how near it was, or where, beyond a racketing of the nerves that was easily confused with adrenaline.

By Evgeny Sakirko's recollection, they hadn't walked ten yards from the entrance road before they ran across Markov's knife, which he described as the kind one would use to chop vegetables. Onofreychuk quietly absconded with it as he had the gun. Its location, so close to the site of the attack, troubled Sakirko, leading him to wonder if it represented Markov's last attempt to save himself as he was being dragged into the woods. When they came across a dog's paw, Onofreychuk recognized it immediately: it belonged to Strelka ("Arrow"), Markov's oldest and most experienced hunting dog. No one was able to determine whether she had been killed with Markov or sometime beforehand though it is reasonable to suppose that she may have died trying to protect him. Because of the deadfall and heavy brush, they did not see his body until they were almost upon it, and when they did, Onofreychuk's slow and terrible dream took another turn. This was the first time he had actually set eyes on his friend Markiz: he was lying on his back—headless now, disemboweled and frozen solid. After the initial bolt of horror, the emptiness Onofreychuk felt within himself expanded like a private universe. Unable to help his friend, he felt the least he could do was cover for him—that, and collect his remains.

Although the Russian Orthodox Church had been repressed for eighty years, many of its traditions still persisted around key ceremonies, including funerals. One of the Church's formal requirements for last rites is an intact body. This is important insofar as the body is an offering to God, but it is even more important for the family, as the dead are typically laid out in state for a couple of days before burial so that family and friends may hold a vigil and say their goodbyes. Onofreychuk had hoped to retrieve the body in order to protect it from further harm, but by then Zhorkin had assumed command of the situation, and he told the men not to touch anything. The authorities must be notified, he said. A formal investigation must be made. These were simple men, raised under communism, and Zhorkin was the boss, so nobody argued; it was he who first notified the village clerk in Sobolonye, who in turn contacted Inspection Tiger later that same afternoon. (It was after Zhorkin and his men had left that the tiger dragged Markov's corpse deeper into the forest to the location where Trush would find it the next day.) There was no established protocol for handling tiger attacks, and it may have been a relief that someone seemed to know what to do. However, all these men understood hunting, and each took note of the cartridge belt around Markov's waist and the three missing shells. These men knew Markov, and they were familiar with his weapon: a 16-gauge single-barrel shotgun. This was a midsize field gun—suitable for game birds and even deer, but too light for tiger killing unless the shot was extraordinary. Assuming Markov had fired at all, he would have had only one chance; there would have been no time to reload. Only Markov's friends, who had seen the gun, knew how those last frenzied moments had played out.

On the evening of Saturday, December 6, Trush interviewed the loggers at Zhorkin's camp. The first one he spoke with there was a bulldozer operator named Viktor Isayev, a genial, easygoing man in his late thirties who seemed strangely untouched by his circumstances. Where many of his friends and neighbors bore visible scars and appeared many years older than they actually were, Isayev looked as trim and fit as if he'd just stepped out of a spa. His eyes were bright, his lips full, and his cheeks soft and flushed with health. His secret, whatever it was, was unknown even to him, for in every other way he resembled his co-workers: a marginally employed Bikin valley logger with neither plans nor means to leave.

Isayev had been in the cook wagon when Markov showed up around dinnertime on Wednesday, December 3. The sun had already been down for several hours, and it was pitch dark in the forest; only a thumbnail moon was visible through black-fingered trees. Markov had been on the trail all afternoon. Apparently, he was on a circuit, having just come over from Ivan Dunkai's cabin, about four miles away on the lower Amba. Isayev recalled that Markov had left his gun somewhere outside, which was standard operating procedure for a poacher, particularly at that time of year, and noted that he was wearing a knife and cartridge belt. When the men offered him dinner, Markov refused despite having been on the trail for hours in minus thirty degree weather. "He looked a little scared," Isayev recalled. "Usually he was very chatty, but not this time. He wasn't in a good mood."

Zhorkin wasn't present that evening, but Markov told Isayev, Luzgan, Sakirko, and two other loggers gathered there that he was searching for his dogs and that he couldn't stay long. He had at least three hunting dogs, but only one of them, a shaggy, black-haired mutt named Jack, was with him now. At that point, Strelka and Belka ("Squirrel") were still at large. Apparently, Dunkai hadn't seen them either. There was a certain amount of confusion around the dogs—which ones and how many, and, ordinarily, one could ignore such details, but not in the case of a hunter. It is hard to overemphasize their importance, especially when the hunter is destitute. Dogs are the poacher's assistants, colleagues, companions, and guards. No one keeps a secret better. Often, they will keep each other warm at night, and their perennial optimism offers a reason to get out of bed in the morning. But in the case of a tiger, dogs can also get a man killed.

Sakirko, Luzgan, and Isayev, who were interviewed separately, each recalled Markov being anxious about his dogs, being unwilling to eat despite the fact that hot food was being served, and refusing their offers to put him up for the night though it was bitterly cold out. They all remember him being agitated and in a hurry—not himself. Sakirko alone remembered Markov mentioning his concerns about a tiger and saying, "I'd better get home because the dogs will get killed." He also remembers being amused by Markov's worries. After all, many in the Panchelaza saw tigers, and who hadn't lost a dog or two over the years?

In fact, on the same day Markov stopped by, Sakirko and Isayev had both seen fresh prints of a tigress and cub about half a mile from camp. All of Zhorkin's men knew this tigress because she was a regular, tending, as tigers do, to orbit through her territory every week or two. For those so inclined it presented an ideal poaching scenario. There was opportunity, motive, minimal risk of discovery, and a nearly foolproof way to get the carcass out of the forest: hidden in a load of logs. And yet these men let her be. It wasn't so much because they respected the law; rather, they respected her. They and most others in the Bikin valley lived by the motto "If I don't touch her, she won't touch me." Such was the stability of human-tiger relations in the Panchelaza that the possibility of a person getting attacked—much less eaten—by a tiger was, literally, laughable—like getting hit by a meteorite. But an analogy to cars may be more useful: everyone knows they are deadly and that people can get killed by them, and yet most people have reconciled themselves to this danger in a way that allows them to live in daily harmony with motor vehicles.

———

At some point, possibly on Sunday, December 7, Sasha Lazurenko was sent off on foot to interview the Nanai elder Ivan Dunkai at his cabin on the lower Amba. This was a crucial interview because Dunkai was someone Markov might well have confided in. But, unbeknownst to Trush, something went awry: it seems now that the interview never took place. Like Trush, Lazurenko is tall, lean, and industrious. His face is round and bisected by a trim mustache; pale blue eyes hide behind heavy, hooded lids. Born and raised on the Ussuri, in a village south of Luchegorsk, Lazurenko is a fully integrated tayozhnik and, like most of his kind, he dresses in camouflage or forest green. It was specifically because of his local knowledge that he was selected for Inspection Tiger's Bikin squad. Sasha Lazurenko was Trush's right-hand man, and Trush trusted him with his life. Despite the lack of a written statement, Trush was convinced that Lazurenko had met with Dunkai, and this may well be because Lazurenko told him he had. Nobody knows now. Lazurenko has had some serious health problems of late and his memories of this event have become a landscape partially obscured by clouds: some details are vivid while others are lost to view.

Nonetheless, Ivan Dunkai's account of his last meeting with Markov survives. "He came to me [on December 3]," Dunkai explained to the filmmaker Sasha Snow, "and it was getting dark when he arrived. He said, 'There's a tiger about.' I asked him, 'Where?' Markov said that the animal was hiding. 'When are you going to visit me?' he asked. 'Come now, and we'll go hunting together.' I asked him, 'How can we go hunting at night? Look, I've made a soup. Let's eat together.' But he kept insisting, saying that he had to go now! I asked if he would come back the next day, but he said he had a lot to do."

Dunkai offered him a bed for the night, but Markov refused; though it was already dusk, he headed off through the forest to Zhorkin's camp. Apparently, he made no mention of a search for lost dogs. Rather, it seemed to Dunkai that the dogs were searching for Markov: "What was curious," Dunkai noted, "was that, after he left, his dog came by. It was strange because a dog usually stays with its master, and that one was a hunting dog."

Markov was not in the habit of chaining up his dogs (in part due to the risk of tigers), and there was no reason for him to become separated from them unless something extraordinary had happened. When one considers the keen senses of a good hunting dog, its familiarity with its home territory, and its loyalty to its master, it becomes clearer just how difficult it would be for one of them, much less all three, to "lose" not only their master but one another. In the Panchelaza, there was really only one thing that could cause this to happen.

Markov's dogs, it seemed, were on a circuit of their own and, like all good trackers, they searched in steadily widening rings around the place they had last seen what they were looking for. They also checked in with the neighbors. The only person located closer to Markov than Zhorkin's loggers was a small, curious hermit of a man with a tobacco rasp and a nickname he had picked up in prison. Kopchony ("Smokey") was about fifty years old and barely five feet tall, with a hairstyle and mustache identical to Joseph Stalin's. He lived a mile southwest of Markov and worked part-time as a watchman for Zhorkin; the rest of the time he lived off the land in a state of solitude much like Ivan Dunkai's, interrupted only by occasional trips to Sobolonye for supplies and a steam bath. Lacking the resources to build a proper cabin, Kopchony lived in what was, essentially, a hole in the ground. It was surrounded by low walls and a shed roof and, were a Muscovite or a Petersburger to encounter it, they would scarcely recognize it as a dwelling; it looked more like a root cellar. Surrounded as it was by undisturbed forest, and accessible only by a faint and winding footpath, Kopchony's hovel looked like something from a fairy tale—the kind of place where a witch might live, or maybe a gnome. The only way to find it was to be led there by someone who knew the way. Markov took tea there on occasion, and at least one of his dogs went there to look for him.

Not surprisingly, tigers were a fairly regular occurrence in Kopchony's world. "Sometimes, I would see one on the way to the outhouse, sometimes when I went fishing," he explained. He was well acquainted with the tigress that frequented the logging base: "I often saw her on the way to the village," he said. "Once, I was walking on the road and noticed something up ahead. I came closer, and there she was—her paw big like *that.*" He put his hands up to frame his face. "She had stood there for a long while, and I said to her, 'You have been waiting for me for quite some time, haven't you? You noticed me from far away.'"

Ivan Dunkai described these experiences, too. "There is something hypnotic in a tiger," he explained. "She has that quality. She treads so softly that there is no sound, and you won't know she's there at all. But if she doesn't like something, she'll stop and hold your gaze. There's a kind of psychological ballet: who will outstare who? In such cases, you should not suddenly turn tail because the scent of fear passes quickly. You must back off slowly, slowly— especially if the tiger has a kill, or if she's a mother with cubs: she makes a step, you make a step—you must not run away. And only when you leave the territory she thinks is hers, only then can you run."

Tigers, incidentally, have been observed doing the same thing: sauntering casually away from a car and then, once they believe themselves to be out of sight, bolting for their lives. But for Kopchony, as small and solitary as he was, fear didn't seem to be a factor; he had found a comfortable niche for himself within the ecosystem of the Panchelaza. "I never had any conflicts with them," he said of the local tigers. Kopchony's world was a peaceful one, governed in part by a pragmatic but circular logic reminiscent of a Laurel and Hardy sketch. When asked if he had ever discussed the Markov incident with Ivan Dunkai, he replied, "No, we never talked about it because he knew about it without me telling him about it, and I knew about it without him telling me, so what are we going to talk about?"

———

Deadly attacks by tigers are rare events in Russia, and Trush had handled only one such incident before. Most of Inspection Tiger's work involved poaching incidents and related infractions, and so weren't usually this involved or this deadly. Typically, interviews were restricted to immediate suspects and possibly a middleman; local informants also played a role. The Khomenko incident had been Trush's first case involving the death of a person. As upsetting as it was, it had fit the typical profile of an animal attack on a hunter: clearly provoked, quickly resolved, and with no third parties attempting to conceal evidence. In human terms, Khomenko's death was a third-degree murder: a spur-of-the moment defensive reaction in which death was incidental rather than intended. By contrast, the attack on Markov was far more sinister. It resembled something closer to a first-degree murder: premeditated, with malice aforethought, and a clear intent to kill. However, at this early stage of the investigation, neither Trush nor anyone else had fully grasped the threat this tiger posed to the general public. Trush was hoping that Markov, like Khomenko, would be a one-off and, now that the score was settled, the tiger would return to its usual prey. But it was too late for that now; this tiger was beyond recall.

Trush's last interview that day was with Pyotr Zhorkin, and Trush certainly didn't endear himself to the man when he confiscated the bullets for his unregistered gun. Zhorkin, in return, issued a warning that Trush transcribed word for word: "I can tell you one thing," he said, "if a tiger decides to hunt somebody, you're not going to stop her." Zhorkin was a man who held his own opinions in high regard, regardless of their grounding, but in this case he was prophetic. By the time Trush got back to Luchegorsk and typed up his notes on Sunday afternoon, the tiger was hunting again.

11

The story of cats is a story of meat.

ELIZABETH MARSHALL THOMAS,
The Tribe of Tiger

MARKOV'S BURIAL SUIT ARRIVED FROM LUCHEGORSK ON SATURDAY, December 6. That afternoon, Zaitsev, Dvornik, and Onofreychuk gathered a load of firewood and drove down the road to the grave-yard. The tiger, never far from their minds, was moving, too, but they had no idea where. Far away, they hoped. Until now, tigers had been more of an abstraction than a fact in these men's minds. There had always been stories and tracks and missing dogs, but now the tiger's presence was personal, visceral—as if the animal had reached some kind of critical mass whereby it shifted into a new and more immediate dimension. None of them had felt a tiger the way they did at Markov's cabin, and it was crowding their consciousness now—waking and sleeping—in a way it never had before. The woods still looked the same, but they did not feel the same. It made a man think about his children differently, and wonder where they were.

After clearing the snow from Markov's gravesite, the men built a fire there to thaw the ground. The temperature in the Bikin valley had not risen above minus ten in a month or more and, lately, it had been much colder, dropping to minus forty. The ground was as hard as cement, frozen to a depth of about three feet. The fire would need to burn all night. The next morning, they would return with picks and shovels to dig the grave. That evening, in an alcoholic fog, the three men, along with a couple of neighbors, took what little remained of the joker Markiz and laid him in his coffin, arranging him the best they could in relation to the clothing provided. Then they slipped a pack of cigarettes into his breast pocket, covered him with a white sheet, and nailed the lid down hard.

The following morning—Sunday—most of Sobolonye's dwindling population joined in the procession to the cemetery. Markov's coffin rode in a truck while the villagers followed on foot. It was thirty below zero. There were no songs, horns, or banners as there might have been before Soviet times. "No one said anything," recalled the huntress Baba Liuda. "After what that tiger did, everyone was speechless. We came; we cried; we buried him."

Tamara Borisova could barely stand. There is no church in Sobolonye and, while there was a practicing shamanka (a female shaman) down the river in Krasny Yar, there wasn't a priest for sixty miles in any direction—three generations of communism had seen to that—so the townspeople took it upon themselves to lay Markov to rest. With no overarching cosmology to guide them, only vestigial formalities, each would have to decide for himself what their friend and neighbor's eternal fate might be.

In fact, Markov had already transubstantiated: he had become energy in one of its rawest, most terrifying forms. Even as his friends and neighbors lowered that disturbingly light coffin into the ground, Markov's flesh and blood were driving a hungry, wounded tiger through the forest, directly toward Sobolonye.

———

Tigers on the prowl may look like the embodiment of lethal competence, but looks are deceiving: in order to survive, they need to kill roughly one large animal each week, and they miss their mark between 30 and 90 percent of the time. This relative inefficiency is extremely costly in terms of energy expenditure. As a result, injured or not, there is no rest for a tiger—no hibernation as there is for bears, no division of labor as with lions, and no migration to lush pastures as there is for many ungulates. Time, for the tiger, especially the male, is more like time is for the shark: a largely solitary experience of hunting and digesting followed by more hunting, until he dies.

The tiger's life is enlivened by breeding, but only briefly. These moments of courtship and intimacy, which typically take place in the dead of winter, can produce behaviors recognizable to any human. Arthur Strachan, a British tiger hunter, author, and artist, described the following encounter between a pair of Bengal tigers at a kill:

> ... The male strode slowly as if in studied indifference to her presence, while the body of his spouse seemed to sink gradually into the ground as she flattened herself as a cat does on the near approach of its prey.
>
> With blazing eyes, ears laid back, and twitching tail, her attitude for the moment was anything but that of the loving wife. Waiting till the tiger was within a few paces, she sprang towards him as if bent on his annihilation, lifted a fore-paw, and gently patted him on the side of his face. Then she raised her head and obviously kissed him.
>
> To these symptoms of affection the male at first seemed rather indifferent, but when she rubbed herself against his legs and playfully bit them, he condescendingly lay down, and a mock battle ensued between the two beautiful animals. This was conducted in absolute silence, save for the occasional soft "click" of teeth meeting when the widely opened jaws came in contact with each other.
>
> Sometimes locked in a close embrace, playfully kicking each other with their hind-feet, sometimes daintily sparring with their fore-paws, they rolled about thus for nearly a quarter of an hour ...

Such tender moments are, however, few and far between. Once the cubs are born the tigress must keep hunting on her own, only twice as hard now because she has cubs to feed—and to protect from infanticidal males. A tiger's taste for meat may be innate, but its ability to acquire it is not, so the tigress must also teach her cubs how to hunt. Tigresses typically bear from one to four cubs in a litter, and they will spend one to two years with the mother, during which time she must keep them warm, safe, and fed. In addition to all her other tasks, she must engineer predation scenarios that demonstrate stalking and killing techniques and then allow the cubs to safely practice them without getting injured or starving due to their own incompetence, *and* while taking care of her own prodigious appetite. The learning curve is long and steep and, in the taiga, the combination of hard winters, hunting accidents, and hostile males takes a heavy toll on cubs, especially young males.

By the time tigress and cubs go their separate ways, the cubs will be nearly adult-sized though still a couple of years away from sexual maturity. Some cubs will stay close by, but these are usually the females who control smaller territories and are more likely to be tolerated by their mother, and by the area's dominant male. A two- or three-year-old male, however, is on his own; for both genetic and competitive reasons, the mother doesn't want him around. A male cub's exile is comparable to sending a barely pubescent boy out onto the street to fend for himself: he might make it, but there's a good chance he won't for any number of reasons. He could be gored by a boar or have his jaw broken by an elk; he could be attacked by a large bear. The dominant male tiger may kill him outright or run him off and, with no territory of his own, he will have to make his living on the margins.

Living as an amateur in this sylvan purgatory is catch-as-catch-can, and one accident with a car, an animal trap, or a hunter—not to mention one bad stretch of deep snow and minus forty weather—could finish him off. Unfortunately, this combination of landlessness and semi-competence can often lead to dog and livestock killing: if the taiga doesn't get him, a farmer may well. In any case, it can require several years of this dangerous, liminal existence before a male tiger acquires the skill—and the will—to stake out and defend his own territory. But as strong and able as he may be, the battle for that territory—even if he wins it—can leave him grievously injured. So lethally designed are these animals that a battle between them can be compared to a hand grenade contest: there is virtually no way to come away from that combination of points, blades, and combustive energy without incurring serious damage. In short, the gauntlet of trials and initiations a male tiger must endure is long, arduous, and deadly, and the survivors are truly formidable specimens.

———

By Tuesday morning, December 9, the Markov attack was front-page news. LAW OF THE JUNGLE, crowed the headline in the Primorye edition of *Komsomolskaya Pravda* ("Young Communist Truth"), a venerable but now ironically titled propaganda-organ-turned-tabloid. Next to a stock photo of a tiger's face ran the sub-head: "Tigress Avenges Dead Offspring."

The Markov investigation was barely three days old, but already fact, rumor, and human error had been woven into a tangled braid, the individual strands of which would be hard to tease apart. Inspection Tiger was trying to do the right things, but with conflicting information. Trush and his team had been patrolling the area, making inquiries, and mining established local informants, and the rumors they were hearing about Markov's activities had the ring of truth. They also had a common theme—that, prior to the attack, Markov had been having trouble with a tiger: something had happened and it wouldn't leave him alone. Confounding matters was the fact that there wasn't just one tiger; nor was there just one story. Over the previous year, Markov had been spending progressively more time at his cabin in the Panchelaza, during which time he had had encounters with several tigers. Maybe they were attracted by his dogs, maybe it was something else, but it seemed that the Panchelaza was becoming a vortex of tiger activity.

It was believed by some who knew him well, including a long-time resident of Yasenovie named Sergei Boyko, that Markov had killed a tiger cub recently. Boyko is a huge and bearded former logger, now in his mid-forties; though a teetotaler, he still manages to project the mass and manner of a Slavic Bacchus. "You cannot hide things in the taiga," he explained in his driveway-barnyard. "The police might not find out about it, but we always do." Boyko had worked with both Markov and Onofreychuk, and he knew the tayozhnik's life firsthand. "I have lived in the taiga all my life," he said. "I have been in many situations, including poaching. I won't lie to you about that."

Boyko was luckier than most in that he had managed to find steady work on a maintenance crew at one of the new highway bridges about six miles west of Markov's cabin. Tigers prowl around their flimsy barracks on a regular basis, and watchdogs don't last long there. One of Boyko's co-workers, a gaunt older man who could have stepped out of a daguerreotype, keeps an aluminum canteen pocked with finger-sized holes made by the fangs of an inquisitive tiger. Boyko believed there was a connection between the attack on Markov and an attempt by him and some other locals, including Onofreychuk, to wipe out an entire family of tigers earlier in the winter. "They were together there," said Boyko. "One had a sixteen-gauge; another had a twelve [a more powerful shotgun]. They seriously injured the tigress and she ran away upriver, but it snowed and they couldn't find her. The cub was left behind, and they killed it. They traded the skin for a Buran" (a brand of Soviet-era snowmobile).

Dmitri Pikunov, the tiger researcher, who had extensive contacts along the Bikin, had heard this version, too, and found it credible. True or not, it formed a tidy narrative, much as Khomenko's story had: Markov, a known poacher, blatantly hunting tigers in violation of federal law, kills a cub and is himself killed by the wounded and vengeful mother. Case closed. It was this version of events, provided by people close to the source, but not eyewitnesses, that inspired the headlines and raised Trush's hopes for a peaceful resolution in which the tigress would simply disappear into the forest.

There was an eerie reciprocity energizing this scenario, and it was that, prior to being eaten by the tiger, it seemed Markov had been eating them. "Tastes like chicken," Markov had once quipped to Denis Burukhin.

"I couldn't tell if he was joking or not," Burukhin said. "It was always hard to tell with Markiz."

But Evgeny Smirnov, a hunting inspector living in Krasny Yar, had also heard this rumor, and it didn't strike him as odd at all.

According to Smirnov, tiger is delicious—not quite as good as lynx, but a bona fide forest delicacy for those so inclined. Yuri Trush even has a recipe. When he and some local villagers were skinning out the Khomenko tiger, the understanding had been that they could keep the meat, but Trush would take the skin and bones. However, when he turned away to attend to something, someone made off with the tiger's head. When Trush found out who it was, he confronted the man in his home and asked him what he was doing. "I was going to make an aspic," the man said sheepishly.

Those were lean years in Primorye, and they still are. Many of the people who live on the Bikin are hungry—and resourceful—in ways that can be hard to imagine. For someone in Markov's situation, it is totally reasonable—righteous, even—to eat what you kill, whatever it may be. "I've tried tiger," said Trush. "My whole family tried it. It's quite unusual—slightly sweet, but I don't care for it anymore—not since I saw a tiger eat a rotten cow in 2000. He ate the meat with worms and everything."

In addition to the story of the avenging tigress, there were other, equally plausible rumors involving Markov and tigers circulating through the valley, but at this early stage of the investigation, Trush ignored them. It was here that Trush's combination of authority and lack of extensive tiger tracking experience betrayed him, if only briefly. The confusion centered on a crucial inconsistency between the emphatic but fallible accounts he was hearing from informants and the far steadier record kept by the snow. The truth lay in the paw prints: soon, it would become painfully clear that the tracks around Markov's cabin were far too big to have been made by a female.

Nonetheless, the avenging tigress theory gained traction when a tiger trap was discovered a quarter mile east of Markov's cabin. The device was all business and whoever built it had known exactly what he was doing. It consisted of a sturdy wooden corral six feet high, four feet wide, and twenty feet long. At the closed end was a stake with a chain, and this was for the bait: a live dog. Between the entrance and the bait was a series of buried wolf traps, rigged in conjunction with heavy cable snares. In the taiga, such a contraption has only one conceivable purpose, and its discovery confirmed for Trush and many others that Markov had made the jump from subsistence poaching to the big leagues of black market tiger hunting.

———

When Ivan Dunkai found out what had happened to Markov, he was flabbergasted: "After he hadn't showed up for four days, I decided to go look for him," Dunkai explained. "I arrived there [Zhorkin's camp], and they told me: 'Markov's been eaten by a tiger.' How could that happen? It seemed such nonsense to me! We've never heard of such a thing! What do you mean 'eaten'? Literally, *eaten*?"

Sergei Boyko, however, wasn't so surprised, and this may be because he knows what it is to run afoul of a tiger. "Another hunter and me, we once took some of a tiger's kill," he began. "We saw the tiger running away and cut some meat for ourselves. We didn't take it all because you can't take everything. It's a law in the taiga: you have to share. But when we came to check the next day, the tiger hadn't touched what we'd left for him. After that, we couldn't kill anything: the tiger destroyed our traps, and he scared off the animals that came to our bait. If any animal got close, he would roar and everyone would run away. We learned the hard way. That tiger wouldn't let us hunt for an entire year. I must tell you," Boyko added, "the tiger is such an unusual animal: very powerful, very smart, and very vengeful."

Boyko's experience is not unique. The Amur tiger's territoriality and capacity for sustained vengeance, for lack of a better word, are the stuff of both legend and fact. What is amazing—and also terrifying about tigers—is their facility for what can only be described as abstract thinking. Very quickly, a tiger can assimilate new information—evidence, if you will—ascribe it to a source, and even a motive, and react accordingly.* Sergei Sokolov is a for-

———

* For example, tigers are adept at distinguishing between the engine sounds of airplanes and helicopters; the former are no threat and are ignored, while the latter may be used for tracking and are responded to with evasive or aggressive action.

mer hunting inspector who now works as a researcher for the Institute for Sustainable Resource Management in Primorye. "Based on the scientific approach," Sokolov explained, "you can say that the more diverse the food of an animal, the more developed his intelligence is."

In an effort to demonstrate the sophistication of the tiger's thought process, Sokolov described the following incident involving a hunter in his management area on the upper reaches of the Perevalnaya River, due south of Tiger Mountain in central Primorye:

"There was little food for wild boar there so boar were scarce," Sokolov began. "In addition, a tiger was visiting the hunter's territory on a regular basis, scaring away any boar that were left. So the hunter decided to kill this tiger by installing a gun trap. The first time, the rifle was not installed properly and it fired but didn't kill the tiger—just grazed his fur. The hunter reset it, and later, based on the tracks, observed that the tiger touched the tripwire, heard the sound of the gun misfiring, stepped slowly backward, and immediately went after the hunter. The tiger understood who was there, who installed the trap, and who was trying to kill him. He didn't even follow the hunter's tracks; he went directly to the hunter's cabin—like he was using a compass.

"The hunter told me, 'I was near the cabin, chopping wood, when all of a sudden I felt like somebody was watching me. I turned around and saw the tiger about a hundred feet away with his ears back, ready to attack.' The hunter ran into his cabin and, for three days, didn't go out, not even to pee—he had to do it in the basin. The hunter was not an educated man and usually didn't write even a letter to anybody, but during those three days, as the hunter said, he became a writer 'like Lev Tolstoy—writing a whole novel about what happened,' because he thought that the tiger was definitely going to kill him and, at the very least, he wanted to let people know what had happened to him. After three days, the hunter finally ventured out, checked the area, and found the spot where the tiger had been waiting. Based on the amount of melted snow, he guessed the tiger had been there for several days. After that, the tiger left his territory."

Vladimir Schetinin, the former head of Inspection Tiger, and an expert on Amur tiger attacks, has accumulated a number of stories like this over the past thirty years. "There are at least eight cases that my teams and I investigated," he said in March of 2007, "and we all arrived at the same conclusion: if a hunter fired a shot at a tiger, that tiger would track him down, even if it took him two or three months. It is obvious that tigers will sit and wait specifically for the hunter who has fired shots at them."

The caveat here is that each of these eight cases met the following conditions: namely, that the tiger was able to identify its attacker, had the opportunity to hunt him, and was temperamentally disposed to do so. In its brief reference to tiger attacks on humans, *Mammals of the Soviet Union* states that "Usually animals shot and wounded or chased by hunters attacked, and only very rarely did an attack occur without provocation." Such responses are, in themselves, examples of abstract thinking: tigers evolved to respond to direct physical attacks from other animals; they did not evolve to respond to remote threats like guns. Nor do they innately understand what guns are or how they work. So to be able to make the multistep connection between a random explosion in the air, a pain it can feel but often cannot see, and a human who may be dozens of yards away is, almost by definition, an abstraction. While many higher animals are capable of making this association, very few will respond like a tiger. If you combine this with a long memory, you can have a serious problem on your hands.

Chris Schneider, an American veterinarian based in Washington state, has had personal experience with the tiger's capacity for holding a grudge. Over the course of his career, Schneider has treated many circus animals, including tigers, sometimes giving them sedatives in the form of a painful shot in the rump. A year might go by before these tigers passed through town again; nonetheless, the moment he showed up, their eyes would lock on him. "I'd wear different hats; I'd try to disguise myself," Schneider explained, "but when I'd walk into the room, the cat would just start following me, turning as I walked around them. It was uncanny." He described the impact of these tigers' gaze as "piercing." "They looked right through you: a *very* focused predator. I think most of those cats would have nailed me if they could have."

John Goodrich and Dale Miquelle, the American field biologists who run the Wildlife Conservation Society's Siberian Tiger Project in the Sikhote-Alin Zapovednik, have had the opposite experience. For more than fifteen years, both men have been living and working in Terney, on the east coast of Primorye, and, over the years, they have caught, sedated, examined, and collared dozens of tigers, some of them numerous times. Despite the fact that both of these men have spent years in these tigers' territories, there have been no cases of tiger vengeance. "As a biologist, I have a hard time believing it," explained Miquelle when asked about such behavior, "but as a type of myth and local perspective on tigers I find it intriguing."

"If tigers are vengeful," said Goodrich, "I should be dead."

It is not known if tigers are capable of distinguishing between humans who intentionally cause them pain or injury, and humans who trap them and manipulate them but release them into their home territory unharmed. Because of this, there is no tidy way to reconcile these differing views, all of which are based on extensive firsthand experience. In the end, it may simply come down to context and character—of all concerned. This, and the fact that, as Miquelle puts it, "What tigers usually do, and what they *can* do, are very different things."

———

A more useful way to understand a tiger's capacity for vengeful behavior may be in the context of territory and property, i.e., prey. As they are with human hunters, these are hard to separate in the tiger's mind. Tigers, particularly males, are well known for their intense and reflexive possessiveness; it is a defining characteristic, and it exerts a powerful influence on their behavior, particularly when it comes to territory, mates, and food. Both males and females can be ferocious boundary keepers, but a male tiger will guard his domain as jealously as any modern gangster or medieval lord. An Amur tiger's sense of superiority and dominance over his realm is absolute: because of his position in the forest hierarchy, the only force a male will typically submit to is a stronger tiger or, occasionally, a large brown bear. Nothing else ranks in the taiga, and this is why, if threatened or attacked, these animals have been known to climb trees to swat at helicopters and run headlong into gunfire.

Fights between animals are rarely to the death because killing a powerful adversary is dangerous and takes an enormous amount of energy. Death for its own sake is seldom an objective in nature anyway: the reason prey is killed is not to kill it per se, but to keep it still long enough to be eaten. Likewise, in the case of a territorial dispute, the goal is not to terminate but to establish dominance and persuade your competitor to go elsewhere. In general, animals (including tigers) avoid conflicts whenever possible because fighting hurts, and the margins in the wild are simply too tight. Most predators—leopards or solitary wolves, for example—will abandon a contested kill rather than risk an injury. But tigers are different: when dealing with its subjects, the male Amur tiger can be vicious, shrewd, and vindictive. In addition to his Herod-like response to other cubs and young males, he may even kill his own. Based on the observations of hunters and biologists, it appears that Amur tigers will occasionally kill bears solely on something that we might recognize as principle. Communal animals sometimes engage in wanton attacks, but it is hard to imagine any other solitary animal capable of a tiger's ambitious and intelligent savagery.

In Primorye, tigers attack and eat both black and brown bears on a fairly regular basis; this is striking because, ordinarily, no animal in its right mind would take on a bear. Russian brown bears belong to the same species as American grizzlies and can weigh a thousand pounds; their ferocity and power are legendary. In spite of this, they have been known to flee at the sight of a tiger. "In January 1941, I encountered the prints of a very large brown bear," wrote the tiger biologist Lev Kaplanov. "This animal, which had accidentally come across a tiger family on the trail, abandoned this path at a gallop."

Practically speaking, even a modestly sized brown bear would be a match for any tiger. So why would a tiger pick a fight with such a dangerous opponent? And why would it then prosecute the battle—as sometimes happens—to the point of tearing the bear limb from limb and scattering its appendages across the battleground? While the motives can never be fully understood, the discovery and description of such scenes would go a long way toward explaining why indigenous people like Ivan Dunkai's son Mikhail refer to the tiger—not the larger brown bear—as the "Czar of the Forest."*

———

Prior to the arrival of Chinese gold miners and Russian settlers, there appeared to be minimal conflict between humans and tigers in what is now Primorye. Game was abundant, human populations were relatively small, and there was plenty of room for all in the vast temperate jungles of coastal Manchuria. Furthermore, the Manchus, Udeghe, Nanai, and Orochi, all of whom are Tungusic peoples long habituated to living with tigers, knew their place; they were animists who held tigers in the highest regard and did their best to stay out of their way. But when Russian colonists began arriving in the seventeenth century, these carefully managed agreements began to break down. People in Krasny Yar still tell stories about the first time their grandparents saw Russians: huge creatures covered in red hair with blue eyes and skin as pale as a dead man's.

Some of these newcomers were Orthodox missionaries and though they were unarmed, their rigid convictions took a serious toll on native society. The word "shaman" is a Tungusic word, and in the Far East in the mid-nineteenth century, shamanism had reached a highly evolved state. For shamans and their followers who truly believed in the gods they served and in the powers they wielded, to have them disdained by missionaries and swept into

———

* Tigers notwithstanding, the bear occupies a place of high honor in the pantheon of Primorye's first peoples. The Nivkh (aka Gilyak), a coastal tribe whose historic lands abut those of the Udeghe and the Nanai, took this reverence the furthest by developing an elaborate bear cult in which a bear would be captured alive, housed, and fed— sometimes for years—and then ritually killed and eaten. There is no record of any indigenous people attempting to do this with a tiger.

irrelevance by foreign governments and technology was psychically devastating—a catastrophic loss of power and status comparable to that experienced by the Russian nobility when the Bolsheviks came to power.

In Primorye, this traumatic process continued into the 1950s. The Udeghe author Alexander Konchuga is descended from a line of shamans and shamankas, and he grew up in their company. "Local authorities did not prohibit it," he explained. "The attitude was, if you're drumming at night, that's your business. But the officials in the regional centers were against it and, in 1955, when I was still a student, some militia came to my cousin's grandmother. Someone must have snitched on her and told them she was a shamanka because they took away her drums and burned them. She couldn't take it and she hanged herself." The drum is the membrane through which the shaman communicates with, and travels to, the spirit world. For the shaman, the drum is a vital organ and life is inconceivable without it.

Along with spiritual and social disruption came dramatic changes to the environment. One Nanai story collected around 1915 begins, "Once upon a time, before the Russians burned the forests down . . ." In this and many other ways, Russia's expansion into the Far East reflects the American expansion into the West. On both frontiers, it was fur traders, gold seekers, and explorers who led the way by land and sea, followed by settlers, soldiers, industrial resource extractors, the navy, and the railroad. However, Russia is almost twice the width of the United States, so even though Russians had a head start of more than a century, a combination of economics, politics, and sheer geographic enormity slowed the pace of progress. Nonetheless, by 1850, it was clear that nothing would ever be the same on either coast of the North Pacific.

If one were able to unfold the globe and view the recent histories of Eurasia and the Americas simultaneously, one would see an explosion of ideological, technological, viral, and alcoholic energy radiating outward from Europe and sweeping across these regions. In Russia, the first vehicles for these world-changing forces were the Cossacks. They were the conquistadors of Eurasia, a legendary class of horsemen, warriors, and explorers who guarded the czars

and endured extraordinary privations in order to open Siberia—
first to the fur trade and later to colonization. The indigenous peoples they encountered on their epic journeys to the Arctic and
Pacific coasts suffered enormously at their hands. Many natives,
along with Manchus and Koreans, were simply killed outright
while the survivors became victims of crippling extortion, mostly
in the form of furs, but nothing was off limits: when Manchus got
wind of a Cossack advance, their first response was to evacuate all
the women.

After Russia lost the Crimean War in 1856, the Far East was the
only direction it had left to turn with its imperial ambitions, and it
was the Cossacks who established settlements on the Amur River in
direct violation of a two-hundred-year-old treaty with China.
From these forward bases, or *ostrogs*, Russia launched its formal
annexation of Primorye. By the turn of the last century, Cossack
soldiers had gone on to occupy most of northern Manchuria.
"They are semi-savages, black-eyed, fierce-browed, the finest
horsemen in the world, caring little for your life, little for their
own," wrote Sir John Foster Fraser, a British correspondent who
spent time among the Cossacks in 1901, en route to Harbin, a
Russian-built city two hundred miles inside Chinese Manchuria.
Fraser came away as moved by the soldiers' hospitality as he was
impressed by their headlong courage. "For a [cavalry] charge there
are no troops that could equal them. . . . And who that has heard a
Slav song, crooning, pathetic, weird, sung by a Cossack at night in
the middle of a plain silent as death, can forget it?"

Some Cossack leaders, so far removed from any law or consequence, degenerated into piratical warlords who would have given
Cortés or Kurtz a run for his money. Even after something approx-
imating the rule of law had been established in Primorye, extortion, shakedowns, cross-border banditry, and racially motivated
murder remained common into the twentieth century (since perestroika, all of these problems have resurged).

———

The few Russians who journey to Primorye voluntarily, or who
stay and embrace it as Arseniev, Trush, and Markov did, tend to

possess an adventurous curiosity that borders on the romantic. They feel their surroundings intensely and one reason they choose to live in Primorye is that, in Russia, there is no other natural environment that is so complex, exotic, or stimulating to the senses. But there is no question that the boreal jungle is an acquired taste, and it defeated people regularly. Many early settlers found life there so strange and difficult that they simply turned around and went back, a retreat, it must be remembered, that could take years. The leopard specialist Vasily Solkin, who was taught to hunt in western Russia, could appreciate the newcomers' disorientation: "I had the feeling I'd walked into a botanical garden," he said. "The forest did not look natural or normal to me; it was too exotic, there were all these different species. I felt like a child in kindergarten: the hunting skills I had were of no use to me here."

However, more often than not, once a Russian had made it to the coast—often as an exile—this was where he would remain; everything he had previously known would exist in memory only. In 1870, Vladivostok had a population of about seven thousand from all over Russia and the Pacific. In those days, the future capital resembled a smaller, more primitive San Francisco: not only was it beautifully situated, but natural resources were abundant, the Pacific offered access to the world, and grandiose dreams were encouraged. A number of those dreamers came from overseas. In addition to China, Russia had managed to beat out England, France, and the United States in its race to lay claim to this strategically situated and physically perfect port where, it was said, all the navies of Europe could be safely hidden. It was a harsh but hopeful time. It was also an inebrious time. In 1878, tax revenue from alcohol sales in the Maritime Territory exceeded all other sources combined by a factor of twenty.

As in all frontier towns, the gender ratio in Vladivostok was hopelessly skewed, so surplus bachelors were forced to find alternative amusements for themselves. One of these resembled a cross between Duck, Duck, Goose and Russian Roulette. Around 1895, an elderly survivor of this game was interviewed by a Russian researcher and travel writer named Dmitri Shreider whose book, an early profile of the region entitled *Our Ussuri*, was "approved by the Czar's censors" in 1897. The following excerpt makes Gogol look like a documentarist.

"Some years ago [c. 1870], at the time of all those fruitless hopes for unity and cohesion, an institution appeared here, 'The Lancepupov Club.'"

"What kind of club was it, and what were its goals?"

"Goals? Why, to combat the fragmentation and alienation in our society, and to gather its members for conversation and the exchange of ideas. But it wasn't long before the Lancepupov Club degenerated into something absurd, something that is shameful to remember."

My companion was quiet for a time, and then, hesitantly, he continued: "For example, how do you suppose you would like to play a game called 'Tiger Hunting'?"

"Tiger Hunting? I didn't know such a game existed."

"I didn't either, but after I lived here for a while, I found out about it. I remember that game very well, especially when it rains or snows . . ."

The narrator rolled up the sleeve of his frock-coat and bared his arm. I looked at it and noticed traces of a large wound above the elbow. The wound had obviously been inflicted by a firearm and, for the first time, I noticed that my companion could not move his arm very well. "Listen," I said to him, "so far, all this doesn't explain anything. And what do tigers have to do with it?"

"You don't understand? Of course," he muttered in embarrassment, "how can you . . . games like this don't exist elsewhere. *I* was the Tiger!" he exclaimed suddenly, and a broad smile lit his sincere face.

"You?!"

"Yes. You seem surprised, but it's all very simple: first, we would appoint someone—let's say me—to be the 'Tiger.' Then, we would take all the furniture out of the room, cover the windows with mats, and turn out the lights. The other club members would be the 'Hunters,' and they would sit in the middle of the room (facing outward), armed with revolvers. Thus arranged, they would shoot in any direction where they heard the Tiger (that is, me). Obviously, I'd taken my shoes off and emptied my pockets of anything that might jingle. I would be running along the walls in my socks, trying to step as softly as I could—like a tiger. But one time, the rôle proved too much for me: I stumbled and got a bullet in my arm. I was lucky it wasn't my heart."

I couldn't believe my ears. "Listen," I said, "this is not a game. It's murder! To cover the windows, turn out the lights and shoot at a human being? You could have been killed."

"Not exactly. As you can see, I'm still alive. Anyhow, we saw it differently: it was amusing, in its way. Of course, with the lamps lit, death was a real possibility, but, in the dark, the Tiger could become 'the Tiger!' Besides, according to the rules, you could only shoot at the legs."

"But you were shot in the elbow."

"It was an accident—I fell down."

"How could you agree to participate—forgive me for saying so—in such an insane game?"

"How? Now, of course, I can't think about it without feeling terrified. But back then, it was nothing. Back then, life was cheap."

"And were your other pastimes so . . . amusing?"

"No, they were more what you'd expect."

At the same time that members of the Lancepupov Club were hunting human tigers, the Yankovsky family were after the real thing. Mikhail Yankovsky was a descendant of Polish nobility who had fought on the wrong side of the Polish Rebellion of 1863. For his crimes, he was sentenced to eight years in Siberia, the first eighteen months of which were spent walking to prison. At that time, the railroad was still forty years away, and the road was barely passable—at any time of year. It was essentially a caravan route, only with fewer camels and none of the romance. Processions of exhausted, lice-infested exiles could be seen slogging eastward, while wagon trains bearing Chinese tea trundled west, wheels often buried to the hubs in mud, the horses and drivers

Liuty at Vladimir Kruglov's
wildlife rehabilitation
center *(John Goodrich)*

(Above)
Cossacks with tiger, c. 1885
(Courtesy of Vladimir Trofimov)

(Left)
Arseniev and Dersu, c. 1907
(Courtesy of Amur Region Research Association)

Nikolai Baikov with tiger, c. 1925
(Unknown)

(Above)
Sobolonye, with Sikhote-Alin
Mountains in background
(Author)

(Above) Main Street, Krasny Yar *(Author)*

(Above right) Kung with ginseng plants *(Author)*

(Right) Luchegorsk *(Sasha Snow)*

Yuri Yankovsky with tigers, c. 1930 *(V. Yankovsky)*

Manchuria, 2008 *(Author)*

(Below)
Tiger wine, Harbin Tiger Park
(Author)

(*Above*)
Markov's cabin *(Y. Trush)*

(*Left*)
Markov's grave *(Author)*

(*Right*)
Yuri Trush, 2004 *(Sasha Snow)*

(Left) Ivan Dunkai (Sasha Snow)

(Below) Vladimir Schetinin,
c. 1997 (David Higgs)

(Above) Evgeny Smirnoff (Author)

(Center left) Dmitri Pikunov (Author)

(Left) Danila Zaitsev (Author)

(Left)
Vladimir Shibnev *(Author)*

(Above)
Anatoli Khobitnov *(A. Khobitnov)*

(Center left)
Kapchiony *(Author)*

(Left)
Yuri Pionka on patrol, Bikin River
(David Higgs)

Pionka, Shibnev, and Gorborukov, taken from a video shot moments after the killing of the tiger, December 21, 1997 *(Y. Trush)*

Author's hand with female tiger track
(Author)

Tiger tracks *(John Goodrich)*

alike besieged by mosquitoes and biting flies. During the winter, it was so cold that the horses' nostrils would become clogged with ice from their own breath, and drivers had to stop periodically to clear them in order to keep the animals from suffocating. Even so, horses died and axles broke on a regular basis. "It is heavy going," wrote Chekhov during his own cross-country journey in the spring of 1890, "very heavy, but it grows heavier still when you consider that this hideous, pock-marked strip of land, this foul smallpox of a road, is almost the sole artery linking Europe and Siberia!"

Mikhail Yankovsky won an early release when Czar Alexander II declared an amnesty, but only on the condition that he never return to western Russia. Yankovsky honored this restriction and went on to lead an extraordinary life in the czar's most recent acquisition, first managing a gold mine on an island in the Sea of Japan, and then traveling down to Korea by junk and returning up the coast on horseback where he discovered a windswept (and mosquito-free) peninsula south of Vladivostok. Not long after staking his claim there, he became involved in a turf war with Manchurian bandits known as the *hong huzi* ("Red Beards") who had burned down the home of another recent settler, hung his wife's corpse on a lamp hook, and kidnapped his son. Yankovsky and his grieving neighbor banded together with local Korean hunters and pursued the gang to the Chinese border where a gunfight took place in which Yankovsky killed the bandit chief. He then went on to build a virtual fortress with bulletproof adobe walls, and began breeding horses and deer.*

In addition to the meat, young, soft deer antlers (*pantui*) are highly prized by Koreans for their rejuvenating properties; some took it to such an extreme that they would stand in line by the Yankovskys' paddock while the antlers were sawed off live deer in

---

* Mikhail Ivanovich Yankovsky (Jankowski) was also an amateur naturalist who discovered many species of Far Eastern bird, beetle, and butterfly, some of which bear his name to this day, and many more of which he sold to European museums and collectors. His son, Yuri, made a name for himself as a tiger hunter and published two memoirs, including *Fifty Years of Tiger Hunting* (in Russian, 1944).

order to suck the blood directly from the pulsing stumps. A tiger's appetites are not so different, and the Yankovsky family hadn't lived in their new home a year before they registered their first losses. Between 1880 and 1920, tigers killed scores of the Yankovskys' animals—everything from dogs to cattle. Once, a tiger dragged one of their hired men from his horse.

In the eyes of Russian settlers, tigers were simply four-legged bandits, and the Yankovskys retaliated accordingly.* Unlike the animist Udeghe who were native to the region, or the Chinese and Korean Buddhists who pioneered there, the Christian Russians behaved like owners as opposed to inhabiters. As with lion-human relations in the Kalahari, the breakdown began in earnest with the introduction of domestic animals. But it wasn't just the animals, it was the attitude that went with them. These newcomers arrived as entitled conquerors with no understanding of, or particular interest in, the local culture—human or otherwise. Like their New World counterparts across the Pacific, theirs, too, was a manifest destiny: they had a mandate, in many cases from the czar himself, and they took an Orthodox, Old Testament approach to both property and predators.

Accompanying this was a siege mentality that was exacerbated by the real threats posed by bandits and predatory animals. In addition to killing livestock, wolves really do kill people in Russia, and no one who had made it as far as the Pacific coast was going to put up with them, or with tigers either. They had been through too much already.

Over the course of sixty years, three generations of Yankovskys hunted tigers in Russia, Manchuria, and North Korea, where some of the family fled after the Russian Revolution. They began by hunting them in self-defense and, in later years, they hunted for sport, sometimes working as guides for other hunters. When they could, they sold the carcasses and the buyers were invariably Chinese. Mikhail Yankovsky's grandson Valery participated in some

---

* "Sixty-five tigers were said to have been killed in the [Vladivostok] district the year before my arrival," wrote the British evangelist and traveler Henry Landsdell in 1879.

of these expeditions and, in 2008, at the age of ninety-seven, he still recalled them vividly. Like the long-dead veteran of the Lancepupov Club, Valery Yankovsky offers a keyhole view into a world that no longer exists. "The Russians were probably the most aggressive tiger hunters out there, but after us it was the Koreans," he explained in a candid letter recalling his early days on the coast.

> We hunted in winter, using dogs and carbines, never traps or poison.* But tiger hunting was incidental rather than intentional; it wasn't a stable trade. When we had a tiger, Chinese apothecaries would buy it from us whole; they were particularly interested in the meat, heart, and bones. Of course, it was believed that the tiger's meat had supernatural powers; the heart, especially, was thought by all to make one more courageous. We didn't eat the meat ourselves, but I did try it once in 1943—boiled and cooked with miso. It was fatty and surprisingly tasty—a bit like mutton.
>
> In Korea, tigers would occasionally kill people in the deep forest, and when that happened the hunter's family would abandon the area. I have personally seen cabins there with the doors knocked in by tigers, and I have heard of tigers digging up fresh graves, but I never witnessed it.
>
> The tiger's character is very wily, cautious, and bloodthirsty; when walking in a tiger's tracks, you could always feel his presence, his menacing danger. Once, my father was attacked by a wounded tiger, and my brother saved him by shooting it. In those early days around Vladivostok, they were the principal killers of livestock. [Like my grandfather,] my father declared war against the tigers, and he bagged seven of them on his own. They were our vicious enemies.

Yankovsky's is a worldview caught in amber. Although he was born in the generation between Dersu Uzala and Ivan Dunkai, his experience of tigers is so radically different that he might as well

---

* As some Asian hunters did and do.

be describing another animal. Even a hundred years later, Ivan Dunkai's son Vasily's description of his relationship to the local tigers stands in stark contrast to a Russian settler's: "You know, there are two hunters in the taiga: a man and a tiger," he explained in March 2007. "As professional hunters, we respect each other: he chooses his path and I choose mine. Sometimes our paths intersect, but we do not intrude on each other in any way. The taiga is his home; he is the master. I am also a master in my own home, but he lives in the taiga all the time; I don't."

This disparity between the Yankovskys and the Dunkais is traceable to a fundamental conflict—not just between Russians and indigenous peoples, but with tigers—around the role of human beings in the natural world. In Primorye, ambitious Russian homesteaders operated under the assumption that they had been granted dominion over the land—just as God had granted it to Noah, the original homesteader:

> 1: Be fruitful, and multiply, and replenish the earth.
> 2: And the fear of you and the dread of you shall be upon every beast of the earth.

Implicit in these lines from Genesis 9 is the belief that there is no room for two on the forest throne. And yet, in a different context, these words could apply as easily to tigers as they do to humans. In so many words, God puts the earth and all its creatures at their disposal:

> 3: Every moving thing that liveth shall be meat for you; even as the green herb have I given you all things.

In 1857, when Primorye was still technically Chinese territory, the governor of East Siberia (who was the czar's, and therefore heaven's, agent in the Far East) said much the same thing to a crowd of outbound settlers: "God be with you, children! You are free now. Work the land, make it Russian, and start a new life." The Yankovskys, like so many other pioneers, took these words to heart and applied them to the forests of Primorye. This was unfor-

tunate, because the tigers had already claimed these gifts for themselves. It is only in the past two hundred years—out of two million—that humans have seriously contested the tiger's claim to the forest and all it contains. As adaptable as tigers are, they have not evolved to accommodate this latest change in their environment, and this lack of flexibility, when combined with armed, entitled humans and domestic animals, is a recipe for disaster.

———

This may well be what got Markov into trouble. It is safe to say that had he not been carrying a firearm, he would still be alive. And had he not been so tightly linked to animals that trigger the tiger's wolf-killing instincts, the likelihood of conflict would have dropped to nil. Remove guns and dogs from the equation and Markov would not have felt as bold, while the tiger would not have felt as threatened or protective. Even if there had been a dead boar lying in the snow between them, both parties would have responded to the situation very differently. Tigers will bluff-charge the same way bears do and, in most cases, all the tiger wants is an indication of submission. Under those circumstances, Markov would have deferred to the czar, and everyone would have lived to hunt another day. But guns and dogs are central to the tayozhnik's identity; for someone like Markov, life here would be impossible without them. Furthermore, submission of this kind doesn't come naturally to European Russians. Even had Markov wished to avoid a conflict with the tiger, seeing his dogs threatened or injured may have been too much to bear. Ivan Dunkai might be willing to sacrifice his dogs to the tiger, but not Markov.

A graphic example of the lengths to which a hunter can go to protect his dogs occurred in October of 2008, in south-central British Columbia. There, in the forest outside the town of 100 Mile House, a forty-five-year-old hunter and tree faller named Jim West was out with his two Labrador retrievers, searching for moose sign. West explained to Carole Rooney of the *100 Mile House Free Press* that he was unarmed and traveling upwind when "All of a sudden I heard a kind of a huff and a growl off to my right, and when I turned around there was a bear six feet away." It was a black bear with two cubs. Caught by surprise, the bear, which weighed about 250 pounds, attacked. "I had no opportunity to hit the ground like I should," West explained, "so I just started to kick her in the face. She jumped up and took a snap at my face, split my upper lip, and then I hit the ground, and she jumped on top of me, tore my scalp and bit my left arm."

At this point, the dogs entered the fray and attempted to draw the bear off. The bear abandoned West to pursue them, but as soon as West attempted to rise, the bear turned and attacked him again, this time biting his right arm. Again, the dogs intervened, and again, the bear went after them. Lying on the ground, bleeding from his head and arms, West tried to fathom what to do next. It was his dogs that gave him the motive and clarity to act: "I heard one of my dogs yelp," said West, an intense and wiry man who stands about five-foot-nine (shorter than the bear, had she been standing upright). "I thought, 'Well, you're not gonna kill my dog.' So I stood up; there was a stick at my feet. As I picked it up and looked, the bear was running at me full tilt and I in effect said, 'Let's go, bitch.' So I swung the stick, hit her between the ears, stopped her dead in her tracks. And she shook her head and she was stunned, and I realized that if I didn't continue, that bear would attack me again because I knew if I went down a third time I would never stand up. So, I just pretended I was driving spikes with a sledgehammer 'til that bear hit the ground, I saw blood coming out her nose. I then dropped the stick, wrapped my shirt around my head and told my dogs, 'It's time to go, kids.'"

West was treated for shock and required sixty stitches in his scalp, face, and arms.

"None of us had ever heard of anything remotely like this," said Darcy MacPhee, the field supervisor who oversaw the investigation with British Columbia's Predator Attack Team. "A bear is a pretty robust animal so we approached this from a very skeptical point of view."

Due to the extraordinary circumstances, an exhaustive necropsy was done and, in the end, it confirmed that West had indeed crushed the bear's skull. "In that sort of situation, you only have one choice," West said later. "It's live or die. Most people are too scared to think about living."

There is every reason to suppose that, in the heat of the moment, Markov believed he faced a similarly stark choice. It was well known that Markov loved his dogs, and the motive to act decisively may have been identical. Had Jim West been in Markov's situation with a loaded gun, there is no question what he would have done. "There are two categories of people when it comes to extreme situations," said the leopard specialist Vasily Solkin. "One gets scared first and then starts thinking; the other starts thinking first and gets scared after the fact. Only the latter survive in the taiga."

Markov was certainly one of the latter, but sometimes that isn't enough.

———

Because of the early evidence supporting the theory that Markov's death was an act of revenge by a tigress, Trush had not given much thought to the possibility that this attack might have stemmed from a confrontation between a tiger and Markov's dogs. But he had his hands full: following his investigation of the Markov site on Saturday the 6th, and his return to Luchegorsk, Trush spent the 8th and 9th fielding reporters' questions and issuing bulletins on radio and television, warning people who lived in the Bikin valley to be on their guard, and urging everyone else to stay away. However, once this was done, Trush went back to work, patrolling and responding to calls in other parts of his district.

Meanwhile, life in Sobolonye had changed dramatically. In addition to being in mourning, many residents were justifiably terrified: who was going to be next? "Will the tigress leave the area, having completed her revenge?" wondered the news commentator on a local television station. "Or, God forbid, will she inflict more sorrows?"

12

The only beasts that enter the myth complex are
those that kill the hunter and those into which he is
transformed.

JOSEPH FONTENROSE,
"Orion: The Myth of the Hunter and the Huntress"

FROM THE START, THERE HAD BEEN NO QUESTION IN THE MIND OF
Trush's squad mate, Sasha Lazurenko, that the tiger was a male—
not just any male, but an exceptionally large one. He had deferred
to Trush, his superior, and to the circumstantial evidence pointing
toward the avenging tigress because, initially, the tiger's gender
hadn't seemed that important. The most reliable way to determine
the size of a tiger without the tiger being present is by the paw
prints. Typically, hunters and biologists will measure the forepaw,
specifically, the relatively narrow "heel" which in Russian is called
the *pyatka* (*pyat*-kuh). The value of a pyatka measurement lies in
its consistency: physiologically, it is composed of a single heavy pad
so it won't spread or clench from step to step the way the broader
and more flexible toes can. The pyatka also takes the most concentrated weight of each step and thus leaves the deepest and clearest
impression. A large female Amur tiger will have a pyatka measurement of three and a half to four inches across the back of the heel,
while males will start there and can go as high as five inches or
more. Six inches is, at least by the standards of modern Amur tiger
data, a giant. A tiger with a pyatka that size could only be a male
and would probably weigh in the neighborhood of five to seven
hundred pounds—bigger than any wild lion.

Measurements were taken at the Markov site under favorable conditions; it wasn't a heavy snow year, so everything, as the hunters say, was on the surface. The pyatka measurement that is burned into Lazurenko's mind is 13.5 centimeters (about five and a half inches). Trush remembers the measurement as twelve centimeters. In the end, these differences would become moot. What mattered was that this was not only the biggest tiger in the Panchelaza, but for fifty miles around, and somehow Markov had crossed him.

Born shortly after perestroika, the tiger was roughly six years old—just entering his prime mating years—and wherever he chose to live he would likely be the dominant male. After a good feed, he could weigh close to five hundred pounds, and yet he had the explosive power to make a standing leap over a ten-foot fence, or across a residential street.

It is possible to determine a tiger's gender, and even his identity, simply by looking him in the face; a male's head is noticeably bigger and broader with a manelike ruff about the neck and tufty muttonchops running along the lower jaw. As with male humans, the male tiger's nose is also bigger and heavier—in the case of some tigers, almost snoutlike. The Panchelaza tiger had a big nose, and, like a male athlete's heavy brow and jaw, it was a clear indicator (among several) of this animal's fully developed masculinity and natural inclination toward dominance. A tiger's nose carries other clues, too: because the hair on it is so short and thin, it is one of the few places where battle scars will show, and this tiger's nose was crisscrossed with them. He bore other wounds as well, and these would come to light in time. As young as he was, he was already a veteran and, as such, was perfectly poised to be the czar of his domain for years to come.

When the tiger met Markov, he would have been in full arctic mode: thickly furred in a way that his southern counterparts would never be, he was insulated by a dense, woolly undercoat laid over with long, luxuriant guard hairs. From certain angles, he appeared as bushy as a lynx. His tail was a furry python as thick as a man's arm. This was the winter tiger: not the svelte, languorous creature of long grass and jungle pools, but the heavy-limbed sovereign of mountains, snow, and moonlight, resplendent and huge in his cool blue solitude.

———

Driven off Markov's corpse by Trush and his men on December 6, the tiger limped eastward, halting periodically to nurse his wounded leg. Each time, he would lick and gnaw at the wound, cleaning away the blood and pus, but above all, trying to soothe that incessant, searing pain. A tiger's tongue appears pink and soft from a distance, but it is actually covered in thornlike barbs, which are angled back toward the throat. They are so abrasive that they can pull out an animal's hair and excoriate its hide like a rasp; it would have the same effect on the tiger's own foreleg. Over the coming days, this cycle of travel and recovery would ebb and flow, but at this early stage, the tiger, crippled as he was, was otherwise perfectly fit. He had been well fed on forest game and could draw on the reserves he had built up during the fall and early winter before these latest encounters changed not only his diet but his modus vivendi.

The tiger's route led directly to the gravel highway and a road workers' camp where the raucous stench of feces emanating from the outhouse would have manifested an almost physical presence in the still and icy air. To the tiger, it would have been as arresting as a siren. Because it was the weekend, the soldiers drafted to work on the highway had been trucked back to their base in Khabarovsk, and two watchmen had been left behind to look after the cabins and equipment. The outhouse was plainly visible from their caravan and they were terrified by what they saw.

The tiger was following a human trail, but he was also, intentionally or not, reconstructing a story—a crime of sorts. This animal was now intimate with every nuance of Markov's scent, an elemental mélange of blood, sweat, intestines, and dogs combined with gunpowder, woodsmoke, vodka, and cigarettes. In a very real sense, these two beings were now fully integrated. It wasn't only Markov who had been irrevocably transformed; so, in his way, had the tiger: he had never had this kind of contact with a human before, and as a result he was no longer the same animal he once had been. His focus had shifted in a fundamental way. Now he was highly sensitized to the smallest trace of Markov, and to those who smelled like him, whatever form they might take.

Markov had been a regular at the road workers' camp just as he had been at Zhorkin's. Both bases had resident crews and were stocked with supplies that Markov needed: cooking oil, rice, potatoes, and cigarettes; perhaps a little vodka. What these remote camps lacked was a steady supply of fresh meat, so when Markov bagged something big he would pack a haunch down the trail to barter. Trush interviewed the watchmen, and according to them, Markov had come by earlier in the month with some boar meat. Trush had a strong suspicion that Markov had robbed it from a tiger kill.

One of a tiger's jobs as keeper of a territory is to take inventory; a tiger needs to know who is around and "available." When speaking of local tigers, Andrei Onofreychuk described them coming by periodically "to count us." One of the most efficient ways to do this is at an outhouse. It may reek to high heaven, but it is precisely because of this that it is a gold mine of information. Tigers mark their territories in a variety of ways: by clawing trees, scratching the ground, defecating, and also by spraying a durable and redolent combination of urine and musk. When doing the latter, they often select sheltered areas—the undersides of bushes, leaning trees, and angled rocks—to ensure their sign lasts as long as possible. A camp latrine is a kind of human equivalent: a communal scent tree, and it is to a tiger what a compressed personnel file is to a CEO. From its concentrated off-gassings a creature so attuned may glean the latest information about who is present, how many, their gender, disposition, health, and, of course, their diet. In the midst of that olfactory cacophony at the road workers' camp there may well have been two scents in particular that leaped out from the others: those of Markov and boar meat, specifically, meat from the tiger's last wild kill. Whatever was in there was rank and ruined, but the tiger considered it his, and he tore that outhouse down to get at it, board by shrieking board.

Under normal circumstances, a tiger's menu is based on a handful of local prey species, but it can expand almost limitlessly to include lizards, snakes, turtles, frogs, crocodiles, crabs, fish, seals, grass, berries, pine nuts, livestock, eggs, monkeys, cow dung, bones, carrion, maggots, termites, locusts, birds, porcupines, pangolins, badgers, sables, squirrels, cats, dogs, dholes, wolves, rats, mice, rabbits, bears, lynxes, leopards, and other tigers. But even with such catholic tastes, it is hard to understand what would compel a tiger to rip the walls off a locked outhouse and devour the contents. This is a decidedly strange thing for a tiger to do. It may even be unprecedented. But if one of the last people to use it was Markov, and Markov and others had been eating meat that the tiger recognized as his, then there was a motive. Trush, for one, felt sure the tiger had scented Markov or its stolen meat. The tiger researcher Dmitri Pikunov believed the tiger was driven to such an extreme by hunger, but the tiger had been gorging on Markov and his dogs only a day earlier, and the scats left by his cabin were ropey with boar hair. This tiger wasn't starving—not yet anyway. A sick or injured tiger can lay up for a week or two without food if it has to, and there was other potential prey around. With this in mind, the notion that the tiger smelled something in there that belonged to him, that enraged him, becomes more plausible. "Throughout the investigation," said Trush, "we kept wondering why the tiger was pressuring the man so intensely, why he had been stalking him. It seemed that he wanted to settle accounts." And, perhaps, to reclaim that which he knew to be rightfully his.

Unarmed and without a vehicle, the camp watchmen could do nothing but piss in a bucket, gape through the glass, and pray the tiger didn't do to their caravan what it was doing to the stoutly built privy thirty yards away. In the end, the tiger held them hostage for about twenty-four hours after abandoning Markov on Saturday the 6th and making the six-mile trek east. The watchmen had neighbors at the nearby Takhalo bridge maintenance camp, but no way to communicate with them. However, Sergei Boyko was on duty there that weekend and, having gotten wind of the Markov attack, paid a social call on Sunday. When the tiger heard Boyko's vehicle approaching, he retreated into the trees to watch. The watchmen heard it, too, and they cracked the door, signaling Boyko to stay inside. "There is a tiger!" they shouted.

Boyko ignored them and strode across the lot, went inside, and had a cup of tea. He knew what it was to have tiger trouble, but he had no issue with this tiger, so in his mind there was no possibility of a conflict. Many of his neighbors felt the same way. But his hosts, being city dwellers from Khabarovsk, weren't aware of this unspoken agreement; in this case, their ignorance probably saved their lives.

———

During the previous four days, the tiger had crossed over into a realm from which there was no returning. This was a one-way trip through uncharted territory—for the tiger and for the humans around him. A new model had been created; whatever bonds had held this tiger in relationship to his human neighbors, indeed, to his own nature, were broken. Now, anything was possible. When a domestic animal goes wild—a sheep-killing dog, for example—it is referred to as feral, but there is no name for what happens when a wild animal goes in the other direction and becomes dangerously familiar with the world of domesticated creatures. What should one call it when a tiger starts eating people and shit, and injures itself demolishing man-made things? Is it rage? A loss of bearing? Or simply adaptation to a new order? Perhaps some things are best left unnamed.

In any case, this tiger was now linked to the world of men in a way no animal should ever be. In the metabolic sense, at least— contaminated by both the bullets and the blood of his enemy—he had become something that doesn't exist in the West, something, if one had to put a name to it, akin to a weretiger. In the narrative canon of the southern Udeghe, whose current population is centered on Krasny Yar, there exists a kind of specialized amba called an *egule*. An elder named Martina Nedezhda described it as an enormous fur-covered creature, "like a tiger," that eats people. It is impossible to say now whether entities of this kind are recognized in the environment and given a name, or conceived by the collective imagination to serve a particular purpose, but suffice to say that things are described and named for a reason. In the Udeghe tale, "Uza and the Egule," Uza and his older brother, both of whom were legendary heroes, were hunting on the Bikin when they were attacked by an egule in the river; their boat was destroyed and Uza was eaten. Miraculously, Uza survived and managed to escape from inside the egule. He then killed the beast, fashioned a tent from its skin and bones, and made it his home.

But Uza was a hero and, in the Panchelaza, in the 1990s, heroes were in short supply. And so, this latter-day egule roamed at will. Stranded between the worlds of animals and men, at once fixated and unhinged, there was no law to hold such a creature, and no known words to recall it. When the tiger left the road workers' camp on Sunday, the 7th, he crossed the gravel highway, and made his way down the Takhalo toward the Bikin. In this animal's chest was a heart the size of a child's head, and it was pounding away, blending the bad blood with the good and driving the tiger on.

13

But ask now the beasts, and they shall teach thee.

Job 12:7

If a lion could talk, we would not understand him.

Ludwig Wittgenstein

Nevertheless the difference in mind between man and
the higher animal, great as it is, certainly is one of
degree and not of kind.

Charles Darwin

Him all same man, only different shirt. Him know
everything, know traps, know angry, know all
around . . . all same man.

Dersu Uzala

IN 1909, AN ESTONIAN-BORN BARON-TURNED-PHYSIOLOGIST NAMED
Jakob von Uexküll introduced the concept of *Umwelt* to the world.
Uexküll is considered one of the fathers of ethology, which is also
known as behavioral ecology. It is a young discipline whose goal is
to study behavior and social organization through a biological lens.
"To do so," wrote Uexküll in "A Stroll Through the Worlds of Animals and Men," "we must first blow, in fancy, a soap bubble
around each creature to represent its own world, filled with the
perceptions which it alone knows. When we ourselves then step
into one of these bubbles, the familiar . . . is transformed."
Uexküll called this bubble the umwelt, a German word that he

applied to a given animal's subjective or "self-centered" world. An individual's umwelt exists side by side with the *Umgebung*—the term Uexküll used to describe the objective environment, a place that exists in theory but that none of us can truly know given the inherent limitations of our respective umwelten. In addition to being delightful words to say, umwelt and umgebung offer a framework for exploring and describing the experience of other creatures.

In the umgebung of a city sidewalk, for example, a dog owner's umwelt would differ greatly from that of her dog's in that, while she might be keenly aware of a SALE sign in a window, a policeman coming toward her, or a broken bottle in her path, the dog would focus on the gust of cooked meat emanating from a restaurant's exhaust fan, the urine on a fire hydrant, and the doughnut crumbs next to the broken bottle. Objectively, these two creatures inhabit the same umgebung, but their individual umwelten give them radically different experiences of it. And yet these parallel universes have many features in common: both dog and mistress must be careful crossing the street, and both will pay close attention to other dogs, if not for the same reasons. One way to envision the differences between these overlapping umwelten is to mentally color-code each creature's objects of interest as it moves through space; the graphic potential is vast and fascinating, and it can be fine-tuned by the intensity of the given color, the same way an infrared camera indicates temperature differences. For example, both dog and mistress would notice the restaurant exhaust fan, but the dog would attach a "hotter" significance to it—unless the mistress happened to be hungry, too.

Uexküll had a broad romantic streak, but it was tempered by discipline and scholarship and, at the University of Hamburg, where he was a professor, he founded an environmental research institute (Institut für Umweltforschung) in 1926, which was the first of its kind to apply these methods.* The umwelten Uexküll

* It was closed in 1960. In 2004, an archive of the institute's holdings was established at the university.

sought to describe and illustrate covered the living spectrum from
humans and jackdaws to ticks and sea cucumbers. Based on the
latest information about these creatures' biological processes, his
narrative descriptions are not only fascinating reading but
remarkable feats of empathic thinking: "The eyeless tick is
directed to [her] watchtower by a general photo-sensitivity to her
skin," he writes. "The approaching prey is revealed to the blind
and deaf highwaywoman by her sense of smell. The odor of
butyric acid, that emanates from the skin glands of all mammals,
acts on the tick as a signal to leave her watchtower and hurl herself downwards." Uexküll was, through science and imagination,
trying to put himself inside the body and experience of another
creature, much as the wizard Merlin enabled the boy King Arthur
to do by transforming him into different animals in T. H. White's
The Sword in the Stone. Uexküll's exhaustively detailed descriptions and analyses are all the more remarkable when one considers
his contemporaries' general lack of interest in, and understanding
of, the subjective experience of other species. "These different
worlds," wrote Uexküll in 1934, "which are as manifold as the
animals themselves, present to all nature lovers new lands of such
wealth and beauty that a walk through them is well worth while,
even though they unfold not to the physical but only to the spiritual eye."

These ideas became more mainstream in the 1960s when, in
the wake of the civil rights movement, the individual experience,
and even the rights, of animals began to be considered more
seriously (one result being the Animal Welfare Act of 1966).
Nonetheless, there remains a schism between strict behaviorists
and ethologists. The former reject the notion of animal consciousness and firmly believe that they are merely biological machines:
bundles of instinct and base reaction that are all but unconscious
in any measurable sense of the word. It is here that language,
arguably the signal difference between us and our fellow creatures, becomes our greatest liability. As the science writer Stephen
Budiansky wrote in *If a Lion Could Talk*, "we have no means of
describing cognitive processes that do not involve words." Ultimately, the problem comes down to umwelt; we are such prisoners

of our subjective experience that it is only by force of will and imagination that we are able to take leave of it at all and consider the experience and essence of another creature—or even another person.

In fact, the ability to step inside the umwelt "bubble" of another creature is not so much a newfound skill as it is a lost art. Successful hunting, it could be said, is an act of terminal empathy: the kill depends on how successfully a hunter inserts himself into the umwelt of his prey—even to the point of disguising himself as that animal and mimicking its behavior. It was our ancestors' skill at not only analyzing and imitating the nature of a given animal, but identifying with it, that enabled them to flourish in dangerous environments, both physically and psychically. In hunting societies, such as the Udeghe, the !Kung, the Haida, or the Sioux, animals were not merely food, they were seen as blood relatives, spiritual companions, hunting guides, and sources of power and connection to the surrounding world. The boundaries between the umwelten of humans and animals were, of necessity, much less rigidly defined. Many residents of the Bikin valley maintain these skills and relationships to this day; there are hunters there who speak with tigers and who can identify game by scent alone. In the predominantly Russian village of Yasenovie, a random winter scene in 2007 revealed a circle of men in forest green and camouflage, in the center of which a man charged and wheeled while holding a rack of elk antlers to his head.

"All species have been shaped by the forces of evolution to meet immediate needs," wrote George Page in his companion to the television series *Inside the Animal Mind.* "The more a given species needs to be conscious of, the more it *is* conscious of. Either that or it becomes extinct." Georges Leroy, a naturalist and gamekeeper to Louis XV at Versailles, had ample opportunity to observe predator-prey relations and he speculated that the reason wolves seemed so much smarter than deer was that they would starve to death if they weren't. While deer forage is stationary and abundant, wolf prey, by contrast, is not only highly mobile but doing its utmost to avoid being eaten. In order to succeed, predators must actively—and consciously—contrive successful hunting scenarios by adapting to, and manipulating, random events within a constantly shifting environment. This, as any hunter or businessperson knows, is hard to do, and these conditions favor the prey almost every time.

Ivan Dunkai's son Vasily, a lifelong hunter who has shared his territory with tigers all his life, has come to a similar conclusion. On a bitterly cold day in March 2007, he tried to put the tiger into a context an outsider could understand. "A hunter can only rely on himself," he said. "If anything happens, there is no one to help him, and all of us who live this way have a very advanced intuition. We also carry the experience of our ancestors in our heads: that's how a man functions in taiga. The tiger is a hunter, just the same as a man is a hunter. A hunter has to think about how to get his prey. It is different for boar and deer: if leaves or cones fall down from a tree, that's what they eat; there is no need to think. Tigers think."

Clark Barrett, a professor in the anthropology department at UCLA and an expert on predator-prey dynamics, describes the deer's advantage as the *anywhere but here* principle: all a prey animal needs to do is be anywhere the predator isn't—it doesn't matter if it's a foot away, or a hemisphere—and it will live another day. The predator, on the other hand, must be *exactly* where its prey is, and at exactly the same moment, or it will starve. Thus, for a predator, mastery of both time and space—in addition to a thorough understanding of terrain and prey behavior—are crucial. Pack hunting, of course, increases the odds enormously, but unlike the wolf or the lion, the tiger is a solo stealth hunter and, thus, has a far more challenging task. Possessing neither the endurance to run its prey down, nor the numbers to surround and harry it, the tiger's method must instead resemble that of the lone assassin: it must insert itself almost intravenously into its prey's umwelt—an umwelt, it must be noted, that has evolved over millions of years to be exquisitely sensitive to the presence of felid predators. Making matters still more difficult is the fact that tiger prey typically travel in herds. With their dozens of eyes, ears, and nostrils, and their decades of collective tiger-evading experience, a herd of deer or boar can be as vigilant and jumpy as a Secret Service detail. In order to subvert this, the tiger must embody a contradiction: this large, pungent, extraordinarily charismatic animal must achieve a state of virtual nonexistence while operating *inside* the sphere of its prey's highly attuned senses. Witnesses, native and Russian alike, agree that there is something almost metaphysical about the tiger's ability to will itself into nonbeing—to, in effect, cloak itself. In the Bikin valley, it is generally believed that if a tiger has decided to attack you, you will not be able to see it. With the exception of the polar bear, which also hunts by stealth, there is no other land mammal this big whose survival depends on its ability to disappear.

———

Yuri Trush appreciated and respected these qualities in the tiger. While investigating the site of the Markov attack, and while writing his report that weekend, he had made a sincere effort to understand this animal—to place himself inside the tiger's umwelt and imagine his world as it pertained to Markov and those around him. He did the same with Markov, working hard to reconstruct both his umwelt and his last days. Trush is generally cautious and disciplined in his thinking and, when he is not sure, or just guessing, he is not afraid to say so. However, on one particular point, he was unequivocal: "I am one hundred percent sure," he said, "that Markov shot at the tiger from the caravan at close range."

It would have looked something like this: on December 1 or 2, a day or two before his death, Markov went out hunting with his dogs. He could have been alone or with Andrei Onofreychuk; the possibility of other people being present as well is not out of the question. The dogs would have been running up ahead, searching for a scent trail, and may well have been following one when they came upon a freshly killed boar. Markov is in hunting mode, so he is traveling with a gun, a rucksack, and perhaps a hatchet. When he catches up to the dogs, he sees the boar, and it is obvious that it has been killed by a tiger. He looks around, takes note of the dogs' behavior, and decides the coast is clear. He can't take the whole carcass, and he knows better than to do so, but he takes a haunch—maybe two, if he can carry that much. Then he hurries back to his cabin, feeling lucky: in the Panchelaza, this windfall was more fungible than mid-1990s rubles. Upon his return, Markov stores a portion of the meat in the beehive wellhead, which doubles as a food cache and is a safe distance from his cabin. Then he packs the rest of it down to the road workers' camp to trade, returning home at dusk.

Meanwhile, the tiger returns to his kill. It is clear that it has been tampered with, and the tiger takes umbrage. Perhaps the tiger has a feed and a rest, or he may set off immediately on the trail of these interloping competitors. There is no ambiguity about who the tiger seeks: the scent trail of several dogs and a man is easy to follow. The tiger arrives at Markov's sometime after nightfall, which, in early December, means anytime after 4:30 in the afternoon. He approaches from the east, from the Amba River, and the first thing he comes across is the meat cache.

When Trush investigated the meat cache wellhead in the stream, east of Markov's cabin, he saw that it had been knocked over and that something had been dragged away from it, something that could have been a frozen boar leg. Trush didn't spend a lot of time there, just long enough for him and Lazurenko to ascertain that the tiger had come from that direction and that the wellhead had been the first thing he investigated. However, they did note that this was the site of a resting place where the tiger spent a particularly long time—perhaps while he ate the recovered meat.

Following this, the tiger continues on toward the cabin, stopping briefly by Markov's log latrine. By now, the dogs, wherever they are, are sounding the alarm. The tiger makes his way down to the cabin where he scours the area, knocking over Markov's belongings and chewing them up in his angry search for Markov, his dogs, the rest of the meat, or all of the above (this damage could also have been done when the tiger returned later for the final stakeout). Meanwhile, Markov is inside, probably cooking up some of the boar meat (which the tiger may have scented already), and he may understand perfectly why the tiger is there. He realizes now that he has a serious problem on his hands. The tiger circles the caravan, searching for a way to get in, or at the dogs, which may be inside if they're not hiding underneath. Markov is growing increasingly nervous; the caravan is a flimsy structure, sheathed only in boards, the cracks between them stuffed with rags to keep the wind out. By now, he may have realized that he has taken meat from the wrong tiger, and he is going to have to do something besides chain-smoke. Markov gets his gun.

Here, a problem arises in this scenario: where does he get the gun from? Because of condensation issues, poachers' guns are usually stored outside, in order to maintain a stable temperature. However, since it was late, and a patrol was unlikely, Markov may have simply leaned it up outside the door along with his cartridge belt. If that is the case, then he has a chance of retrieving it—so long as the tiger is on the far side of the caravan. Another possibility is that he has the gun inside on the floor. When it is this cold—minus thirty or so—poorly insulated cabins may stay ice-cold below knee height because the heat from the stove rises and dissipates so quickly. In any case, Markov now has his gun. His dogs are whining and barking, and he is going to have to do something decisive. However, as soon as he brings the gun up to window height, there is a significant change in temperature and the steel components start sweating, as do the brass shells. At this rate, it won't take long for the gunpowder to be compromised, if it isn't already. There is a new moon so visibility is poor, but Markov can hear the tiger, which at this point is making no effort to disguise its presence. Perhaps it has already killed one of his dogs, an offense many tayozhniks would consider just cause for shooting a tiger. At least one of his dogs is a trained hunter, a "breadwinner," and his livelihood depends on it. Markov is frightened, angry, and maybe a little drunk. Humble as it is, this is his castle, and there is a tiger at the gate.

In addition to a couple of small windows and the door, Markov's caravan also had openings cut specifically for shooting in case deer or boar should wander into range. In this way, his trailer doubled as a kind of live-in hunting blind. From one of these openings, Markov finds his angle, thrusts the barrel through, and takes his shot from point-blank range, aiming for the tiger's chest or head. There is a furious roar and a thrashing of brush, and the tiger is gone. For now. Markov reloads immediately. His heart is pounding. No one who has been challenged by a tiger comes away unmoved, and it is hard to tell who is more frightened now, Markov or his dogs. Once he has determined that the tiger is gone for the moment, Markov finds himself overcome with the need for a cigarette. If his dogs are outside, maybe he calls them in—if they haven't already fled. He smokes, strokes his dogs if they are around, and gathers himself, assessing the damage, and trying to figure out what to do. He has just committed a federal offense, but it may not be his first and, if the tiger lives, federal laws will be the least of his problems; it is the tiger's law he will need to worry about. He is going to have to come up with a strategy for dealing with this conflict, and he will have no peace until he does.

———

As confident as Trush is in his interpretation of these events, there are other credible versions and one of them comes from Ivan Dunkai's son Vasily, who discussed the incident with his father at the time. "Markiz had killed a boar not far from my father's cabin," he recalled. "The tiger found it and was eating it. When Markiz saw the tiger eating it, he shot at him. Naturally, the tiger ran away. The tiger was injured, and he could not kill anything for a week."

For a hunter on foot, dismantling a dead boar can take days, which means that, even after Markov packed his first load home, there would have been hundreds of pounds of meat left in the forest. Just as a human may help himself to an unfinished tiger kill, a tiger may do the same to a half-butchered human kill. It wasn't clear if Markov's dogs had been mixed up in this, but one of the downsides of hunting dogs is that, when confronted by large, dangerous animals, they have a tendency to run back to their master, thus putting him directly in harm's way. Had this happened, or had his dogs been attacked, Markov might have felt it necessary to shoot at the tiger. In any case, he would have had mere seconds to make a decision.

This version squares with that of the local hunting inspector Evgeny Smirnov, who headed a small agency called Field Group Taiga. Even though Smirnov was an ethnic Russian, the fact that he lived in Krasny Yar and was married to a respected native gave him access to information that could easily elude an outsider like Trush. Between his daily presence on the river and his direct pipeline to local gossip, Smirnov had his finger on the pulse of the local hunting and poaching scene. Smirnov counted the Dunkai clan among his neighbors and, shortly after Markov's death, he got on his Buran and rode out to Ivan Dunkai's cabin at the confluence of the Amba and the Bikin.

"The first thing I wanted to know," Smirnov began, "was where the tiger came from. Uncle Vanya [Dunkai] showed me boar tracks going down along the Bikin, and the tiger had followed these boar tracks. He said, 'Zhenya [a diminutive form of Evgeny], that's not my tiger. He must have come from up the river.' Then I knew the tiger had ventured out of its home territory. Uncle Vanya got scared when I told him that Markov was involved in trapping tigers and selling their skins. He understood very well that, if Markov had injured the tiger or harmed him in any way and then visited his [Dunkai's] cabin, the tiger could come for Markov and might not spare him either."

It seems now that Evgeny Smirnov was the only person with a forensic interest in this case who actually spoke with Ivan Dunkai at the time of the incident. What must be taken into account here is that Russian citizens, particularly older ones, have learned through painful experience that information is a weapon that can and will be used against them. Therefore, people protect their friends and neighbors, and information about them is shared carefully, being limited or altered according to who is asking. Shooting a tiger is a serious offense; if it came down to a choice between Inspection Tiger, foreign journalists, and a known and trusted local like Smirnov who had married into the tribe, the latter stood the best chance of getting good information. This is why

Smirnov's account must be considered, even though it differs substantially from Trush's piecemeal one, which depended heavily on his (often excellent) powers of deduction.

"The thing is," Smirnov explained, "that particular year was a bad year for tigers in terms of prey. Boars are very susceptible to disease and the boar population was in decline. That was the main reason this tiger came down the river: he was forced to expand his turf because there was not enough food and, while chasing boars, he ended up in someone else's territory. As it happened, the tiger killed this boar very close to a road. At the same time, Markov was passing by with his dogs. The dogs ran toward the tiger, the tiger killed a dog, and, either because he was scared or because he didn't know what else to do, Markov shot at the tiger. The misfortune was that the tiger memorized the smell of that man and started hunting him. There were many people in the area—soldiers, loggers, beekeepers—but the tiger moved around them and did not touch anyone. He was looking for a particular person. When Markov realized that the tiger was pursuing him, he fled.

"He was afraid to go home then because he knew that he had not killed the tiger. He ran four miles to Uncle Vanya's, and stayed there, hoping the tiger would go away. Uncle Vanya saw that Markov was not himself: he was constantly deep in thought, and he seemed scared, but Uncle Vanya did not ask him any questions. Only after several days did Markov tell him that he had shot at a tiger and injured him. That's when Uncle Vanya said, 'Listen, you have to go to the village or somewhere else; you have to leave the taiga. The tiger will not let you live.' And that's when he left.

"In the meantime, the tiger had finished off what was left of the boar. Then, he found Markov's tracks, found his apiary, and waited there for him. Tigers are very well insulated so, if a tiger lies down somewhere overnight, his body heat does not melt the snow completely. It was obvious that the tiger waited for a long time because the snow had melted to the ground where he was resting. He waited for a long time; he waited long enough."

As Smirnov understood it, Markov had stopped in at Zhorkin's logging camp in the hope of getting a ride back to his cabin. However, by the time he arrived that evening, all the heavy vehicles

had been put away for the night and their radiators drained.*
Zhorkin had already driven home, and there were no other vehicles available. For some reason—very likely his dogs, who may
have run ahead—Markov was unwilling to wait.

————

As much as these accounts may differ from one another, there is,
running through them all, the common theme of dogs and
meat—the two things humans and tigers are most likely to have
conflict over in the forest. In this sense, the incident was a text-
book case, and is completely consistent with the behavior of all the
creatures involved. Markov for his part was certainly familiar with
tigers and with the local lore, both native and Russian, but the
only tiger attacks he is likely to have known much about were two
local incidents, both of which were spontaneous retaliations to
human attacks. In the mid-1980s, a woman from Yasenovie had
her arm mauled after she tried to chase a tiger out of her barnyard
with an axe; the man who came to help her was also injured before
the tiger was shot. On the Bikin River, in 1996, there had been
another incident in which a native man named Evgeny Nekrasov
shot at a family of tigers from his boat, whereupon the tigress
jumped into his boat and attacked him. He survived only because
his partner, who was also in the boat, shot the tigress and killed
her. That same year, about a hundred miles to the east, on the
Pacific slope of the Sikhote-Alin Mountains, two poachers were
killed and eaten within days of each other by a tiger whose right
foreleg had been crippled by a snare.

According to Evgeny Suvorov, a journalist and author from
Primorye who has studied the subject exhaustively, the mid-1990s
were bad years for tiger attacks. In 1996, at least five people were
killed, and several more were seriously injured. Some of these
attacks were provoked, but others clearly weren't. In his book

———

* In remote areas like the Bikin, antifreeze is hard to come by, so at night the radiators
in heavy machinery will simply be drained into a bucket. The following morning,
before dawn, a worker will build a fire, thaw the water out, and refill the radiators for
the workday.

Zapovednoye Primorye, Suvorov quotes the following verse by a game warden who had to face this uncertainty on a daily basis:

> *I've read a tiger's not dangerous,*
> *They say the tiger won't attack*
> *But one thing's not clear to me.*
> *Has he read this, too? Does he know?*

In Primorye, between 1970 and 1994, there were six recorded tiger attacks that were classified as "unprovoked"; in four of them, the tiger appeared to hunt the victims as if they were prey. However, it is difficult to ascertain from the data how the prior history, or momentary desperation, of these animals might have predisposed them to hunt people. According to Suvorov, attacks on patrolling border guards were "entirely ordinary occurrences" during this period.

Earlier data—from mid-century and back—is patchy at best, but for what it's worth no incidents of man eating were recorded anywhere in the Russian Far East from the 1920s through the 1950s (probably because the Amur tiger population was at an all-time low). In any case, most early attack reports are anecdotal accounts collected by travelers and, with the exception of the German lepidopterist whose remains were identified only by his butterfly net and jacket buttons, they tended to involve solitary Russian hunters, or Korean and Chinese ginseng collectors and railway workers, some of whom were reportedly snatched from their own beds. Chinese gold miners would also have been among the victims of an atypical rash of attacks reported by the famed Russian explorer Nikolai "Give me a company of soldiers and I'll conquer China" Przhevalski. According to Przhevalski, twenty-one men were killed and six more were wounded by tigers on the Shkotovka River in southern Primorye in 1867.

———

Regardless of whether Trush's, Smirnov's, or Vasily Dunkai's scenario is closer to the truth, Markov had reason to believe the tiger might pursue him. It is not known exactly how long he remained sequestered after shooting the tiger, but on the morning of December 3, something emboldened—or compelled—Markov to leave his cabin and make the risky journey over to the Amba River, three and a half miles away. Perhaps he was searching for his dogs, or he may have been looking for backup to finish off the tiger. Whether the profit motive entered into his calculations is not known. However, Markov did not go immediately to see his friend Ivan Dunkai, but instead went northeast, to visit Dunkai's son (and Vasily's brother) Mikhail. Mikhail was never interviewed by Inspection Tiger, but in May 2008 he described the last time he saw Markov.

Mikhail Dunkai is in his early fifties, and he is a hunter and trapper like his father and brother. He is short and thickly set with a shock of black hair that falls across his forehead in bangs, the only straight line on an otherwise round face. Dark eyes glimmer through folded lids. Like his father, he had a good relationship with Markov and, over the years, they had shared meals, vodka, and each other's cabins. Markov arrived at Mikhail's cabin on the Amba shortly before noon on the 3rd, and he was clearly upset. "He was angry with the tiger," Mikhail recalled as he stood in a recently thawed dirt track dotted with puddles and cow pats that serves as one of Krasny Yar's main streets. "He was swearing at him; he was saying that we should kill, destroy, and wipe out the tigers. 'There are too many of them,' he said. I could see that he was really worried: he didn't want to drink or eat anything; he didn't even have tea. He was just smoking cigarettes—one after another, one after another, and complaining that they were too weak. 'Let's roll them with *makhorka*,'* he said. He was smoking constantly for a half an hour."

Many Udeghe and Nanai, including Mikhail Dunkai, feel about tigers the same way Pyotr Zhorkin did: that if one has set its sights on you, there is little you can do to alter the outcome. "He was doomed," Mikhail said simply. "You could tell by looking in his eyes. They were strange and empty when I was talking with him: dead-looking. This tiger was probably angry and vindictive,

---

* Slang term for strong, loose tobacco.

and Markiz probably struck a wrong chord with him. Personally, I think he was trying to shoot the tiger, and this tiger didn't forgive him. If the tiger had felt that it was his fault—if he had killed a dog or done something else wrong—then he would have gone away."

———

Anthropologists who write about indigenous peoples often note their tendency to anthropomorphize the animals around them. Even though !Kung and Nanai hunters (among countless others) have used this approach to great effect while hunting, the ascription of recognizable emotions and motives to animals causes problems for Western scholars, not least because they are awfully hard to prove in a lab or defend in a dissertation. Such claims are what lawyers and philosophers refer to as "arguments from inference": anecdotal and unprovable. Under these circumstances, the potential for hair-splitting, semantic quibbling, and "definition objection" is endless, but it also misses the point: these feelings of trans-species understanding and communication have less to do with animals being humanized, or humans being "animalized," than with all parties simply being sensitized to nuances of the other's presence and behavior. If you spend most of your life in a natural environment, intimately connected with, and dependent upon, the animals around you, you will undoubtedly— *necessarily*—feel a certain kinship with those creatures, even if you have no conscious intention of doing so.

A striking example of this unintended intimacy occurred in present-day Namibia in 1940. In May of that year, two German geologists, Henno Martin and Hermann Korn, having already fled Nazi Germany, chose to disappear themselves in the desert rather than risk being interned in their host country (South Africa) as enemy aliens. The two men were experienced desert travelers and, after making careful preparations, they loaded a truck with bare necessities, including a dog named Otto, and descended into the vast and labyrinthine Kuiseb River canyon, 120 miles southwest of Windhoek. Always fearful of discovery, and at the mercy of hunger and thirst, they crept about like persecuted anchorites, living in caves and stone shelters, hunting game with strictly rationed ammunition, and sleeping by their kills to keep the hyenas away. For two and a half years, they survived in this desiccated underworld, an environment in which neither the plants nor the animals had changed significantly in a million years.

The Kuiseb canyon contained reservoirs of last resort and, when the waterholes on the plains above went dry, leopards, jackals, hyenas, ostriches, antelope, and zebra would descend to the canyon floor in order to search among the stones for springs and sumps. For Martin and Korn, a by-product of this self-imposed exile in a place devoid of other humans was total immersion into the animal world. As trained scientists, both men took a disciplined and energetic interest in their new circumstances, which Martin recounted in great detail in his memoir, *The Sheltering Desert* (1957). In it, he describes how they were forced to adapt to an elemental existence, which centered on a trinity of basic needs: safety, food, and water. But it had a surreal twist: a wind-powered generator enabled them to listen to the radio. There, in the desert fastness, where the Southern Cross gave shape to the night sky, herds of zebra clattered by in the dark, and thirst trumped all other concerns, news of the war in Europe intruded like distress calls from another planet. These men were, quite literally, caught between worlds. As wanted men, and refugees from twentieth-century fascism and war, they were forced to rediscover skills and instincts that had lain dormant since the Stone Age.

The Namib Desert is barren for much of the year, save for a few scattered bushes and trees, so Korn's and Martin's diet was heavily dependent on meat. As a result, animals became a central focus; they were mobile hubs around which their own lives revolved. Because their bullets were old and weak—to the point that they would bounce off the skulls of their prey—Martin and Korn had to creep within bow and arrow range to be assured of a kill. But even as their lives took on an increasingly savage and desperate cast, they were able to step back and observe their own behavior—as if they were researcher and subject rolled into one. "Our clothes, always stiff with blood and sweat, were torn and frayed from crawling over the sharp hot rubble," wrote Martin.

"After a while we gave up wearing trousers and stockings. . . . Using towels as loin-cloths we sat there and tore apart the ribs of an antelope . . . and gnawed away like carnivorous beasts. But our thoughts were freer and less oppressed than they had ever been, and later that evening Hermann's violin sang triumphantly into the dark night around us." At one point, Korn was moved to say, "My paleolithic soul feels at home here."

As they settled into the Namib's ancient rhythms of flood and drought, hunting and repose, Martin and Korn studied the animals around them, and their social bonds, hierarchies, and inter-species dynamics became a source of fascination. Inevitably perhaps, both men began to identify with them. "They were like people you meet constantly in the street without knowing their names," wrote Martin, "and we soon began to look on them as neighbors." In essence, this desolate but surprisingly lively maze of boulder and scrub was a kind of communal umwelt and, in it, Martin and Korn developed a sense of deep, empathic familiarity with their cohabitants: "We learnt to recognise their mood and intentions from the way they held their heads, or set their hooves. We got to understand them and their behaviour as you get to understand your friends without the need of speech. . . . The longer we lived with animals the clearer it became to us that human and animal behaviour were very closely related."

Martin was continually impressed by the subtlety of interaction and awareness he witnessed all around him: rival zebra stallions spelling each other at the same hole as they pawed away stones to access water; an ostrich hen spreading her wings to block the progress of other ostriches after detecting a remote hazard; a baboon dismantling a pair of binoculars by carefully unscrewing all the component parts; a hyena giving way to a leopard on the trail and, once the leopard was safely past, shrieking and yelping after it like a coward hurling insults. "It struck me," Martin observed, "that the 'all too human' behaviour of men was in reality 'all too animal.' "

However, Martin's most surprising discoveries concerned the changes taking place in his own psyche: when they had first descended into the canyon, he found that his dreams focused on the people and places he had left behind. But as the months turned into years, "Animals began to play an increasing part in them and the distinction between human beings and animals became blurred." Martin's subconscious—his interior umwelt— was gradually recalibrating itself to match his new, if atavistic, reality. It was the kind of real-time immersion experiment that psychologists and anthropologists can only dream of, and it may shed some light on why the painted caves of southern Europe and the wall art of the Kalahari are so heavily weighted toward animals. "Perhaps," speculated Martin, "this was the origin of mythology . . . in which human beings and animals mingle and merge into each other."*

Considering that it took a German-born urban academic only two years to (re)discover this connection at an impressively deep level (in an African canyon, no less), one can only imagine the profound sense of intimacy and understanding an indigenous hunter like Ivan or Mikhail Dunkai would possess after a lifetime in his native taiga. When one adds to this the fact that the Dunkais are drawing on centuries of communal memory and experience with local animals, their interpretation of human-tiger dynamics takes on a certain weight. "The tiger is strong, powerful and fair," Mikhail Dunkai declared. "You have to respect him. You think he doesn't understand the language, but he understands everything; he can read a person's mind. So, if you start thinking, 'He's a bad tiger; I am not afraid of him,' well, something bad will happen to you, and you'll have only yourself to blame. The tiger will warn

---

* In September 1942, Henno Martin and Hermann Korn were forced to return to civilization when Korn became seriously ill with beri-beri (caused by a deficiency of vitamin B). Although they faced multiple charges, the presiding judge was impressed by their story and they were not interned. Instead, the authorities put them back to work, using their intimate knowledge of the land to locate water sources for farmers. Korn died in a car accident in 1946, but Martin lived until 1998, during which time he did pioneering work in geology, including plate tectonics, taught as a university professor, published several more books and monographs, and was awarded numerous international honors. A road has since been built through the Kuiseb canyon, which is now part of the Namib-Naukluft National Park.

you first, but if you still don't understand, then he will seriously punish you."

Mikhail had an interesting take on the sharing of prey in the forest, and things might have gone better for Markov if he had known about it. "Once, a tiger killed a wild boar about ten yards from my cabin," Mikhail began. "In the morning, I saw the dead boar and the tiger sitting nearby. So, I started talking to him: 'The taiga is big,' I said. 'Why would you kill a boar right here? Go, enjoy the rest of the taiga, but don't do this near my cabin.' The tiger was sitting, listening, and then he left. Afterward, I saw that a part of the boar—the haunch—had been left for me; the rest of the boar was eaten and everything was cleaned by the tiger.

"But I didn't take the meat," said Mikhail, "because, if you take it, then you are in debt and have to give something back. So I said, 'Thank you, but I have meat now. Don't be insulted that I don't take it. It was good of you to share with me.' If you take meat from the tiger," Mikhail explained, "you will feel that you owe him, and then you will be afraid of the tiger."

The way Mikhail Dunkai saw it, accepting meat from a tiger is like accepting a favor from the Communist Party, or the mafia: once obligated, it can be very hard to extract oneself. Markov may not have fully grasped the nature of the contract he was entering into if, indeed, he helped himself to that tiger kill. Ivan Dunkai, being from an earlier generation, seemed to accept these rigorous terms, but his son clearly did not. That the tiger researcher Dmitri Pikunov was able to scavenge so successfully, and so safely, from tiger kills was most likely due to the fact that he didn't go near a kill until he was sure the tiger was completely finished with it. The czar always eats first.

That Markov had become so entangled with this tiger seemed genuinely to surprise Mikhail Dunkai. "Markiz was a strong, good man," he said in sum. "He was always optimistic, always kept his spirits up. He was honest. It's hard to understand how it happened, but this situation with the tiger diverted him from the path of life. I tried to tell him that he should stay overnight, that he should take it easy, stop worrying, and think it over. I said, 'If you didn't do anything bad to him, he won't do anything to you. *Just don't do*

anything bad to him. Remember: you are living in the taiga. He can crush you.'"

But by then, the die was cast, and a facet of Markov's own character may have sealed his fate. "If Markiz started something," Mikhail said, "he usually finished it."

"Look at it from the tiger's point of view," Trush said later. "The tiger challenged Markov. From his point of view, either you leave, or you sort it out face-to-face and see what happens. Markov accepted that challenge. Volodya Markov had a chance to leave the taiga; had he done so, he would still be alive. He had that choice."

The question remains: why did Markov go for a long walk in the forest, alone, if he knew there was an angry tiger looking for him? Was it pride? Was it concern for his dogs? Or was he intending to finish what he had started? Mikhail Dunkai believed it was something else altogether. He had the sense that Markov was already in the tiger's thrall when he saw him that morning. "The tiger had already taken his soul," he said. "I had this dog once," he explained, "and one day the dog became nervous, angry, irritated; it started to bite me, and was running away. The next day, a tiger killed him. The dog was angry, irritated, and scared because the tiger influenced his mind: the dog didn't see the tiger, but the tiger attracted him from a distance—like a magnet. It's like hypnosis: putting thoughts in somebody's head. The person, or the dog— they don't understand what is happening or what they are doing. They are going somewhere without thinking clearly."

There are other explanations, but none more satisfactory for why Markov behaved as he did: why he struck everyone who saw him as "not himself," why he refused their food and shelter, why he walked alone, in darkness, back to a place the tiger knew well. But it is the tracks that are most unsettling: the way they lead, mile after mile, down the Amba and through the taiga, directly into the path of the tiger. This, and the way the tiger did not hunt him, but waited patiently outside his door, as if he was expecting him, like a dog—or a hit man. A human being could not have engineered a more bitter revenge scenario.

14

When we look at nature, we are only looking at the survivors.

STEPHEN BUDIANSKY,
If a Lion Could Talk

THE TERMS OF THE BIG CAT–PRIMATE RELATIONSHIP HAVE BEEN amazingly consistent over time: it doesn't matter if the primates in question are gun-wielding tayozhniks, !Kung hunters, preverbal australopithecines, or baboons through the ages. As far as our immanent fear of predatory cats goes, virtually nothing has changed in five million years beyond our techniques for managing it. Because of this, there are striking similarities between the behavior of Trush's Inspection Tiger team at Markov's cabin and that of a troop of baboons on the African savanna: formed into defensive groups by day, both man and monkey will travel in the open, even going so far as to confront predatory cats. But as soon as the sun goes down, each group will retreat to safe quarters where they huddle together until dawn.

In order to get an idea of how we coped with big cats and other predators prior to the acquisition of tools and fire, some paleoan-thropologists have looked to savanna baboons for comparison. One of the most diligent and respected of these researchers is the South African paleontologist Charles K. Brain. In the course of his work excavating hominid and animal fossils from caves in the Transvaal's Sterkfontein valley during the 1960s and '70s, Brain spent time observing a troop of cliff-dwelling baboons that lived nearby. On particularly cold nights, the troop of about thirty baboons would retire to the caves that run deep inside the cliffs. One night, Brain did something no modern human had ever done: "I hid inside the cavern," he wrote, "making my presence known only after the baboons had taken up their sleeping places. Although pandemonium broke out in the cave, the baboons could not be induced to leave the place in the dark."

Brain did not go into much detail about that wild night, and this may be because the experience of being trapped in a dark, confined space with dozens of fear-crazed baboons is something best left to the imagination. But he came away with some valuable information. Brain was struck by the fact that darkness and whatever it contained was, for these baboons, so frightening that it overrode their panicked response to a large intruder in their midst. What, one wonders, did they think was out there? In the mid-twentieth century, when Brain paid his surprise visit, it would have been leopards, lions, and hyenas. Three million years earlier, however, an even more daunting array of predators would have awaited them—and our own ancestors—beyond the mouth of that cave. Hunting both by day and night, these would have included several species of wolf and hyena, some of which were the size of lions. Out there, too, were big cats and catlike predators—saber-toothed and otherwise—all in far greater numbers and variety than exist today. As if that wasn't enough, there were also eagles that preyed on the young until they reached three or four years old when they would have been too heavy to carry off, but not to kill.

Another detail that Brain found noteworthy was the stark corollary between savanna baboons and safe sleeping areas: where there were no cliffs or caves, there were no baboons. When one compares the baboon's idea of safety with a Hopi pueblo, a medieval castle, or an apartment building, the similarities are uncanny. Wherever we go, whatever the medium or terrain, our concept of sanctuary remains essentially the same. Lacking height, we'll make do with a hole. In this way, a cave, an igloo, a bunker, and a surplus Russian army truck would be universally recognizable across geography and time.

———

C. K. Brain is significant, not just for the baboons he has observed and the fossils he has found, but for the fact that, in doing so, he refuted the Killer Ape theory. He challenged Ardrey and many of his own colleagues with his seminal work, *The Hunters or the Hunted?: An Introduction to African Cave Taphonomy** (1981). In it, Brain described his exhaustive study of fossils he and others found in the Sterkfontein valley, a place that has since been dubbed the "Cradle of Humankind." Brain's conclusions were radical for the time: our ancestors were neither hunters nor gratuitously homicidal; if we were fighting, he asserted, it was for our very lives against a host of predators far better equipped than we were.

From a paleoanthropologist's point of view, the Sterkfontein and neighboring Swartkrans valleys represent the motherlode; for nearly a century now, paleontologists have been excavating the caves and quarries that pock these arid valleys west of Johannesburg. Over the years, hundreds of fossils of baboons and early hominids have been found here, including nearly intact skeletons, some of which are more than three million years old. The region, which is now a World Heritage site, has also yielded some of the oldest known evidence of controlled fire (one million years BCE). Of particular interest to Brain was the fact that many of these fossilized bones, hominid and otherwise, bear evidence of predation. Big cats and hyenas haunted these caves, too; they still do, and they offer valuable clues to our formative experiences with large, dangerous animals.

There is no question that the world inhabited by our hominid forebears was a perilous place at ground level: we were smaller and just about everything else was bigger than today. Our carnivorous neighbors, in whose eyes we would have been considered relatively small game, were superior to us in every way that mat-

———

* Taphonomy is the study of an organism's decay and related processes over time, including its fossilization.

tered. This long and precarious phase in our early development, before we mastered tools and fire, may well have inflicted the "wound" Robinson Jeffers alluded to in his untitled poem, which also begged the pressing question:

> *But whence came the race of man? I will make a guess.*
> *A change of climate killed the great northern forests,*
> *Forcing the manlike apes down from their trees…*
> *They had to go down to the earth, where green still grew*
> *And small meats might be gleaned. But there the great flesh-eaters,*
> *Tiger and panther and the horrible fumbling bear and*
>   *endless wolf-packs*
>   *made life*
> *A dream of death. Therefore man has those dreams,*
> *And kills out of pure terror.*

These lines were written more than fifty years ago by a non-scientist; nonetheless, this secular story, combining banishment from Eden with a traumatizing fall from arboreal grace, remains consistent with what many paleontologists and paleobotanists believe today. Judging from discoveries made in the Transvaal, the Olduvai Gorge, and elsewhere, we landed hard, and there was no going back. Until about two and a half million years ago, when the australopithecines' successors, *Homo habilis*, began using tools, we had few natural defenses beyond those we carried in our heads: stereoscopic vision, decent hearing, a reasonably sensitive nose, and a brain only a third the size of ours today. In other words, we weren't all that far ahead of baboons or chimpanzees.

Conceivably, there could have been generations—maybe thousands of generations—of cats that taught their cubs to hunt primates. Just as the lions Elizabeth Marshall Thomas encountered on the Kalahari appeared to have been "acculturated" to not eating humans, the reverse is equally possible. The most notorious modern case of inherent man-eating occurred in the Njombe district of present-day Tanzania between 1932 and 1947. During this period, a single pride of fifteen lions killed approximately 1,500 people before George Rushby, a legendary British elephant-

hunter-turned-game-warden, exterminated the pride, one by one.
It took him a year. "If a man-eater continues to kill and eat people
for any length of time," wrote Rushby in his memoir, *No More the
Tusker,* "it develops an almost supernatural cunning. This often
makes the hunting down and killing of such a lion a lengthy and
difficult task."

There is a related phenomenon among predators, large and
small, that is politely termed "surplus killing," but which manifests as a kind of spontaneous, frenzied slaughter. This is not what
the Njombe lions were engaged in, but lions have been known to
do it. So have leopards, tigers, wolves, hyenas, polar bears, and
killer whales, among others. Shortly after the Njombe man-eaters
were killed, one of Rushby's colleagues observed such an incident
at the Kruger National Park, 250 miles east of the Sterkfontein
valley. Colonel James Stevenson-Hamilton was working as a warden there when he witnessed what he described as a "massacre of
baboons" by a pride of lions. Apparently, a baboon troop had been
approaching a water hole and failed to notice the lions napping
nearby. The lions awoke and two lionesses rose and quietly hid
themselves by the trail. When they leaped out, the baboons panicked and fled—directly into the larger body of lions. "The
baboons were apparently too terrified even to try to escape up any
of the surrounding trees," wrote Stevenson-Hamilton, "and hid
with their faces in their hands while the lions simply struck them
down right and left with blows from their paws."

The colonel might as well have been describing peasants
falling before berserkers. The most painful detail in this anecdote
is the baboons' resignation: with no hope of escape, they fashioned
a refuge of last resort from the darkness in their own hands. The
image is so poignant, in part, because those hands could so easily
be ours. Perhaps it was the possibility of such catastrophes that
kept the Sterkfontein baboons from fleeing that night when Brain
frightened them so badly: better to lose one or two than risk the
whole troop.

Even from millions of years away, it is upsetting to visualize
the fate of a family of australopithecines caught out on the veld, a
bit too far from a climbable tree, and it wouldn't have had to hap-

pen often to put a chill on everyone in the vicinity. To this day, entire districts have been paralyzed by the presence of a single man-eater, to the point that life-sustaining crops are left to rot in the fields. A similar kind of paralysis overcame the village of Sobolonye, even though most of the populace there was armed. When faced with threats of this kind, the loss of morale can be profound. If one imagines those hands over the face as a metaphorical hiding place, perhaps that is what sleep and shelter once meant to us: a more sustainable way of blocking out the horrors that stalked our waking lives, a way of thinking them into the world of unbeing, at least until the sun lit up the world again.

This is a humbling scenario to contemplate. On the other hand, if one could manage to survive and multiply in an environment like that, it stands to reason that nothing could stop you. Given enough time, such creatures could colonize the earth, and we have. Seen from this point of view, Southern Africa was not so much the Cradle of Humankind as it was the crucible. If the savanna was as Brain and others believe, it would have been a kind of ultimate proving ground for slow, weak, thin-skinned but increasingly quick-witted creatures like ourselves. In the view of evolutionists, such a challenging environment would have provided the necessary selection pressures for us to evolve, a prime and primal example of what Arnold Toynbee called the "optimum challenge."

Brain has found fossil evidence to support this in the caves of the Transvaal, and can roughly identify the moment when the same caves into which we were once dragged and consumed became the refuges from which we actively drove predators away. It took a new species to shift this balance of power, and it almost certainly occurred at the hands of our direct ancestor, *Homo habilis*. It is a transition that would have been thrilling, and agonizing, to witness. Brought about by larger brains, tools, and, eventually, fire, it would have profoundly altered the relationship between early humans and the creatures who preyed on them, however occasionally.

All of us, whether predator or prey, are opportunistic and creatures of habit. Thus, if a leopard or a pack of hunting hyenas failed enough times in its efforts to capture us, or was effectively intimidated, its menu preferences would shift accordingly—perhaps to baboons, where they remain today. Once this new configuration had stabilized, the offspring of such "reformed" predators would presumably reflect these dietary changes. There is good reason to suppose that, like the !Kung among lions, and the Udeghe among tigers, early man became an active, if cautious, cohabitant with these animals rather than their chronic victim.

In any case, it would have been a close call—most likely, a long series of them. It is noteworthy that it took roughly five million years before hominids—probably in the form of *Homo erectus*—finally developed the brains, the tools, and the legs to get out of Africa alive. There were big cats, hyenas, and wolves all along the way, and this may be one reason most of our hominid relatives never made it. It is striking, too, that, unlike so many other species—cats, for example—we are the only branch of our family (Hominidae) who survived the journey. In this sense, we are evolutionary orphans—a broken family of one, and it puts us in strange company: we share our genetic solitude with the platypus, the gharial, and the coelacanth.

———

Today, the ghosts of our ancestors continue to haunt us, manifesting a host of old family traits that have persisted through the ages, and that continue to influence our behavior and inform our responses and attitudes toward the world around us. In an effort to test some of the instinctive connections between modern humans and our primitive forebears, Richard Coss, a psychologist at the University of California, Davis, conducted a study in which he created a virtual savanna with typical features including a thorn tree, a boulder, and a rock crevice. After showing this empty, primordial landscape to a group of American preschool children, he introduced a virtual lion. Then he asked the children where they would go to find safety. Most of them chose the thorn tree or the crevice; only one in six picked the boulder. With no prior experience of savannas or predation, and a rudimentary, possibly cartoon-based, understanding of lions, more than 80 percent of these children understood the risk and the appropriate response to it. The small percentage who chose the boulder would not have escaped the lion, and to this day, despite millions of years of natural selection, there remains that small percentage of humans who make fatal choices.

The UCLA anthropologist Clark Barrett approached this question from another angle and, like Coss, he sought the help of children to answer it. It has been observed that infants as young as nine months understand the concept of pursuit and can distinguish between the chaser and the chased. But Barrett wanted to know at what age children were able to ascribe motives to different animals in hypothetical situations that didn't involve them personally, as Coss's lion experiment had. In other words, he wanted to know at what age we develop a "theory of animal mind," the same mental tool hunters like the !Kung and the Udeghe use to anticipate the behavior of game and avoid predators. In order to do this as objectively as possible, Barrett assembled two groups of children aged three to five; one group was made up of German preschoolers and the other was composed of Shuar, a tribe of subsistence hunter-agriculturalists from Ecuador's Amazon basin. Needless to say, these two groups of children had radically different cultural reference points and experience with animals. The experiment was elegant in its simplicity. Using a toy lion and a toy zebra, Barrett asked each child, "When the lion sees the zebra, what does the lion want to do?"

The results were surprising: 75 percent of the three-year-olds in both groups answered with some variation of "The lion wants to chase/bite/kill the zebra." (It must be remembered that these children had only just learned to speak and had vastly different levels of exposure to media and information about the wider world.) When Barrett posed the same question to the four- and five-year-olds, every single child anticipated the predatory intentions of the lion. Barrett then took the scenario a step further, asking, "When the lion catches the zebra, what will happen?" In this case, 100 percent of the Shuar three-year-olds answered with some version of "The lion hurts/kills/eats the zebra." Only two thirds of the more sheltered and media-saturated German three-year-olds gave this answer, but when Barrett got to the four- and five-year-olds, every child understood that the zebra was in serious trouble.

What is remarkable about this experiment is that very young children, regardless of culture, learning, or living conditions, understand fundamental rules of predatory behavior, even when they have never seen a live lion or zebra and know nothing about life in sub-Saharan Africa. Barrett believes their innate grasp of these primordial relationships is a genetic legacy based on millions of years of hard-won experience, and that this is why young children continue to be fascinated by dinosaurs and other monstrous creatures. He calls this "Jurassic Park syndrome"; the implication is that, in ages past, this was information one absolutely had to take an interest in if one was to survive to breeding age.

As we get older, our skill at motive discernment grows increasingly sophisticated, and several studies have shown that we are adept at determining an animal's behavior and intention simply by being shown spotlit portions of its limbs and joints with everything else blacked out. This ability is crucial for distinguishing friend from foe and predator from prey when only fragmentary information is available, as is often the case in tall grass, dense forest, or at night. Today, this same visual acuity enables fighter pilots to distinguish between ally and enemy aircraft in a split second, and it is also what keeps us alive in heavy traffic. But the full perceptive range of these ancient gifts is most easily appreciated in a crowded bar as we assess potential mates, no matter what they may be wearing.

Researchers from the Center for Evolutionary Psychology at the University of California, Santa Barbara, wanted to refine this idea and test whether people pay preferential attention to certain categories of things like, for example, animals, over others. To determine this, they showed undergraduates pairs of photographs depicting various scenes in which the second image varied slightly from the first and included a single specific change. The students' only instructions were to indicate when and if they noticed a change and what it was. There were animate and inanimate categories so the second image might introduce a pigeon, a car, or a tree. It quickly became apparent that students were more successful at noticing animals, and they did so 90 percent of the time. When something like a wheelbarrow or even a large silo was added, only two thirds of the students noticed. The success rate spiked when the changes involved a human or an elephant, with 100 percent of the participants noticing. These relative success rates held even when it came to introducing a distant, well-camouflaged elephant or a bright red minivan into scenes on the African savanna: fewer than three quarters of the participants spotted the added van.

Joshua New and his colleagues published their findings in *Proceedings of the National Academy of Sciences*, concluding that "the results herein implicate a visual monitoring system equipped with ancestrally derived animal-specific selection criteria." Which is to say, we seem to be hard-wired to spot animals. "People develop phobias for spiders and snakes and things that were ancestral threats," Dr. New told a journalist in 2007. "It's very infrequent to have somebody afraid of cars or electrical outlets. Those statistically pose much more of a threat to us than a tiger. That makes it an interesting test case as to why do tigers still capture attention."

Evidence suggests that the reason tigers and their kind continue to capture our attention is because, over time, this has proven the most effective way to prevent them from capturing *us*. Maybe this is why it is impossible not to wonder what Markov and Khomenko saw and felt in their last moments—an experience so aberrant and alien to us, and yet strangely, deeply familiar: there is a part of us that still needs to know.

———

Ongoing in the debate about our origins and our nature is the question of how we became fascinated by monsters, but only certain kinds. The existence of this book alone is a case in point. No one would read it if it were about a pig or a moose (or even a person) who attacked unemployed loggers. Tigers, on the other hand, get our full attention. They strike a deep and resonant chord within us, and one reason is because, as disturbing as it may be, man-eating occurs within the acceptable parameters of the tiger's nature, which has informed *our* nature. If the pig or the moose did such things, they would simply be abhorrent and weird; it wouldn't resonate in the same way.

As long as they are carnivorous and/or humanoid, the monster's form matters little. Whether it is Tyrannosaurus rex, saber-toothed tiger, grizzly bear, werewolf, bogeyman, vampire, Wendigo, Rangda, Grendel, Moby-Dick, Joseph Stalin, the Devil, or any other manifestation of the Beast, all are objects of dark fascination, in large part because of their capacity to consciously, willfully destroy us. What unites these creatures—ancient or modern, real or imagined, beautiful or repulsive, animal, human, or god—is their superhuman strength, malevolent cunning, and, above all, their capricious, often vengeful appetite—for us. This, in fact, is our expectation of them; it's a kind of contract we have. In this capacity, the seemingly inexhaustible power of predators to fascinate us—to "capture attention"—fulfills a need far beyond morbid titillation. It has a practical application. After all, this is the daily reality of many savanna baboons, and it has been ours as well. In southern Tanzania, in the Sundarbans of Bangladesh, and in many war zones around the world, it still is.

Over time, these creatures or, more specifically, the dangers they represent, have found their way into our consciousness and taken up permanent residence there. In return, we have shown extraordinary loyalty to them—to the point that we re-create them over and over in every medium, through every era and culture, tuning and adapting them to suit changing times and needs. It seems they are a key ingredient in the glue that binds us to ourselves and to each other. Without our social networks and the fragile carapace of technology with which we shield ourselves, Khomenko's and Markov's fate could be our own. And neither our psyches nor our stories will allow us to forget it.

PART TWO

| | |

POCHEPNYA

15

It is quite in the order of things in folk-tales . . . that a
parent should purchase his own safety by sacrificing
his son to a ferocious animal or to a supernatural
enemy.

C. F. COXWELL,
Siberian and Other Folk Tales

SOBOLONYE WAS A PLACE FAMILIAR WITH MORTAL TRAGEDY, BUT IT
tended to be accidental or self-inflicted, and alcohol was often a
factor. One side effect of these repeated blows was a caustic graveyard humor, and not even Markov was spared. Some in the village
felt sure he had invited his own death by robbing the tiger of its
kill. "It became a bit of a joke," said one local resident, "that he
brought that meat to his own funeral."

True or not, this assumption was also a way of deflecting such
a fate away from oneself, a corollary to the widely held belief that
tigers never attacked unprovoked. Without this psychic armor,
how could one dare to make one's living in the taiga? Nonetheless,
the possibility that there might be exceptions to this rule had been
preying on people's minds during the week following Markov's
death. By then, news of the tiger's behavior at the road workers'
camp had also spread through the valley, and there was little
doubt that this was the same tiger that had killed Markov. Regardless of their other feelings about tigers, the residents of Sobolonye
had great respect for their intelligence and hunting prowess, and
the idea that these powers might be directed against them—at
random—was terrifying. This tiger's presence had cast a pall over

the village, not just for its own sake, but for what it implied: the forest was Sobolonye's sole reason for being, and Mother Taiga was the closest thing to a deity its inhabitants had. When all else failed—and it had—she alone had stood by them. If the taiga should turn against them, too, where else could they go?

———

During those few days following Markov's funeral, nothing much had changed for Denis Burukhin or his best friend, Andrei Pochepnya, save for the emptiness left by the death of their "Uncle" Markiz, a man they had known and liked. Both Denis and Andrei were twenty years old and fresh out of the army; they had lived in Sobolonye for most of their lives. Where Denis was short, dark, and compact, Andrei was tall and fair-haired; he was a quiet young man, even shy, but like Denis, he was a competent tayozhnik. The two of them had been hunting and trapping together since they were boys; they trusted each other implicitly, and trust among fur trappers is like trust among gold miners—a rare and precious thing. In many respects, their fates appeared to be linked; they even left for the army on the same day. Denis, the better marksman of the two, drew the short straw and was sent to the front in Chechnya, and that was the last his family heard of him. After a few months, his mother, Lida—short, dark-haired, and densely packaged like her son—gave him up for dead. "There were no letters," she said. "Nothing. We stopped waiting. And then he came back." But he wasn't quite the same. "He became aloof—like a different person. It must have affected him to see all those people die."

Andrei, meanwhile, spent his entire tour at a base in Khabarovsk, the tough, historic city of half a million on the left bank of the Amur River, only 150 miles north of Sobolonye. But even so far away from the front line, the Russian army can still be a brutal environment. The hazing of new recruits is entrenched, systematic, and often barbaric, and morale was abysmal: soldiers could be seen standing at the edge of their fenced compounds begging for money from passersby. For teenaged boys from a remote village, either experience would have been a rude awakening and, after two years away, both of them were having trouble readjusting to village life. On the one hand, they were free at last; on the other, they were effectively marooned with no prospects in this broken, isolated outpost.

There was also tension at home, and it was exacerbated by the lack of work and money. Andrei's father, a former logger and market hunter, had managed to get a job as the night watchman at the elementary school, but it paid a pittance, and now Andrei, the third of five children and the oldest boy, was one more mouth to feed. It didn't help that he was at loose ends and chafing at the confines of the cramped family house. The slow-motion implosion of this community, which had been going on for years, was playing itself out in microcosm inside the Pochepnyas' home. Andrei's father was profoundly demoralized; his mother was moody and combative and had strained relations with many of her neighbors. The negative synergy was almost palpable, and Andrei spent as much time out of the house as he could.

With so much time to kill, Denis and Andrei went back to what they knew best: hunting and trapping. The two of them had parallel traplines running down either side of the Takhalo River, near its confluence with the Bikin. It was a twenty-five-mile round-trip from the village and the boys would travel there together. When they couldn't catch a ride with a logging truck, they would go in on horseback. The Pochepnyas had an apiary on the Takhalo with a well-built cabin where the boys would often stay for days at a time. Prior to Markov's death, this had been a casual outing, but now everything had changed; everyone was on edge, and it wasn't just for safety reasons.

Outside of logging and the relatively small poppy and marijuana cultivating industries, ginseng hunting, beekeeping, fur trapping, and pine nut gathering were the most lucrative "crops" in the forest. The latter two, along with meat (and tiger) hunting, are pursued in winter, and every day that a villager was prevented from going into the forest meant money taken from her pocket and food taken from her table. A hand-to-mouth existence is, for most people who have the time and inclination to read books like this, nothing more than a quaint and vivid turn of phrase. But for many in the Bikin valley, it is a factual description of their reality. Denis Burukhin summed it up bitterly: "In Sobolonye, you go into the taiga for a week, come back, eat what you've got, and then it's back into the taiga. What kind of life is that? It's no life at all."

A century ago, many Russians lived this way in the Far East, and most natives did, too. Then, there wasn't an alternative, but the expectations for what life can and should be have changed radically in the past twenty years. Under communism, there was room, albeit strictly controlled, for aspiration, and there was a State guarantee of basic security in terms of education, employment, housing, and food. But most of these assurances disintegrated after perestroika. Replacing them, along with crime, alcoholism, and despondency, were satellite dishes offering multiple channels that allowed you to see just how far behind you really were. Nowadays, in many parts of the world—not just Sobolonye—it is possible to starve while watching television.

Neither Denis nor Andrei saw the village as part of their future, but for now, this was their lot and they focused on those things over which they had some measure of control—namely, their traplines. In spite of recent events, both boys kept their faith in the tayozhnik's dictum "If I don't touch her, she won't touch me." Shortly after Markov's funeral, they went back up the Takhalo with the horses, figuring that if the tiger was around the animals would scent it and warn them, and that together they could handle whatever came next. They weren't the only ones venturing into the forest that week, and there may have been an element of bravado to their casual demeanor. They were young soldiers after all, skilled with guns and brimming with testosterone; they knew these woods like the backs of their hands, and hadn't Denis survived Chechnya? Traveling through the forest, as tall as giants on their shaggy, steaming mounts, emboldened by all that heat and power between their legs, these two close friends may have said to each other the same thing Markov said to his fretting wife: "Why should I be afraid of her? She should be afraid of me!" Either of them would have relished the opportunity to avenge themselves against the tiger that killed their friend and neighbor.

But their parents felt differently. After the boys made it safely back that evening, Denis's mother and father flatly forbade him going into the taiga again. "He wanted to go," said the huntress Baba Liuda, "but we talked him out of it. We said, 'Denis, you did not die in Chechnya. Your mother cried day and night waiting for you.' "

Their neighbor Leonid Lopatin felt the same way about his son. Lopatin is a rare Jew among the Slavs and natives along the Bikin. A thoughtful man and a skilled hunter, he had worked as a truck driver for the logging company before it closed down. Despite his rugged circumstances, Lopatin's ability to articulate psychological and interpersonal nuance stands out among his blunt and forthright neighbors. In the West, a certain level of psychological awareness—and the language to go with it—is taken for granted now, but in Russia, with the exception of some in urban, educated circles, this is virtually nonexistent. Stoicism isn't so much a virtue as it is a survival skill. Of the people in rural Primorye, a longtime expatriate said, "Those folks are tougher than nails and hardened from horrors." A Russian-American author once quipped that what Russians needed after perestroika wasn't economic aid but a planeload of social workers, and this seems painfully true. One reason people find it so difficult to describe how they feel is that they have never been asked. It is understood that life is hard and men, especially, are expected to suck it up and gut it out. If you need a counselor, confessor, or escape hatch—that's what vodka is for. Lopatin makes his own and keeps it handy in a ten-liter milk can by his kitchen table. "You've never had vodka like this," he assures his visitors. "It gives you better memories."

Lopatin's son, Vasily, was the same age as Andrei and Denis, and he, too, had just returned from the army. Like them, he was an avid hunter and trapper, but his father laid down the law: "As soon as I heard about Markov," Lopatin explained in his kitchen in Yasenovie, where he works now as a scrap metal dealer, "I said to my son, 'Vasya! We have no business in the taiga any longer. It doesn't matter how careful you are; this animal can sneak up on you in the blink of an eye. Do not take *one step* toward the taiga.' My son was saying, 'But we already put the traps out; this is the best part of the season.' I said, 'Let it be. Life is more important.' "

The situation at Andrei Pochepnya's house was more complicated. The Lopatins lived next door and they knew the family
well. "I know what Andrei's father told him when he came back
from the army," Lopatin said. "He said, 'I fed you. I raised you.
Now, you look after me; feed me.' He liked to drink, you know. It
was a tough time, and Andrei was just a young boy out of the army
who didn't know how to live his life. He had talked to the supervisor of a logging crew who sort of promised him a job, but it wasn't
a sure thing and both his parents were on his back, 'sawing on
him.'"

Andrei was in a bind: his parents didn't want him to risk his
life in the forest, but he was the oldest son and was expected to
contribute. At that point, no one was hunting the tiger and no one
knew where it was, what its intentions were, or how long this
paralysis would last. For Andrei, this uncertainty combined with
the situation at home was intolerable. At least the taiga was quiet
and he could be his own boss, and if he got lucky and caught some
mink or weasel, he would have something to show for himself.

———

On Friday, December 12, Tamara Borisova held a ninth-day vigil
for her husband. Vigils were a holdover from the days of the
church: nine days after a person's death, the soul is believed to still
be wandering, searching for its place; at that time, friends and
family gather to drink, eat, and remember the deceased. On the
fortieth day, there would be another vigil and by then the soul is
expected to have settled. "Markov's son came and woke me up,"
Denis recalled. "He said, 'Let's go; people are gathering.' I told
him, 'I'll go get Andrei and we'll come right over.' I went to
Andrei's, but they said he had gone to the forest. We hadn't
planned on going anywhere that day because it was Markov's
ninth-day vigil. I don't know what happened; I think Andrei had
an argument at home or something. His parents told me he had
gone out to look for a job."

"I will tell you how it happened," said Denis's mother, Lida.
"Andrei dropped by the night before. He said, 'The tiger hasn't
smelled my bullets, so she won't touch me.' Denis wanted to go,

too, but we wouldn't let him. Then, Andrei argued with his parents and left in the morning."

Leonid Lopatin saw Andrei as he was heading out on the morning of the 12th. "I was with my son sitting and talking at my kitchen table," he explained, "and through the window we saw Andrei coming out of his house." This image remains vivid in Lopatin's mind: "He was a tall fellow," Lopatin continued. "He would make a good man. . . . Anyway, he had a small knapsack on and was headed toward the taiga. My son and he were school-mates, so my son asked him, 'Where are you going?' Andrei said, 'I have a few traps; I have to go and check them.' My son and I both told him, 'The cannibal tiger is out there. Don't go!' Andrei said, 'Don't worry, I stink so bad that she wouldn't want to touch me anyway.'

"I knew that he had only a crappy rifle," said Lopatin, "an old Mosin carbine*—some rusty, prewar nonsense. I had used it before: it was not a rifle—it was a stick. I wanted to give him my own rifle, and if he would have stopped for a moment, I would have. But he was unstoppable—like a torpedo. He left about ten or eleven a.m. and as soon as he stepped out onto the road, Sergei Boyko drove by, so Boyko gave him a lift out to the apiary."

Denis Burukhin was puzzled by his friend's sudden departure, but at first he wasn't overly concerned; after all, the tiger was far away. "His parents said he had gone up to First Creek, which is in a completely different direction," he recalled, "and that he would be home in the evening. I thought, why should I go looking for him? He would come back soon anyway. So, I went to the ninth-day vigil, and then here and there. The next day, I went to see him, and they said he was still not back. What to do? I figured he had stayed in the cabin overnight and that he would be home that evening. I went to see him the day after: again he was not there."

Burukhin still had faith in the law of his jungle, and this may have been because he had been spared seeing Markov's remains or

---

* A bolt-action infantry rifle whose design had changed little since it was introduced in 1891.

the scene at his cabin. As a result, the threat this tiger posed was still abstract for him—more of a parental fear than something that could actually happen. "She hides well," Burukhin said. "I have seen all the other animals, but I have never seen a tiger—not once." Nonetheless, with each passing day, he grew more uneasy. "That was the only time he went by himself," Burukhin said of his friend's unannounced departure. "Always we would go together. Always."

———

The tiger had eaten Markov over a three-day period, but that had been more than a week ago and, once again, the animal was ravenous. His routine had also been disrupted; he was no longer making his usual rounds. Instead, he was moving in a linear fashion, steadily downstream. In doing so, he may well have been poaching on other tigers' territories. Though this tiger was in his prime, and large, he was now seriously wounded and vulnerable to attack by another dominant male.

The tiger was hunting constantly as he moved down the valley toward Sobolonye, and every step was painful. In the tiger's left forepaw was a deep, fresh laceration through the pad—possibly sustained when the tiger destroyed the outhouse. Far worse, though, was the wound to his other leg. A small handful of pea-sized buckshot had raked his right paw and foreleg, separating it at the cubital joint (the equivalent of our elbow). The only way buckshot could be so tightly concentrated is for it to have been shot from point-blank range. A factory load shot from that distance would have shattered the tiger's leg and crippled him fatally, but Markov's homemade shell, possibly compromised by condensation, didn't have the same punch. It had only succeeded in making the tiger extraordinarily dangerous.

The tiger's wounds were also becoming infected, but this was a mere inconvenience compared to a much more serious mechanical problem: the damage to the joint was impacting the tiger's ability to hunt. Over and over again, he caught fresh scent, stalked viable game, and set up ambushes that, a week earlier, would have produced life-sustaining results. Now, the boar and deer were getting away. The tiger's speed, agility, and jumping distance were off— not by much, but margins in the taiga are tight to begin with; when measuring a missed kill, an inch might as well be a mile.

The tiger was not a man-eater by nature—Markov had been a special case—but even as the tiger hunted, he was being hunted, too, by his own hunger, and by the unrelenting cold. The tiger understood this instinctively and, with every passing day, his desperation mounted. It is hard to say if it was injury, hunger, or some kind of primordial rage that changed his behavior, but ever since being shot by Markov, the tiger had been acting with a kind of calculated audacity that is not typical of these creatures. In any case, shortly after he arrived at the Takhalo River, some peculiar events took place.

––––––

Andrei Pochepnya arrived at the apiary cabin about midday and, before heading out to check his traps, he made a fire and had some tea and bread. Pochepnya believed himself to be alone there, but he wasn't. The tiger, though he was more than a mile away, sensed the young man's presence. It is impossible to know whether it was the slam of the cabin door, the smoke from the fire, or some other cue that caused the tiger to pause in his tracks there near the foot of the Takhalo, but something did. Whatever it was made the tiger change direction, and he stalked this new information with a single-minded intensity that would have been chilling to behold. A mile downstream from Andrei's cabin, on the right bank, was a crude Udeghe-style shelter made of branches; the only indicator of the century in which it was made was the tarpaper that covered it instead of tree bark. The tiger crossed the river on the ice and broke into this structure, inside of which was a mattress and other camping equipment belonging to a man named Tsepalev. After scavenging some rancid bait that had been sealed inside a plastic jar, the tiger hauled Tsepalev's mattress out of the shelter and dragged it fifty yards across the frozen Takhalo. There, on the opposite bank, he spread the mattress out under a commanding spruce tree, lay down on it in plain view, and waited. The ground was open along this section of the river and visibility was excellent in both directions.

When Pochepnya arrived, as the tiger somehow knew he would, it would have been around two in the afternoon. Hunters are vigilant of necessity, and a four-hundred-pound tiger sitting sphinxlike on a mattress is hard to miss. But Pochepnya was not aware of the tiger until he launched himself off his bed from ten yards away.

Pochepnya's rifle would have been slung over his left shoulder with the trigger facing upward. This arrangement enables a hunter (or a soldier) to grasp the barrel with his left hand and bring the gun up to his right shoulder in one fluid motion. Pochepnya, fresh out of the army and a hunter all his life, was trained to do this in a fraction of a second—and he did. But when he pulled the trigger nothing happened.

———

There are, scattered around the hinterlands of Asia and—increasingly—elsewhere, a small fraternity of people who have been attacked by tigers and lived. Its members find their way in through various means: greed, desperation, curiosity, bad timing, and, in a handful of cases, dazzling stupidity or madness. There is no association that advocates for them as there is for so many other niche populations of afflicted people, and there is no journal that reviews their cases or disseminates information on their behalf. Mostly, they stay at home, often in shacks and cabins a long way from paved roads. If they leave, it is usually with difficulty and sometimes in great pain. Very rarely is there anyone in their immediate vicinity who fully appreciates what happened to them out there and, in this way, the lives of tiger attack survivors resemble those of retired astronauts or opera divas: each in their own way has stared alone into the abyss.

In the case of the hunting-manager-turned-big-cat-researcher Sergei Sokolov, it took years to pull himself back out. Sokolov was in his early forties when he was attacked by a tiger in March of 2002. Powerfully built, with a bull neck and a closely shorn head, he exudes the kind of pent-up intensity that one might expect of a highly trained soldier—the kind that gets dropped alone behind enemy lines and must, somehow, get himself back alive. Sokolov is a rigorously principled and very focused man, made more so, it seems, by his experiences with tigers and leopards. To date, he has spent more than twenty years working and hunting in the taiga. During his thirteen years as a ranger and hunting inspector, two hunters he knew were killed by tigers, and he was personally involved in a hunt for a man-eater (a decrepit male whose fangs had been worn down to nubs). Like so many in this work, Sokolov was drawn to the Far East by the stories he had read, and by their promise of the wild and exotic. Today, there is an urgency about Sokolov, a sense that time is limited and precious, and it may have something to do with coming so close to death. Even so, it took him several hours to recount the ordeal that began, as these incidents so often do, with a roar.

"I will tell you my personal outlook on things," said Sokolov late one evening at the kitchen table in his modest apartment in Vladivostok. "Everybody has his fate and his destiny. It is difficult to escape it: if it is your destiny to die this year, it won't matter if you go into the taiga or not. I never thought that something could happen to me in the taiga, because in the taiga I felt like I was at home."

. Sokolov's purpose on that cold spring day in the mountains of southern Primorye had been to collect samples of Amur leopard scat for DNA analysis, which is one way scientists determine population numbers for this critically endangered cat. He was working with a partner—a novice—who was some distance away, and both men were unarmed as per the regulations for this type of research. It was early afternoon, just below freezing, when Sokolov ran across a set of tiger tracks and stopped to measure them; they were fresh, and it was clear they belonged to a female. He decided to follow them, but did so backward as a precaution. He lost the trail and, as he circled around to find it again, he crested a ridge where he paused to catch his breath. And this was when he heard it. "This sound," said Sokolov, "you cannot confuse it with anything else—God willing you should never hear it. My partner was a hundred yards away, and he said that when he heard that roar he was stunned; it was all he could do not to start running."

Sokolov paused, trying to find words to describe a sensation that is essentially indescribable. Elizabeth Marshall Thomas could have helped him here: on the African savanna, she explains in *The Tribe of Tiger*, when thunder rolls, lions will roar back. What other creature, besides the lion, the tiger, and the whale, can answer Creation in its own language?

"I will use an analogy," said Sokolov, trying his best to articulate what he heard and felt on that ridge. "Every melody is based on the same seven notes, but some melodies make you happy, some make you sad, and some can terrify you. Well, this was a roar which makes your blood go cold in your veins and your hair stand up on your head. You could call it a 'premonition of death.' When I heard it, I thought, 'That tiger is going to kill somebody,' but the wind was blowing and my back was turned, so at first I didn't realize it was going to be me."

Nor had Sokolov realized that there was more than one tiger. The tigress he was tracking was in heat and a large male had been tailing her; while backtracking on the trail of the female, Sokolov had run into the male. When a tigress comes into estrus, a kind of pheromone-induced insanity follows wherever she goes, and this tiger was out of its mind with lust. He had probably fought for his position and he had a lot to look forward to: once the tigress has reviewed and accepted a suitor, the two may copulate twenty times a day for a week or more. Individual encounters are brief and loud and, once consummated, the tigress may wheel around and club her mate savagely in the face. It is hard to tell from the human vantage whether this is a sign of irritation or tigerish affection.

When the tiger spotted Sokolov, it may have perceived him as a competitor, a threat, or simply as an obstacle, but by the time Sokolov realized his mistake, it was too late. "The tiger roared again," he said. "He was about forty yards away and I saw him running toward me. The word 'fear' doesn't really describe the feeling in that situation. It's more like an animal horror—a terror that's genetically inherent in you. Something happened to me then: I went into a stupor; I was paralyzed, and I had only one thought: I am going to die right now. Very clearly, I realized that I was going to die."

The tiger closed the gap in a matter of seconds and, in that moment of arrested consciousness, Sokolov didn't even see the final leap. "I stepped back," he said, "and closed my eyes for an instant—because of my nerves. They say that when a person is in this type of critical situation his whole life rushes through his mind. Well, that didn't happen to me. I remembered Sergei Denisov [a hunter he had known who was killed and eaten by a tiger], and I had just one thought: let this tiger kill me right away so I won't suffer too long.

"The tiger knocked me down; my left leg was bent and he bit into my knee. For an instant, he and I were looking in each other's eyes—his eyes were blazing, his ears were pressed back; I could see his teeth, and I thought I saw surprise in his eyes—like he was seeing something he hadn't expected to see. He bit me once, twice. My bones were cracking, crushing; everything was crackling. He was holding my leg sort of like a dog, shaking his head from side to side, and there was a sound like heavy cloth ripping. I was in excruciating pain. He was eating me, and there was nothing I could do to stop him."

In that moment, Sokolov shifted into a different mode; it was as if the clouds of fear parted to make way for another emotion, much as they had for Jim West when he heard the bear attacking his dog. "I just got mad," said Sokolov. "Instinctively, I punched the tiger in the forehead, between the eyes. He roared and jumped away. Then my partner came to help me."

In the act of coming to his senses, and tapping that deep and ancient vein of self-preservation that flows through all of us, Sokolov had brought the tiger to its senses, too. The tiger had no particular issue with Sokolov; he was simply in the wrong place at the wrong time. But for Sokolov, this was just the beginning. "As soon as the tiger left, I understood that my bones were crushed and shattered, and my ligaments and tendons were torn apart."

And yet, in spite of this, the pain Sokolov felt then was as keen in his heart as it was in his leg: "I have spent so much time in the taiga," he said. "I love the taiga and I treat it like my home—like it is some living creature. I have never violated her law, never killed anything which I shouldn't have, never cut a tree unless I had to do it. So, when I saw that tiger charging me, I felt like I was being betrayed by my own mother."

Andrei Pochepnya may have felt the same way.

Sokolov was now in a grave situation: lethally injured, lying in deep, wet snow, miles from the nearest road, with an inexperienced partner. There was no radio, and walking was out of the question. His knee was so badly damaged he looked, in his words, "like a grasshopper"; it was bleeding profusely. Sokolov's partner managed to bind his upper leg with a tourniquet and ease him into his sleeping bag. "I told him, 'Vladimir, please, cut some pine branches, prepare some firewood, make a fire and run for help.' He gave me what he had, including his knapsack, his sweater, some chocolate, and then he left. There were cigarettes, too—a whole pack. I smoked them all in the first half hour."

By then, it was about three in the afternoon. It was windy and the temperature was dropping, the sodden snow turning to ice. The sun went down, and darkness settled in. Sokolov lay there as the hours passed, and the pile of firewood shrank, but nobody came. The nearest road was three miles away, and the research base was ten more beyond that. In spite of the tourniquet, Sokolov's blood was draining steadily out of him, taking his body temperature down with it. Somehow he stayed alert; it may have been the pain that kept him conscious. Sokolov spent the entire night like that, alone in a traumatized limbo of blood loss, creeping hypothermia, and unimaginable pain. On top of this, there was no guarantee that the tigers wouldn't come back. "I just wanted to lose consciousness and stop feeling that pain," he said. "By three a.m., I understood that nobody was coming."

This was only the second circle of Sokolov's hell; there were still at least seven more to go. Despite his best efforts, he never lost consciousness for more than a few minutes, and there in the dark, in shock, his mind wandered to some frightening places. He could not fathom where his partner was and he imagined he must have had an accident, too; he pictured Vladimir injured at the bottom of a cliff, and his despair deepened. "I don't consider myself a religious man," said Sokolov, "but at that time I was thinking: 'God, please take me, and stop this torture.' Over the course of the night, I passed through different stages of desire to live and to die. I decided I would hang on until noon the next day; if nobody had come by then I would take a knife and slit my wrist—these were the kinds of thoughts going through my mind."

———

Meanwhile, Sokolov's partner was having some serious problems of his own. He made it to the road all right, but when he stopped at the first village, no one was willing to help him so he had to go all the way back to the base. Once there, it took him until around five in the morning before he managed to gather some men with a Caterpillar tractor and a hay wagon. In this, they made the slow trip back. Not even the Cat could get up to the ridge so they made the last mile or so on foot, carrying a stretcher. They didn't reach Sokolov until nine. By then, he had been on his own for eighteen hours, and he was on the threshold, wavering between the living and the dead. "While I was in that suspended, uncertain state," he recalled, "my body understood that it should fight for life and I should be alert. I knew that there was nobody to rely on, except myself. But as soon as I saw familiar faces, all my strength left me. I felt very weak; I was very thirsty. I started to cry.

"I told them that they wouldn't be able to take me to the hospital by tractor. I told them to call a helicopter immediately because I was going to die otherwise. As it was, I almost died on the way to the tractor. It took them six hours to carry me because the slope was so steep. The snow was melting and it was slippery; there were fallen trees along the creek and waterfalls covered with ice. There were only four people on the rescue team and they got exhausted."

The rescue team had a radiophone and they called for a helicopter, but because bills for previous rescue flights were in arrears, the aviation authority refused to fly. They were referred to the governor of the territory. They called the governor's office, and they were told he would have to think about it. Hours passed, and Sokolov was slipping. They made more calls: to a well-connected

Russian tiger researcher and then to his ex-wife, who eventually got in touch with Dale Miquelle, the American tiger biologist in Terney. Miquelle agreed to vouch for the flight and, finally, the helicopter took off. By then, it was late afternoon and, still, the stretcher-bearers had not been able to reach the tractor. Sokolov was drifting in and out of consciousness. When the helicopter arrived, there was nowhere to land so they had to winch him up through the trees in a basket.

By the time Sokolov finally arrived in the hospital, the doctor gave him hours to live. His leg became a secondary concern then; simply saving his life was now the priority. When he was eventually stabilized and conscious again, Sokolov was greeted with the news that his leg would have to be amputated. By then, more than twenty-four hours had passed since the attack, and the wound had gone septic. Even the bone itself became afflicted with an infection of the marrow (osteomyelitis). The mouth of a tiger, even a healthy one, is a filthy place, and Sokolov required massive doses of antibiotics. He had to have a cannula (a semipermanent intravenous device) inserted under his collarbone and, like this, he was parked in the hospital, attached to an IV drip, for months. During this time, close friends managed to find doctors willing to try to save his leg, which they managed to do with multiple surgeries, plates, and screws. Whether he would ever be able to walk on it again was another matter. For months afterward, Sokolov was held together with a stainless steel armature called an Ilizarov apparatus, which gave him the macabre appearance of a human being under construction.

Immediately after the attack, Inspection Tiger examined the site and determined that it was an unfortunate accident and chalked it up to human error; no attempt was made to pursue the tiger. When Sokolov's boss came to the hospital to explain what had actually happened—that he had stumbled on mating tigers— he ribbed him, saying, "You're lucky that tiger didn't try to fuck you instead of the tigress."

"Well, he should have proposed it to me," Sokolov replied. "I'd have let him have his way with me if it would have kept him from biting."

Infected by the tiger in mysterious ways, Sokolov found himself stirred by powerful impulses he had no wish to control. As
soon as he was able to hobble around, he was overcome by sexual
desire. "For a year and a half I had to use crutches," he said. "After
that I had to use a cane. Maybe some strength came from the tiger,
or maybe I understood that I was really alive, but I started fucking
around."

It is the wish to acquire this same form of potency, but at less
personal cost, that drives much of the illegal trade in tiger-based
supplements. The brandname Viagra is derived from *vyaaghra*,
the Sanskrit word for tiger.

————

"I consider this event to be fate," said Sokolov in conclusion. "If
you go to the taiga, you should be prepared to encounter a tiger—
that is where they live. In terms of my feelings toward this tiger, I
have only feelings of gratitude, and I will explain why: if a person
goes through a tough ordeal in his life, he either breaks down or
becomes stronger than he used to be. In my case, it was the latter.
After this incident, I became stronger—not physically, of course,
but spiritually. Maybe it will sound funny, but, possibly, some
strength from this tiger was transferred to me."

All told, Sergei Sokolov's rehabilitation took three years. During that time, he met his wife, Svetlana, and they have started a
family. Their apartment in Vladivostok feels like a cozy, happy
home, and it is clear that this has been a key ingredient in his
remarkable recovery. "I vowed to a friend of mine: 'I will walk,
and I will return to the taiga,'" said Sokolov. "'Even if I have to
use crutches, even with a wooden leg, I will return.' This is what I
decided for myself."

Today, Sokolov's leg bends only slightly, and it is a horror to
look at, but he can walk, and he can work. It is not a miracle so
much as it is a testament to bloody-minded determination and,
probably, love. It takes him twice as long now, and he pays for it in
pain, but Sokolov has managed to return to his Taiga Matushka
(Mother Taiga).

16

Amba, the tiger, said to the father, "Old man, leave me your son here; don't take him with you. If you take him with you I will come and kill you both."

"The Boy and the Tiger,"
NINA VASILIEVNA MUNINA

BY SUNDAY, DECEMBER 14, LEONID LOPATIN COULD STAND IT NO LONGER.

"One, two, three days passed. Andrei is not back, but nobody is doing anything. So I said to my son, 'Let's go to the apiary.' I had a car so we went. Vasily went to look in the cabin, came back to the car and said, 'Something is wrong. Come take a look.' I saw a pot filled with frozen water in the kitchen; the rest of the bread was on the shelf, mostly eaten by a mouse, and I saw pieces of spaghetti eaten by the mouse as well. So everything was telling me: there's trouble. We drove back and I went to Andrei's mother. I asked her, 'How much food did Andrei have? How long was he planning to stay in the forest?' She said, 'He only had a loaf of bread and a package of macaroni—he only left for a day.' I asked her, 'Why aren't you worrying? It's been four days, and the tiger is in the taiga. Where's his father?' She said, 'He is working at the school; he's on the night shift.' I said, 'Tell him to come and see me as soon as he gets off, I need to talk to him.'

"So in the morning, after his shift, Alexander Pochepnya came to see me. And when he came, I told him man-to-man: 'It is your own son, what the hell are you doing? He is not a dog. He's out there somewhere for *four days* and you're not worried about him? If it was me, I would fly over there.' He said, 'I *am* worried. Some-

thing inside tells me that something is wrong. But I can't go there
by myself. Let's go together.' He was confused and upset; he didn't
know what to do, and I said, 'You're his father—gather some
hunters and go with them.' He asked Danila Zaitsev, Denis
Burukhin, my son, and me."

Lopatin stopped speaking and rubbed his eyes. "I am sorry,"
he said, "my vision is bad and my eyes are in pain. That is why
they are watering."

On Monday the 15th, Danila Zaitsev; Denis Burukhin; Andrei
Pochepnya's father, Alexander; Leonid Lopatin; and Lopatin's son,
Vasily, squeezed themselves and their guns into Lopatin's Toyota
sedan. Andrei's younger brother had wanted to go, too, but they
wouldn't allow it because, said Burukhin, "We knew where we
were going. We knew what we were going to find." Leonid Lopatin
was nearly sixty at the time—old for that country—so, after driving them to the apiary, he left on some other business, letting the
younger men go ahead on their own. The men were all armed
except for Alexander Pochepnya, who had only the one rifle, which
Andrei had taken with him. This made Zaitsev the de facto leader
of the party. He was carrying a powerful double-barreled shotgun,
which, formidable as it was, would have been scoffed at by anyone
with experience in shooting big cats. However, this is what he had,
and it was legal.

According to Markov's friend Andrei Onofreychuk, Zaitsev
was dismayed by the younger men's casual attitude. "They were
going down the trail with their weapons on their shoulders as if
they didn't need them," he recalled. "So, Zaitsev said, 'Are you
guys nuts? You have to have your guns ready, right?' But they just
said, 'Whatever happens, happens.'

"Youth is youth," said Onofreychuk. "They don't realize the
danger yet."

Although they were neighbors, Zaitsev did not know Alexander Pochepnya particularly well. A father himself, he accompanied Pochepnya on this dreadful errand, not out of love or loyalty,
but because he had been asked, and perhaps because he could
sense how close to the edge this man already was. Zaitsev had
been born in western China where many Old Believers sought

refuge following the Russian Revolution. Shortly after Stalin's death, Zaitsev's family had moved to Kazakhstan, and later he had moved on to the Far East—first to Chukotka and then south to Primorye, a path similar to Yuri Trush's. Zaitsev was a rarity in Sobolonye, having stayed sober and kept the same job maintaining the village's diesel generator for twenty years. Whatever his other failings, Zaitsev was a calm and sturdy soul whose presence alone was a bulwark against the crushing circumstances of both the era and the moment. And this was what Alexander Pochepnya needed now, more than anything.

———

The day they were given was crystalline, brittle, and bitterly cold. The taiga was at its winter finest and seemed made for the eyes alone: the sunshine was so brilliant, the snow so pristine, the sky so depthless, the stillness of the forest so profound that speech or motion of any kind felt like an intrusion. Here, even the softest sounds carried an echo, and the search party's presence, announced by the irksome, eightfold squeaking of their boots, seemed out of place—an affront to the exalted silence all around them. Burdened as they were by their dark concerns, these men were strangers here.

They did not travel in any kind of formation, or with any particular plan, but they all knew how to decipher winter sign—how, as Russian hunters say, to "read the White Book." The frozen river was a wind-stripped tabula rasa bearing just enough snow to record a track. A steep escarpment rose up from the right bank, guiding the river and pushing the men, first onto the ice and then over to the other side—Burukhin's side, where only his traps were set. The lower ground there carried more snow but was confused by a tangle of grass, shrubs, and fallen trees that soon gave way to full-blown forest. Even with the leaves down, it would be nearly impossible to find anything that didn't want to be found. But the snow missed nothing: a meticulous record keeper, it captured the story and held it fast. Andrei Pochepnya's was a meandering narrative of one line only: a single set of boot tracks leading away, and never coming back. His traps, which were set at the bases of small trees and among overhanging roots along the right bank, lay empty and undisturbed. A mile downstream from the apiary, hunkered down among bare stalks and saplings on the same side of the river, was Tsepalev's tarpaper hovel. As the men drew abreast of it, they noticed a second set of tracks emerging from the low doorway. Under normal circumstances these would have been made by the owner, a trapper and poet who was known to these men. But these tracks weren't made by a man.

It was shortly after noon, a week from the solstice, and the sun hung low over the river, blazing heatlessly. It was so cold and dry that it felt as if every molecule of moisture had been sucked from the air. There was no wind, and the snow sparkled with such fierce precision that each flake appeared distinct from those around it. In the midst of this exultant dazzle, dread turned to certainty. They readied their weapons and followed the tracks—across the river and up the left bank, over to a massive spruce tree, well over one hundred feet tall. There at the base, they found, along with the poet's tattered bed, a story very like the one at Markov's cabin: that of a tiger who made no attempt to hide and who attacked an alert, armed man head-on from ten paces away—as if he was an adversary, as opposed to prey. It was becoming a kind of signature. How, they wondered, could Pochepnya have been so close to something the size and color of a tiger, lying in the snow—on a mattress, no less—and failed to see it?

The site of the attack was clearly marked by the trampled snow, but there was strangely little blood, and Pochepnya's body was nowhere to be found. Only his rifle remained where it had fallen. Denis Burukhin picked it up and the first thing he did was draw back the bolt and look in the breech; it was still loaded. He withdrew the bullet to study it more closely and there in the primer, at the center of the bullet's brass head, was a dimple where the firing pin had struck it. The gun had misfired. Andrei Pochepnya's last fully realized thought may well have been the sickening realization that his father's gun had betrayed him. Burukhin cleared the snow from the barrel, reloaded the same bullet, and pulled the trigger. This time, it fired perfectly. Pochepnya's father was standing next to Burukhin, and there is no way to

know now what went through his mind, or his heart, as that deafening report echoed through the forest. But he took the gun from
Burukhin and, after walking a short distance, heaved it into an
open stretch of the Takhalo where the water ran deep and fast.
Then he went to look for his eldest son.

What Alexander Pochepnya found is something no parent is
equipped to see. Fifty yards into the snowy forest lay a heap of
blood-blackened clothing in a circle of exposed earth. It looked
more like a case of spontaneous combustion than an animal
attack. There was nothing left but shredded cloth and empty
boots. Nearby, a watch and crucifix lay undamaged on the ground.
The remains of Pochepnya himself were so small and so few they
could have fit in a shirt pocket. It is normal for a tiger to leave
extremities as the tiger did with Markov, but Pochepnya was gone,
and this was—like the ransacking of the outhouse—unprecedented. One need only imagine Udeghe hunters discovering a
scene like this two hundred years ago—their astonishment and
terror at the bloody tracks and empty clothes—to understand how
the possibility of a man-eating amba like the egule might implant
itself in the collective mind.

The men searched cautiously in the surrounding forest and
found the tiger's exit trail; it was fresh, perhaps only hours old.
Based on the two sets of tracks, the men deduced that Andrei had
been killed within hours of his arrival on the 12th, and that the
tiger had stayed with him for the next three days; when he wasn't
feeding, the tiger reclined on his padded throne, sheltered by
spruce boughs. Now, with nothing left to hold him there, the tiger
had moved on, sated for the time being.

Andrei Pochepnya had been carrying an army-issue ditty bag
with him in case his traps produced anything, and this is what
they collected him in. Then the four men walked back upstream
to meet Lopatin. Other than Denis Burukhin, who had witnessed
comparable scenes in Chechnya, Danila Zaitsev was the only one
present who had faced anything like this before. He bore it as sto-
ically as he had ten days earlier, and made a point of staying close
by Alexander Pochepnya. The father did not cry and barely spoke,

but in that silence, hooped and bound, he weathered a torrent of subjunctive recrimination that would only intensify with time.

"I came back to the apiary," said Lopatin, "and they were sitting on the porch, waiting. 'Where is Andrei?' I asked. His father picked up a bag from the ground and said, 'He is here.'"

17

Every fact seemed to warrant me in concluding that it was anything but chance which directed his operations; he made two [separate] attacks . . . both of which, according to their direction, were calculated to do us the most injury. . . . His aspect was most horrible, and such as indicated resentment and fury.

Owen Chase,
Narrative of the Most Extraordinary and Distressing
Shipwreck of the Whale-Ship Essex, *of Nantucket*

THERE ARE NO STREETLIGHTS IN SOBOLONYE, AND THE SUN WAS keeping winter hours, so darkness of a profound kind set in around five in the afternoon. People stayed indoors. If they had to go out, they only did so armed, even to the outhouse. Inside, by their massive Russian stoves, people paid close attention to the barking of their dogs and any augury a change in timbre—or a sudden silence—might contain. Daylight, fire, weapons, and wild animals were now determining the shape and schedule of the villagers' lives. It was as if the clock had just been turned back a hundred years—or a million.

Andrei Pochepnya's death had a profound effect on the people around him, and it moved their understanding of this tiger into unfamiliar territory. Never, in the living memory of the Bikin, had there been such a sense of menace emanating from the forest itself. Markov's death had been tragic, but one could still find in it an elemental logic, even justice: Markov, it could be said, had been forgiven his trespasses as he forgave those who trespassed against him.

He had judged the tiger and, in turn, been judged by him. But what had young Andrei done? He had been devoured while checking his traps for weasels. His mother was shattered, out of her mind with grief, and his father was spiraling into a suicidal depression.

"We were neighbors," explained Leonid Lopatin, "but as we say, 'Somebody else's family is like a dark forest.' " Now the darkness in the Pochepnyas' private forest was revealing itself in some disturbing ways. Their anguish was compounded by the fact that all their neighbors had managed to keep their own children home and safe, and this knowledge became a gulf between them. Alone on the far side, the Pochepnyas replayed the previous week in a vicious feedback loop that left them beseeching the cosmos for some way to reclaim those lost days. Their sorrow and discord touched everyone around them, not least because it resonated so closely with their own. Neighbors shook their heads and clucked their tongues, but they also feared for their lives.

"People stopped going into the taiga," said Lopatin, recalling the week of December 15. "Hunters who had been upriver came back to the village; loggers were afraid to work. It had a big impact on the people. Something like this might have happened a very long time ago, but nobody can remember. The relationship between the people and the tiger changed."

"Many people have seen tigers, or bumped into them, but there were never any conflicts," insisted Andrei Onofreychuk. "It might happen that a tiger would snatch a dog right in front of a person, but they never hunted people. They had their standards, so to say."

Once again, Kuzmich was commissioned to build a coffin though there was little to put in it, and once again, a fire was laid in the graveyard to thaw the frozen ground. This time, it was Leonid Lopatin who would bring the wood on his Buran, glancing behind him as he went, a rifle slung from his shoulder. The survivors were clinging to symbol and gesture now because there was little else except for anger and blame. There seemed to be no shortage of these, and both landed squarely on the shoulders of Yuri Trush and Inspection Tiger. "They should have shot the tiger right away!" said Onofreychuk, still bitter after nearly a decade.

"They could have caught her that day, but because they let her go another person died—only then they moved a peg!"

"People were not happy about it," said Danila Zaitsev. "They should have tracked him right away. He killed a man, plus he was injured. They could have done it right away."

"Somebody told me that in India they won't shoot a tiger until it has eaten four people," Sasha Dvornik told the filmmaker Sasha Snow in 2004. "Before then it's not considered a man-eater. Well, I recommend them to bring their own children to feed the tiger. The authorities are responsible for the death of Andrei Pochepnya. It was obvious the tiger was a cannibal; they should have killed it immediately. After Andrei was killed, I thought we should catch those inspectors and beat the crap out of them."

———

When news of Pochepnya's death reached Yuri Trush in Luchegorsk, on the afternoon of the 15th, it upset him deeply. Even now, when he recalls it, he must work fiercely to master his emotions. In Trush's eyes, Andrei Pochepnya was an "innocent," the same age as his own son. As Andrei had said himself, he had no quarrel with this tiger. Khomenko's death, of course, had been impossible to anticipate, and so, even, had Markov's. But Andrei's was preventable, and this fact was like acid in the collective wound. Trush couldn't help revisiting that pivotal moment when he and Lazurenko had that hot track back at Markov's cabin: "The situation was very difficult and tense," Trush recalled. "What we saw there made quite an impression on us: it was like a horror film; we were all in shock. But had I seen the tiger at that moment, I am sure my hand would not have trembled. I was certain that animal had to be killed."

In the end, though, Trush had decided not to pursue it. That had been a tough call and now he had the thankless task of being the go-between for Inspection Tiger and the traumatized citizenry of Sobolonye. Even after reinforcements arrived, Trush was still the point man—the name and face everyone knew. Complicating matters was the fact that Trush and his men had cited so many locals for poaching and possession of illegal firearms. It put him in the impossible position of being both an adversary and a savior; for some, he became a scapegoat. Markov's wife, along with a number of other villagers, was holding Trush personally responsible for Sobolonye's misery. "She was pouring mud on me as if the tiger was my personal property, saying it was all my fault that it got away and that all this happened," said Trush, recalling their first meeting. "She claimed that Markov hadn't shot at the tiger— that the tiger had just attacked him. She was shouting so much that I wasn't able to explain the situation to her properly. I thought she was having a mental breakdown as a result of her husband's death, and she was blaming us for it."

Trush wasn't far off the mark, but that wasn't the end of it. As if on cue, a newspaper article appeared with the nasty headline "Tiger Eats While 'Tigers' Drink," and it wouldn't be the last. Word was getting around. The situation was no longer simply a safety issue: Inspection Tiger's credibility was at stake, and so was Trush's reputation. This tiger was going to die, even if killing it was Trush's final act.

———

Within twenty-four hours of the discovery of Pochepnya's body, two Kungs and a pickup truck filled with armed men had converged on Sobolonye. Multiple checkpoints were established on roads leading toward the village, warning travelers away. The show of force was unprecedented for a tiger attack, and a passerby could have been forgiven for thinking that a terrorist cell had just been discovered in Sobolonye. Not only was this response a clear indication of how serious the authorities were about preventing any further loss of life, it was also a measure of their respect for their adversary. Nobody was underestimating this animal's capability now, nor misconstruing its intention. This was a creature who disappeared and reappeared at will, apparently for the purpose of attacking experienced hunters face-to-face and eating them. In spite of its injuries, it was able to travel day and night through arctic cold. If this had occurred at any other point in human-tiger history, such a creature would have been described as having supernatural powers—an egule if ever there was one.

The reinforcements had arrived from as far away as Vladivostok, a long day's drive to the south. Along with members of other Inspection Tiger units came the boss himself, Vladimir Schetinin, a man known to friend and foe alike as the General. Schetinin had acquired this nickname due to his fondness for military regalia and dramatic officers' hats that made him appear much taller than he was. As the chief of Inspection Tiger, he was the one person in Primorye with the authority to issue a shooting order for an Amur tiger. Schetinin is of the same generation as Ivan Dunkai and Dmitri Pikunov, and the fact that he survived Stalin's purges is a minor miracle. Fully a head shorter than Trush, he has a long pewter gray beard and flowing hair that give him the look of an Orthodox priest—an impression that evaporates the moment he opens his mouth. He takes two tea bags in a four-ounce cup and he doesn't mince words: when a pair of earnest British journalists once asked him how he thought the tigers could be saved, his answer, "AIDS," caught them off guard.

"But don't you care about people?" one of them asked.

"Not really," he replied. "Especially not the Chinese."

China's powerful presence and close proximity are volatile issues in Primorye where many residents feel as Schetinin does. Prior to the reopening of the Chinese border following Gorbachev's rapprochement with Beijing in 1989, commercial tiger poaching was virtually unknown in Russia. Since then, the export of Primorye's natural resources—in all their forms and shades of legality—has exploded while local Russians have found themselves completely overmatched by the Chinese: their hustle, their business acumen, and their insatiable appetite for everything from ginseng and sea cucumbers to Amur tigers and Slavic prostitutes. In the 1970s, after the Damansky Island clashes, a joke began circulating: "Optimists study English; pessimists study Chinese; and realists learn to use a Kalashnikov."

Today, the imbalance between Russia and China is a near total reversal of what it was a century ago when China was referred to as "the Sick Man of the Far East." Now the same is said of the Russians, and it is they who live in fear of being overwhelmed. The hemorrhaging of natural resources from every port and border crossing is one reason Primorye still has the feel of a colonial outpost—one that, despite its wealth and ecological importance, gets short shrift from the distant capital. In Asia today, wildlife trafficking is a multibillion-dollar industry, and roughly three quarters of all trafficked wildlife ends up in China, which has become a black hole for many endangered species. As Primorye's irreplaceable patrimony—the best timber, caviar, and animals—flows out, its citizens eagerly accept second-rate surplus in return: the cars are cast-offs from Japan, the buses are rejects from fleets in South Korea, and China provides cheap polyester clothes and fresh fruit suffused with pesticides and heavy metals. Import regulations put Russians in the humiliating role of mules to bring the dry goods in.

Even as the number of Russians in the Far East decreases steadily due to high mortality and relocation, shabby Chinese border towns that might have hosted ten or twenty thousand people prior to perestroika have mushroomed into gleaming centers of commerce with ten times their former population and more on the way. Carefully coached and chaperoned groups of Russian shoppers—powered by beer breakfasts—make day trips to these emerging cities in order to buy all the things the former Soviet Union's national industry and distribution system now fails to provide. Meanwhile, North Korea, at the very bottom of the pecking order, supplies what amounts to slave labor, much of it to the logging industry. "What went wrong in the Russian Far East?" wondered John Stephan in his comprehensive history of the region. "Why did it not develop like British Columbia or Hokkaido? How did such a rich land and littoral, settled by such talented and hardworking people, and bordering on such dynamic economies, present a spectacle redolent of a Third World basket case?"

There is no easy answer to this question, but the current situation is deeply painful to many Russians who maintain a bittersweet sense of national pride and—for those born before 1970 or so—a belief that they once represented the vanguard of a grand and noble social project. For Vladimir Schetinin, whose history with the State is checkered, to say the least, this erosion of status and order burns like an ulcer in his heart and mind, not least because of the toll it is taking on the taiga. Now, more than ever, his primary concern—with the possible exception of his grand-children—is the fate of the Amur tiger and its far rarer cousin, the Amur leopard. The four-way tension between this, Moscow's tiger killing protocol, his deeply felt responsibility to protect his men, and a need to reassure the public, would determine the fate of this tiger and the people around it.

———

In his capacity as chief of Inspection Tiger, Schetinin had sought to give his men all the tools at his disposal. This is why, moments after first hearing about the Markov attack from Trush on Friday the 5th, he had sent a fax to Moscow requesting a shooting permit for an Amur tiger. Though he had little information about the case at that point, Schetinin was familiar enough with federal bureau-cracy to know that responses from the capital often took weeks, and he wanted to be covered. Even Schetinin's critics were impressed when he received a telegram just four days later, on Tuesday, December 9, from Valentin Ilyashenko, the federal administrator of biological resources. It was brief and to the point: "This is to approve the shooting of the man-eating tiger in the area of the vil-lage, Sobolevka [a diminutive form of Sobolonye]. The official per-mit will be issued upon receipt of the shooting report."

Sometimes, the system worked. On the same day as the telegram, a more formal document arrived by fax; this one bore all the appropriate seals and signatures, but it was inexplicably post-dated, clearly stating that the hunt was to begin a week later, on December 16. Whether this delay was a clerical error, or intended to build in a cooling-off period in which nature could take its course, is not clear and, apparently, never was. While there was real concern for the safety of the local populace, there appeared to be no great urgency—at either end of the fax line—to hunt this tiger down. Ultimately, it was Schetinin's call, and his official mandate was to protect the environment, specifically tigers. The last thing he wanted was to oversee the unnecessary shooting of another tiger, especially at a time when decades of hard work to restore a relict population was being undone before his eyes.

In addition to the logistical nightmare and cost of trying to find one possibly transient tiger among perhaps half a dozen or more living in the frozen wilderness around Sobolonye, there may have been another reason for Schetinin's hesitation, and this concerned his personal history with the State. Schetinin's sympathy for tigers—one could say his identification with them—goes deeper than that of most government employees, and this is because for years he ran the risk of being exterminated himself. Schetinin is a Cossack; his ancestors served in the Amur division of the Cossack army, which was instrumental in the annexation of Primorye.

In return for their service and loyalty to the czars, the Cossacks enjoyed a special status among Russians and were rewarded with land and a large measure of autonomy, but all this changed under communism. After the Revolution, their independence, fighting skill, and tribal solidarity were seen as threats to the Soviet State, and Stalin added them to his long list of enemies. In 1934, Schetinin's paternal grandfather was conscripted to dig a clandestine tunnel under the Amur River, and his family never saw him again. Schetinin's father was next: in 1938, at the peak of the Great Terror, he was relieved of his duties as a village postmaster and charged with "harmful activities related to untimely mail deliveries." For this he was shot. The rest of the family was banished to a concentration camp in the Jewish Autonomous Region, a little known creation of Stalin's intended to serve, oxymoronically, as a Soviet Zion for Russian Jews. It still exists today. Located on the Amur River between China and Khabarovsk Territory, it is hard to imagine a place further removed from the Holy Land. The regional flag depicts not a Magen David but a strangely familiar rainbow band on a plain white background; the regional coat of arms features, of all things, a tiger. At its peak, only about seventeen thousand Jews actually lived there and, during the purges, it became a catch-all for a wide variety of undesirables, including Cossacks. While still a boy, Schetinin was branded a "son of an enemy of the State," a designation that would determine the course of his life. From his one surviving grandfather he received this stern advice: "Never tell anyone that you are a *Kazak*. Forget that word."

"When I was about six, I clued in that we were in exile," Schetinin explained in his cramped apartment near the harbor in Vladivostok. "There was a concentration camp nearby and most of the prisoners there were teachers. Our homeroom teacher had been in jail there for fifteen years, and he was released because there was a shortage of teachers. When I was finishing grade ten, he called us in one by one. He said, 'Tell me your sins.' I respected him so I told him that I was a Cossack and a son of an enemy of the State. He said, 'You can only study agriculture. Forget about everything else.' "

As advised, Schetinin went up the Amur to study agriculture in the nearby river town of Blagoveshchensk ("Glad Tidings") and in this there was a savage irony: Blagoveshchensk is the site of one of the Cossacks' most notorious massacres of Chinese civilians. While Schetinin was studying there, his father was "rehabilitated," a process by which a blackballed Soviet citizen could be exonerated of his crimes and restored to good standing—dead or alive. By way of compensation for the murder of his father, Schetinin now receives 92 rubles (about $3) a month, plus a housing subsidy. Not surprisingly, he never joined the Communist Party. Nor was he cut out for farming (few Cossacks were). Today, the notion of captivity still appalls him. "I can't stand the sight of animals in cages," Schetinin said. "I have never been to see the circus or the zoo."

Instead, he maneuvered himself toward the study of wild animal herds, and in 1964 became the first field ecologist in a recently created national park near Blagoveshchensk. From there, he moved to Vladivostok and into animal protection, discovering tigers in the late 1970s. Schetinin's overarching goal was to protect these animals, but after Pochepnya's death there was no doubt in his mind about what needed to be done with this tiger.

PART THREE

|||

TRUSH

"He is. But he will still be hunted for all that. What is
best let alone, that accursed thing is not always what
least allures. He's all a magnet! How long since thou
saw'st him? Which way heading?"

CAPTAIN AHAB,
Moby-Dick

THE HUNT FOR THE TIGER BEGAN ON THE TAKHALO—THE FIRE RIVER. IT
was Tuesday, December 16, another brilliant, bitter day, and the
hunting party that took charge of it was formidable. Six men
descended the riverbank at the apiary and headed downstream on
the ice, every one of them armed. In addition to Trush and
Lazurenko were three local hunting inspectors who had been
brought in to assist, along with Nikolai Gorunov, the Belarusian
sheriff of Krasny Yar. There were no dubious locals or green cops
this time; these men were all seasoned professionals. Like Trush,
Sheriff Gorunov is a born Alpha, a handsome, fire-breathing
dragon of a man who smokes with an alarming vigor: cigarette
clamped between his canines at the point where filter and tobacco
meet, the act of inhaling fully integrated into breath and speech
such that there is no discernible pause, only billowing smoke that
seems to be a natural by-product of a voice that booms even in the
confines of his quiet kitchen. He bears a striking resemblance to
the hawk-eyed and mustachioed tiger hunter Yuri Yankovsky, and
seems to share the same temperament: he will haul a total
stranger bodily (and effortlessly) through a doorway because it is
considered bad luck to shake hands across a threshold; a map,

when he is done with it, will be scored and pocked with holes from his emphatic pen.

While there was no question in anyone's mind that the tigers that killed Markov and Pochepnya were one and the same, it still had to be confirmed, and this was one of the purposes of this trip down the Takhalo. It was also an opportunity for the new arrivals to take this tiger's measure and see where he was headed. Everyone on the team was a lifelong hunter and this was a good day for hunting; spirits were high. Walking together in loose formation down the river, one had the sense that these men, whom fate had gathered from end to end of Russia, were doing what they were made to do. They were all workers with a deep affinity for the taiga, and there was a certain bracing joy—like that of sled dogs being put into harness—in being presented with a task that was not just worthy of their mettle but bound to test it. They were in Arseniev and Yankovsky territory now, and it was in part the promise of such challenges that had lured most of them or their parents to the Far East in the first place.

Seeing that Trush was filming, they razzed one another: "Aw fuck," said one. "It's too bad I didn't put my gold epaulettes on."

"What were you thinking, you stupid ass?" called another. "You missed your chance."

Of all of them, it was Yuri Trush, alone behind the camera, who bore the day's burden most heavily—not just because he was the mission's now embattled leader, but because, with the exception of Sasha Lazurenko, he was the only one present who truly, viscerally grasped what a tiger could do to a human being. The rest would understand soon enough and, when they got to the site, the collective mood sobered quickly. There was no mistaking the implications of the pale and hairless scat that lay on the ice like a warning at midstream. Nor was there any confusion about the limping tracks: this was the same tiger. The inspectors projected a solemn intensity there as if it was a murder scene, and Trush urged everyone to take special care with the evidence. Together, these six men represented close to two hundred years of hunting experience—most of it in tiger country—and yet none of them had witnessed anything quite like this. Stepping carefully, speaking only in soft tones, they followed the tiger's tracks to Tsepalev's shredded mattress, which was spattered with blood and laced with tiger hair.

As the men pored over the White Book, Andrei Pochepnya's last moments became as clear as if man and tiger alike had been taking notes: the tiger had approached from the east—the direction of the road workers' camp—until he paused, catching wind or sound of Pochepnya. Anticipating Pochepnya's plans to walk downriver—perhaps by scenting the bait in his traps—the tiger turned south, traveling parallel to Pochepnya's future path, just far enough from the river so that Pochepnya failed to notice his tracks. Then the tiger made a loop into the forest, effectively removing any trace of himself from the area, and came up from behind (downstream), a standard stalking maneuver. From here, the tiger spotted Tsepalev's hovel; after exploring it and having his way with it, much as he had done with Markov's cabin and the road workers' outhouse, the tiger found a comfortable, if oddly exposed, spot and settled down to wait for the inevitable.

Standing by the tiger's bed under that big spruce tree, it would have been easy to see why Mikhail Dunkai believes that tigers can read people's minds and influence their thoughts. One had only to observe Pochepnya's tracks: they looked as if the tiger had him on a line and simply reeled him in. Theory of mind is almost always discussed in the context of human interaction and relationships, but tigers use a version of it, too. The tiger's theory of mind is not as sophisticated as ours, but it is as sophisticated as it needs to be, and it is what enabled this tiger to engineer a situation in which Andrei Pochepnya, a far more intelligent animal, all but delivered himself into his jaws.

———

Sheriff Gorunov traced the impressions of the attack leaps. They seemed awfully close together for such a large tiger: a sure sign, in his view, of weakness or injury. A healthy tiger could have covered that distance in a single bound. There was no doubt this tiger was impaired, but he may have also understood from previous experience that there was no rush. It is hard to articulate how overmatched Pochepnya was, how little effort a tiger needs to make in order to subdue a human being. A tiger's jaws can exert roughly a thousand pounds of pressure per square inch, but it takes less than a hundred pounds to crush a windpipe, and only five pounds to block the carotid artery, which causes unconsciousness almost instantly. In other words, a tiger's fangs don't need to puncture the skin in order to immobilize prey; no blood need be let.

Although a tiger's canines may be nearly an inch thick at the base, they still break surprisingly often, and they don't grow back; these losses can be crippling and are one reason wild tigers may turn to livestock killing and man-eating. As menacing as they appear, tiger fangs are actually delicate instruments—literally, bundles of nerves and blood vessels encased in layers of bonelike dentin, sheathed in enamel and somewhat rounded at the ends. With these four surgical sensors, the tiger has the ability to *feel* its way through prey, differentiating between bone and tissue types to find the gap between two vertebrae in order to sever the spinal cord, or locate the windpipe in order to stifle the air supply—all at attack speed. In this sense, the canines are sentient weapons, capable of grasping and puncturing but also of deciphering the Braille of an animal's anatomy. As removed as we are from our own origins in the wild, our teeth possess the same sensitivity, and we rely on it daily whether we are gnawing a T-bone, love-biting a nipple, or detecting rot in an apple by resistance alone.

It was not clear if the tiger simply took Pochepnya in his jaws and carried him off or clubbed him first. The force of a tiger paw strike has never been measured, but given that a tiger weighs two or three times as much as a prizefighter, and is many times stronger with even faster reflexes, one can begin to calculate how devastating a single blow from a tiger's paw might be. Bengal tigers have been observed breaking the necks and skulls of buffalo with paw strikes. Reginald Burton, a British hunter, author, and longtime India hand, observed a tiger clubbing a beater (hunting assistant) so hard that its claws penetrated the heavy brass dish suspended from the man's back.

In the winter of 1960, coincidentally on the Amba River, a ranger and naturalist named Vladimir Troinin witnessed an epic battle between a juvenile Amur tiger and a full-grown Ussurian boar. The tiger, though half the size of the boar, managed to knock it down repeatedly by jumping on the animal's back and clubbing it in the head with his macelike paws. In addition to their bladed tusks, wild boars are built like tanks: covered with wiry bristles and thick hide beneath which is a mantle of cartilaginous armor that further protects their muscular neck and shoulders. The fight on the Amba was to the death and, in spite of the odds, the young tiger prevailed, motivated, apparently, by spite alone. When Troinin inspected the site afterward he found an appalling scene: the abandoned boar had been eviscerated, its throat torn out, and its snout sliced off "as with a razor." Troinin was particularly struck by the scratches in the boar's skull, which were half an inch deep.

———

It was clear that day on the Takhalo that, wounded as he was, the Panchelaza tiger still possessed deep reserves of strength. Furthermore, he had made the most of Pochepnya; at the very least, the young man had bought him some time. When Sheriff Gorunov examined Tsepalev's ransacked hovel, he discovered a collection of topographical maps, but the tiger had gotten to them first. Gorunov noted evidence of the tiger's fangs rending the landscape—perhaps a sign of things to come. There was a notebook in there, too, with Tsepalev's poems inside, lost now, their author long gone. Gorunov then worked his way back across the river, joining the others at the terminus of the drag trail where they were sorting through Pochepnya's clothes. Danila Zaitsev and Andrei's father had gathered up Andrei's meager remains the previous day, but when Gorunov went through his pockets, he found an undamaged pack of cheap unfiltered cigarettes. He would have been craving a cigarette then, but he wouldn't smoke those.

Police are required to attend anytime there is a body in order to determine whether a criminal investigation is necessary, but in this case there was no body. Gorunov's role ended up being to formally witness the absence of Pochepnya. The sight of those empty clothes was something none of these men was fully prepared for.

The horror in a thing is usually derived from its presence, however distorted or fragmentary, but here in the scrub and snow by the Takhalo was a broken frame with no picture in it. Had there been no tracks and no story, one could have thought these things had simply been abandoned—as if, a year or two earlier, some hunter had come down to the river for a swim, left his belongings in a heap, and simply never returned. Over the intervening seasons, animals, weather, and rot would have shredded and stained them, leaving the ruins that lay there now. But these clothes were only a few days old, and their owner had ceased to exist.

To end a person's life is one thing; to eradicate him from the face of the earth is another. The latter is far more difficult to do, and yet the tiger had done it, had transported this young man beyond death to a kind of carnal oblivion. It was clear on this day that, in the taiga, the sacred vessel of a human being has no more intrinsic value or meaning than a wild boar or a roe deer, and no greater purpose beyond its potential as prey. In the jaws of a tiger, one's body is, for all practical purposes, weightless and, in the case of Andrei Pochepnya, it appeared to have no substance at all. This begs an obscure metaphysical question: if the body journeys through the viscera of an animal—if its substance and essence *become* that animal—what happens to the soul? Hurricanes, avalanches, and volcanoes consume people, but such random acts of insensate violence are considered acts of God; they don't pick their targets, nor do they metabolize them. It is rare that one is confronted, as these men were, with such overwhelming evidence of one's own mutability in the face of a sentient natural force. In this way, tigers and their quasi-conscious kin occupy an uncharted middle ground somewhere between humans and natural catastrophes. Under certain circumstances, the tiger can have the same nullifying effect as a long look into the night sky.

As the men studied the cuffs and collars of Andrei's many layers, it was clear that after his gun misfired Andrei had tried to fend the tiger off with his left arm. But the athleticism of these animals is stunning and, in a series of blinding and fluid motions, the tiger caught Andrei's wrist, jerked it aside, and hurtled onto its target. The shredded collar told the rest: there was no further resistance.

What remained looked like the work of paramedics at an accident scene, and the video camera absorbed it all, discreet as a confessor: "The tiger took all the clothing off the individual," murmurs Trush. "The tiger undressed him quite well." The boots, now unseamed, were homemade: a timeless design of felt-soled arctic moccasin that mimics tiger pads with their texture and silence. But stealth is no defense against the hunter who perfected it.

By the time Andrei had drawn even with Tsepalev's shelter, the tiger would have tapered his awareness down to a single taut beam of consciousness, and the intensity of this attention, boring into its target like a laser, would have been an almost palpable thing, imperturbable: a reality unto itself. The hunt—like love-making—occurs in a timeless zone where all external measures temporarily cease to apply. It is a ritual of concentration that determines life and death for all concerned.

Though death was close and breathing, Andrei had other things on his mind. As the gap between the tiger and himself closed to one of seconds, he may have had an inkling that something wasn't quite right; perhaps a bird sounded an alarm; maybe he glanced around, but judging from the tracks nothing in his gait betrayed uncertainty. Meanwhile, the tiger gathered himself, manifesting anticipation in its purest form: his eyes riveted on their target as he flexed and set his paws, compensating for any irregularity in the ground beneath; the hips rising slightly as he loaded and aimed the missile of himself, while that hawser of a tail twitched like a broken power line. There was the moment when impulse and prey aligned in the tiger's mind, and then a roar filled the forest with the force of an angry god.

Caught off guard and off balance, Andrei, whose life was finished though his heart still beat, swiveled slightly to the left. He would have been amazed to hear and see this avatar of doom so unbelievably close and closing fast. More amazing is the young man's composure and muscle memory: left shoulder dropping to shed the gun strap as the left hand twists the rifle forward and up; the right index finger hooking and hauling back the bolt as both hands, together now, guide the rifle butt to his right shoulder. The target is the hardest kind: head-on and airborne, an arcing blur of fire and ice, black and ocher haloed in glittering snow. Andrei's finger on the trigger, squeezing—tighter now—*Yopt!* The bowel-loosening realization that the magic has failed. *Polny pizdets.* Nothing exists now but the tiger, filling his field of vision like a bad accident, like the end of the world: a pair of blazing yellow lanterns over a temple door framed with ivory columns.

———

For most of our history, we have been occupied with the cracking of codes—from deciphering patterns in the weather, the water, the land, and the stars, to parsing the nuanced behaviors of friend and foe, predator and prey. Furthermore, we are compelled to share our discoveries in the form of stories. Much is made of the fact that ours is the only species that does this, that the essence of who and what we understand ourselves to be was first borne orally and aurally: from mouth to ear to memory. This is so, but before we learned to tell stories, we learned to read them. In other words, we learned to track. The first letter of the first word of the first recorded story was written—"printed"—not by us, but by an animal. These signs and symbols left in mud, sand, leaves, and snow represent proto-alphabets. Often smeared, fragmented, and confused by weather, time, and other animals, these cryptograms were life-and-death exercises in abstract thinking. This skill, the reading of tracks in order to procure food, or identify the presence of a dangerous animal, may in fact be "the oldest profession."

Like our own texts, these "early works" are linear and continuous with their own punctuation and grammar. Plot, tense, gender, age, health, relationships, and emotional states can all be determined from these durable records. In this sense, *The Jungle Book* is our story, too: just as Mowgli was schooled by wild animals, so in many ways were we. The notion that it was animals who taught us to read may seem counterintuitive, but listening to skilled hunters analyze tiger sign is not that different from listening to literature majors deconstruct a short story. Both are sorting through minutiae, down to the specific placement and inflection of individual elements, in order to determine motive, subtext, and narrative arc. An individual track may have its own accent or diacritical marks that distinguish the intent of a foot, or even a single step, from the others. On an active game trail, as in one of Tolstoy's novels, multiple plots and characters can overlap with daunting subtlety, pathos, or hair-raising drama. Deciphering these palimpsests can be more difficult than reading crossed letters* from the Victorian era, and harder to follow than the most obscure experimental fiction. However, with practice, as Henno Martin wrote in *The Sheltering Desert,* "you learn to read the writing of hoof, claw and pad. In fact before long you are reading their message almost subconsciously."

Trush and his men had opened the White Book at mid-chapter, and now they had to place themselves in the story. This isn't something one does lightly in the taiga: the reader must commit to becoming a character, too, with no assurance of how the story will end. There, on that blinding winter afternoon at the foot of the Takhalo, began a struggle for control of the narrative. This had happened at least once already, two weeks earlier, when Markov had been drawn into the story; though he had managed to shift its direction, he had failed to control it—the tiger had seen to that. Once again, the tiger was in charge, as he was accustomed to being. There are conventions in the tracking narrative just as there are in any literary form, and tigers employ different ones than deer or boar or humans. While one can usually make predictions, based on these, about how a particular plotline will unfold, this tiger defied the formula to the point that it occupied a genre of its own. To begin with, there is usually no ambiguity in the taiga about who is hunting whom, but in this story, that wasn't the case.

Even as the men read his tracks, the tiger could have been nearby, reading them, deciding how or when to work them into the plot. Tigers, of course, are experts at this game, and they use the same methods humans do: pick up the trail of potential prey by scent, sight, or knowledge of its habits; follow it in order to get a feel for where it is going; and then, in effect, read ahead and wait for the prey to arrive. End of story.

* In order to save on paper and postage, nineteenth-century correspondents would fill a page, turn it ninety degrees, and continue, thus crossing one line of text with another.

As far as the tiger was concerned, Andrei Pochepnya was simply one more episode—like a character in a murder mystery who is introduced and dispatched solely for the purpose of driving the plot forward. Who would be next was a question of some interest to the tiger, but of even greater interest to Trush and Schetinin, who could not allow it to be answered. Ultimately, there was only one way to prevent it. "For a week I had been thinking about it," said Schetinin, recalling the first stage of the hunt. "I was trying to think like an injured tiger, trying to imagine where an injured tiger was most likely to go."

A homicide detective would have been doing the same thing, but the detective operates in a world of coherent social codes where all but the most deranged understand there will be consequences. The tiger's world, by contrast, is not only amoral but peculiarly consequence-free, and this—the atavistic certainty that there is nothing out there more lethal than itself—is the apex predator's greatest weakness. The coyote is a gifted hunter, but it knows that if it fails to take proper precautions it can easily become prey. Even leopards, arguably the deadliest cats on earth, understand that they hunt on a continuum. A tiger, on the other hand, will, with sufficient provocation, charge a moving car. This doesn't mean that a tiger will not learn to be cautious in the face of certain threats, but these hazards typically have more to do with competition than with predation. Trush and his men needed to capitalize on this inborn confidence, even though doing so ensured that conflict was inevitable: once the tiger understood that he was being hunted, his response would not be to flee deeper into the taiga, it would be to confront his pursuers and liquidate them. The one certainty in tiger tracks is: follow them long enough and you will eventually arrive at a tiger, unless the tiger arrives at you first.

————

In February 2002, a former member of Inspection Tiger named Anatoli Khobitnov found the end of a tiger trail not far from Luchegorsk. The subsequent encounter gave him the distinction of being one of the few people on earth who has been literally nose-to-nose with a wild tiger and managed to walk away. The road to Khobitnov's hometown in Terney, a picturesque fishing village on the outer edge of the Sikhote-Alin Zapovednik, is narrow and serpentine, and there are moments among those green ridges covered in birch, oak, and pine when you could swear you were in New England, somewhere between the Berkshires and the White Mountains. But this illusion dissolves as soon as you cross the bridge over Tigrine Creek or pass through villages with names like Transformation and Little Stone by the Sea. Traveling these quiet back roads—the only roads—it is hard to tell what era one is in. Nestled in the valleys are squat villages that, with the exception of cars and the occasional satellite dish, have changed little since Arseniev passed through. The houses are still trimmed in gingerbread and painted in wavering shades of slate blue, mustard yellow, and verdigris. In summer, the picketed yards are still planted to the doorsills with potatoes and, in winter, buried to the windowsills in snow. Their inhabitants may smoke cigarettes rolled with newspaper, and most of the young and disenchanted have left.

Khobitnov is fortunate in that he has, despite multiple puncture wounds and broken bones, managed to live a relatively normal life, though his path to the present has been anything but normal. A former Muscovite who turned sixty in 2008, Khobitnov has been on the Far East coast for more than half his life, working in fishing and hunting management, and also with Dale Miquelle and John Goodrich on the Siberian Tiger Project. During this time, he has had dozens of tiger encounters, his first occurring shortly after he arrived in the spring of 1974. "About three days after I got here," he recalled, "a lot of snow fell and a neighbor invited me to go down to the ocean. We went to the ocean and saw a tiger!" Seeing this storied creature on the edge of his known world evoked "such joy," recalled Khobitnov. "The tiger is the symbol of Primorye."

The courtyard in front of Khobitnov's low-slung house near the beach is the first indication that one is in the presence of a remarkable person. It is strewn with polished beach stones among which stands the bleached carcass of a driftwood tree. In its branches is an assemblage of bear skulls. Hanging from an upended beach log nearby are scores of carefully chosen stones, each meticulously wrapped with string in a variety of crisscross patterns. It is hard to say if these are shamanic devices or exercises in bricolage, but Khobitnov is a complex and gifted man and he has a grasp of both.

Khobitnov is almost exactly the same age as Yuri Trush; they are friends and, for a time, they overlapped in Inspection Tiger under Vladimir Schetinin, a man for whom Khobitnov maintains the utmost respect. Like Trush, Khobitnov developed an affinity for the forest while hunting with his father and, like him, he participated briefly in the commercial slaughter of saiga antelope on the steppes of Kazakhstan. As a young man, Khobitnov found a wolf cub in Moscow's famous Zavidovsky hunting reserve (now a park) and raised it in his apartment, not far from the city center. After getting his degree from the Moscow Institute for Decorative and Applied Arts (now called the Moscow State University of Arts and Industry), he was hired by the Moscow mint, where he worked as an engraver rendering designs for coins, paper money, and government documents. His face looks as if it could have been made there, too: above his salt-and-pepper beard and mustache, the crow's-feet and brow furrows are so deeply incised that they seem more the result of tools than time. It is hard to reconcile the detail and precision required of an engraver with the size of Khobitnov's hands, which look as if they could palm a basketball, and yet evidence of his skill can be found throughout his home. In his free time, he builds hunting knives from scratch, shaping and engraving the steel, bone, and antler into works of art that look as if they should be in a gallery rather than hanging from someone's belt. The number of Russians who have painted the Sea of Japan for its beauty alone can be counted on one hand, but Khobitnov does that, too. His works—mostly landscapes and marines—are distinctive for their detail and a tendency toward the miniature. "There is a high demand for artistry here," wrote Chekhov on his journey to the Far East in 1890, "but God has not supplied the artists." One has the sense that Anatoli Khobitnov could meet that demand single-handedly—in any medium.

Hunting poachers and tigers requires an entirely different skill set than making art; nonetheless, Khobitnov once shot a leaping tiger between the eyes at twenty-five yards, a feat more troubling than impressive until you realize that the tiger was seriously wounded and had been terrorizing a village for weeks, and that Khobitnov was wounded, too: he made the shot having taped his rifle onto the cast covering his broken left arm, which had been mauled three weeks earlier by a tigress.

The tigress that attacked Khobitnov had been asleep in the snow when he and his companion stumbled on her on that snowy afternoon. Based on the fluids they had seen staining her previous rest spots, they thought they had been following a nursing tigress, and they were hoping to locate her den. It wasn't until later that they realized the fluid they were seeing was suppuration from the tigress's mange-ridden skin. It is always a bad idea to surprise a napping tiger, even when that tiger is napping at death's door, but by the time the men realized their mistake, there was only fifteen feet between them. The tigress awoke with a start, let loose a spine-rattling roar, and leaped at Khobitnov's partner. Khobitnov was as surprised as the tigress and he performed one of those instinctive animal acts that make one proud to be human: he sacrificed himself by jumping in front of his unarmed companion. Khobitnov was armed, but with no time to take proper aim all he could do was thrust his rifle butt into the tigress's face. The blow broke one of her fangs and the tigress responded by knocking Khobitnov off his feet with a stroke of her paw, sending his rifle flying. What happened next gave new life to the cliché "staring death in the face." The tigress jumped on Khobitnov's chest, giving him the extraordinary experience of looking *up* a tiger's throat: nothing on the horizon but fangs and tongue and a cavernous black hole—the same picture early Christians painted of hell. What Khobitnov remembers most vividly is not the fear, or the pain, but the temperature—her "hot, hot breathing."

Disarmed and desperate, Khobitnov swung his right fist, but the tigress simply caught it like a dog snapping at a fly and crushed it. Still trying to stave off the inevitable, he jammed his left arm into her mouth and attempted to reach his pistol with his now punctured hand. The tigress crushed his arm as well, impaling it with her remaining fangs and shattering the bones. At that point, Khobitnov's partner hit the tigress with a dose of pepper spray and she leaped off him, fleeing into the forest. The entire encounter lasted less than five seconds.

When the tigress was later trapped, it was discovered that not only was she old and sick, but her teeth were rotten and she was missing several toes. She had been killing livestock because there was nothing else she was capable of subduing. Although she wouldn't have lasted the winter, this sorry creature was still a match for two experienced hunters. She was put down by lethal injection. Meanwhile, in addition to the stitches, screws, and cast, Khobitnov ended up contracting gangrene.

The lesson from this mishap is one the renowned tiger researcher John Seidensticker tries hard to impress upon his students working in the field: "Don't ever assume anything with tigers." Everyone who works closely with these animals emphasizes the importance of approaching them on an individual basis. Tiger behavior is influenced by age, health, history, stress levels, and place in the local pecking order, among numerous other factors, and like us they are capable of very perplexing behavior. Generally speaking, the more intelligent an animal, the more "character" it is likely to have.

In December 2001, John Goodrich, the field coordinator for the Wildlife Conservation Society's Siberian Tiger Project, encountered what he described as an "extreme, crazy tigress" at a logging camp near the village of Pilana. "She chewed up *chainsaws*," he recalled, "stole a gas can and chewed that up, covered herself in gas. Then she attacked a logger." With life as difficult as it is in the forest, and with so many other things to focus on, the motive to do things like this is hard to ascribe to anything other than rage, desperation, or insanity—all of which lie well within the tiger's emotive spectrum. Inspection Tiger was called to the site immediately and the tigress charged them as well. After wounding her, the inspectors tracked her, only to find she had doubled back and set up an ambush. This is where they found her, poised to attack, covered in a light dusting of snow. She had died waiting for them.

———

Trush was concerned that the Panchelaza tiger might be waiting for him, too. The tiger knew Trush and some of his men "personally" now, and, collectively, the team smelled of weapons, cigarettes, and dogs just as Markov and Pochepnya had. It also seemed that his wounds were healing; Trush noted less blood in the tracks on the Takhalo than he had observed at Markov's. At the same time, the right forepaw was still dragging in the snow: the bleeding may have stopped, but the damage was done. Sometime before noon on the previous day—the 15th—the tiger had crossed back over the Takhalo by Tsepalev's shelter and ascended a steep, rocky bluff covered in ice and snow. There were easier routes available, but the tiger chose not to use them. For a person, this would have been a hand-over-hand scramble. The shortest day of the year was less than a week away so night fell early, and, after following the trail for several hundred yards, the men turned back. But they had the information they needed. There is no easier trail to follow than fresh tracks in fresh snow, and now, Trush had the permit, the manpower, and the motive. It was no longer a question of if, just a question of when.

Mountains are the more beautiful
After the sun has gone down
And it is
Twilight. Boy,
Watch out for tigers, now.
Let's not
Wander about in the field.

YUN SŎN-DO (1587–1671),
"Sunset"

HERDED TOGETHER IN THE DARK LIKE BISON, WOODSTOVES BLAZING, the Kungs seemed like conveyances from another age. Just down the road was the village, still but for the chimney smoke and the anxious pacing of the dogs. Behind locked doors, their owners' lives were suspended, minds awash in unsettling thoughts. Meanwhile, in the river below, fish hung motionless in the dark, countering the current beneath two feet of ice, and finding in that dense and steady resistance a perfect equilibrium. But there was more down there besides—subtle disturbances passing through on their serpentine journey out of the mountains: Takhalo to Bikin, Ussuri to Amur, and on to the ice-choked bottleneck of Tartar Strait, past Sakhalin to the open sea. Along with Andrei Pochepnya's rifle was the rippled memory of a tiger Sasha Dvornik once sought to disorient and drown with his motorboat. A standard maneuver in the river poacher's repertoire, it works like a charm with deer. But deer can't leap like dolphins from deep water, and it seems that tigers can.

Up above, the world was frozen hard and waiting. And through it came the tiger, hunting, eyes alight. Stepping gingerly over the ice and plowing through the drifts, there was in its progress something relentless and mechanical: the clouds of steam chugging, enginelike, from its nostrils, translucent whiskers laced with hoarfrost from its own hot breath. Inside Trush's Kung, men sat jammed hip to hip on the makeshift bunks, rifles cleaned and ready in the rack on the wall, a kettle steaming on the woodstove by the door.

Kungs are essentially self-propelled versions of the caravans Markov and the loggers used, and Inspection Tiger's had been modified to serve as patrol vehicles, personnel carriers, dormitories, dining halls, arms caches, and war rooms rolled into one. On the night of the 16th, Trush's vehicle was dedicated to the latter purpose. "Schetinin got us all together and told us to find the tiger and destroy him," recalled Vladimir Shibnev, one of the local hunting inspectors who had been called in to assist. "I argued with him: I said, 'Do you have any idea what it means to follow tiger tracks in December? A tiger is not a sable who walks a few miles and is done. This tiger could be fifty miles away by now; it could be a *hundred* and fifty miles away.'"

Shibnev worked with Yevgeny Smirnov in Field Group Taiga, a small team of dedicated hunting inspectors who, in addition to being skilled hunters and trackers, were based right on the Bikin. They knew the area intimately and took a proprietary interest in it, both personally and professionally. Shibnev was Russian, but he had been raised on the river in close proximity to the Udeghe and Nanai. Shibnev's father and uncle had both done military service in the Far East, and they had been so inspired by the country—and by Arseniev's descriptions of it—that in 1939 they persuaded their entire family to move out to this lush frontier on the far side of Siberia. Shibnev's father worked on the Bikin as a fur and forest product buyer, and his uncle became a respected naturalist and author who specialized in the Bikin ecosystem. Shibnev's mother taught school on a Nanai collective farm. As a result, Shibnev, a wise and handsome man who exudes a calm vitality, has an exceptionally good feel for the area and its inhabitants. At fifty, he was the oldest member of the hunting team, and he could remember the valley before the loggers came, when it was virtually roadless and thick with game. "Children who are born here are like wolf cubs," Shibnev explained. "Our parents would go to work, and we would roam the river. Back then, everyone used to get around in boats."

Tigers were seldom seen in those days, but Shibnev became familiar with Nanai beliefs about them almost by osmosis: "The tiger was considered a protector, a just animal," he said. "If you were to hurt or kill one, it would take revenge against you and your family. There was a story about a man who killed a tiger and then his entire family died. It was perceived that the tiger's spirit avenged itself on that family." It wasn't until the late 1960s, when the first major logging road was pushed through the Bikin valley, that Shibnev saw a tiger for himself. "It was a feeling of joy and exaltation at the same time," he recalled. "It was a sense, not so much of fear, but of respect or awe. I thought it was the czar of all animals."

From childhood, Shibnev had wanted to become a forest ranger, but his parents talked him out of it, and it wasn't until 1992 that he was finally able to fulfill his dream. It was in this capacity that he ran into Markov for the first time: "He was a poacher, but I kind of liked him," Shibnev recalled. "He was reasonable. Later, when he decided to move to the taiga on a more or less permanent basis, that's when I heard he wanted to poach tigers."

For reasons that remain unexplained, Field Group Taiga had been notified of the Markov investigation on December 6, the same day Inspection Tiger arrived, but never formally included in it. "We were alerted," explained Field Group Taiga's leader, Yevgeny Smirnov, "and we sat on our rucksacks for the entire day [waiting to be picked up], but in the end they took a police officer with them. People who'd never seen a tiger in their lives ended up working on that case. They were walking around in the forest with pistols like they were hunting a criminal. Had they come to me right away, it would have become obvious immediately that it was not a tigress [as Trush had originally thought] but a tiger."

To a man, everyone in Field Group Taiga saw Inspection Tiger as outsiders—poachers, as it were, on their territory. One of Inspection Tiger's greatest disadvantages was the size of its teams' jurisdictions. Trush's Bikin unit was responsible for the entire northwest corner of Primorye, which included nearly a hundred miles of the Chinese border along the Ussuri River. This meant they had a general understanding of their region, but sometimes lacked deep knowledge of specific areas. On the middle Bikin, the Tigers' responsibilities overlapped with those of Field Group Taiga. The tensions this created were analogous to those occurring between local police and federal investigators: whereas Field Group Taiga was a small agency with limited power, Inspection Tiger operated on a larger scale with more resources and a higher profile. These imbalances, along with assorted interpersonal dynamics, made for some hard feelings, but after Pochepnya's death there was no more room for turf wars or jealousy; Vladimir Schetinin simply needed the best men he could get, and Field Group Taiga had them. He called Yevgeny Smirnov.

Smirnov is a former Muscovite who exiled himself to Krasny Yar, and he is a force to be reckoned with. After doing hard time in the army under vague circumstances, he took a job as a night policeman in Moscow. This is a seriously dangerous occupation in which violent confrontations are commonplace, and Smirnov— lean, muscular, with a pale, rawboned face enlivened by piercing blue eyes—faced them head-on. However, the combination of this and his experiences in the army took its toll. "My life kind of cornered me," he said in the living room of his airy and immaculate log home overlooking the Bikin. "The military training came back to haunt me, and my nerves gave out: there were occasions when people would come up behind me and, before I knew it, they would be lying on the ground. I realized that the further away I was from people, the better it would be for everyone. That's why I got into hunting management. I found out about Krasny Yar in the Lenin Library in Moscow."

Smirnov married a Udeghe woman and has been living and working on the Bikin since 1979. He has had many encounters with tigers, but his approach to these meetings is radically different from that of his neighbors. When a questionnaire was sent around to local hunters seeking advice on what people should do if they ran into a tiger, Smirnov ignored the list of carefully crafted questions and scrawled SHOW NO FEAR across the blank side. Smirnov approaches tigers the same way he approached hooligans in the back alleys of Moscow. "An animal is an animal," he said simply. "A predator can smell fear very well. If you show fear, you're finished.

"I have four tigers in my hunting area right now," he added, by way of example. "I know them by their faces, and they certainly know me. Well, last year [2006], the younger female thought I was in her way, so she wanted to mess with my psyche a little bit. She started following me all the time, growling at me; she tried to grab my dog. Well, I went fishing in the early autumn; the bushes still had leaves, and my dog went ahead of me. Just as I was approaching a bend in the trail, the dog came running back; I looked up and saw the tigress flying through the air about fifteen feet away. She was after my dog, and I threw myself at her, swearing and trying to smack her with my fishing rod. She changed direction in midair and landed. I tried again to smack her on the nose and just missed her. She ran away and, since then, not only has she stopped showing up at the cabin, she keeps her distance from me. She was trying to get me to leave the area, but when we got face-to-face and she saw that I was not afraid of her, she started avoiding me.

"Over time, I realized that if you have accumulated more anger inside yourself than a tiger has in him, the tiger will be afraid of you. Really, quite literally so. When a tiger is coming at you, you can gauge very well by his facial expression what he wants from you. You can judge by his eyes and ears. One cannot read bears like that. So, a tiger is coming toward you: if you see that his ears are down, that's not a good sign. Then you have to look him in the eye with all the rage you can muster and the tiger will stop and back off. You don't shout or scream—just look him in the eye, but with such hate that he would turn around and go away. After one, two, three times, they leave you alone."

Smirnov may as well have been quoting Henry V:

But when the blast of war blows in our ears,
Then imitate the action of the tiger;
Stiffen the sinews, summon up the blood,
Disguise fair nature with hard-favoured rage.
Then lend the eye a terrible aspect.

This strategy, as combative as it seems, is motivated by pragmatism, not bravado. Like any of us, Smirnov is using the tools at his disposal, and his include the same bestial ferocity that kept him alive in the army and on the back streets of Moscow. 'Smirnov is a protector of the forest and an admirer of tigers, but he has had to find a way to live within the confines of their domain. He summed up this dilemma with a poignant rhetorical question: "So, that tigress—she wanted to kick me out of the taiga. But where would I go?"

Markov, Ivan Dunkai, and their hermit neighbor all shared the same predicament—along with just about everyone in Sobolonye—and each had to make his own accommodation with the tigers. Smirnov had no doubt that Markov's accommodation had involved killing them. "I knew that he was catching tiger cubs," said Smirnov. "He ate the meat and sold the skins. I was trying to hunt him down myself. If it weren't for the tiger, I'd have gotten him sooner or later. The tiger beat me to it."

This tiger, with his appetite, confrontational attack style, and growing comfort in the world of men, now combined elements of both human and animal predators. And so did Smirnov. Each, in his way, was a traumatized refugee caught in a limbo between the human and animal worlds. That limbo had now become a death zone, and Smirnov, perhaps more than anyone else on the team, was ideally suited to function within it.

Along with Vladimir Shibnev, Smirnov also worked with Yuri Pionka. Pionka is an Udeghe from Krasny Yar, an expert hunter, boat builder, and ski maker who knew the Bikin as well as anyone around. He was the only native on either team, and his role was complicated by something his father had impressed upon him since he was a boy: "The tiger is your god."

Until now, this fact had never posed a problem. "I never got involved in any conflict situations with tigers," Pionka explained. "Udeghe people think carefully before they do any harm to a tiger."

But when Field Group Taiga got the call from Schetinin, Pionka's father was far upriver trapping sable and could not advise his son on what to do. As an inspector, Pionka had a responsibility to his team and to his community, and he had to reconcile this with his responsibilities to his father and to his people's beliefs. Fortunately, there was an escape clause when it came to tigers: god or no god, there were limits to what his subjects had to endure. It was clear that this tiger was an amba in its most destructive manifestation and, when such a creature began killing people, blood vengeance was an appropriate response. The same went for human murderers, and this form of justice was practiced by the Udeghe at least into the 1930s.

Depending on the situation, a hero, a shaman, or other clan members might have intervened in a case like this, but such events were extremely rare and any precedents had receded into the realm of folklore. In 1997, there was one surviving shamanka living in Krasny Yar and, though she had the all-important drum, the serpent belt hung with cone-shaped bells, and even a tiger effigy, she was extremely elderly and this situation was beyond her spiritual writ. But there was also the feeling in Krasny Yar that this wasn't an Udeghe problem. "If tigers liked eating people, they would eat us all," said Pionka's neighbor Vasily Dunkai, who is himself an aspiring shaman. "This tiger knew who injured him. The tiger is a very clever predator with a very big brain; he can tell apart who is darker and who is lighter, plus every man has his own distinct smell. That's why he didn't eat my dad [Ivan] or my brother [Mikhail]. He ate the people who harmed him: he ate Russians."

Vasily Dunkai had a point: even though there were plenty of Udeghe and Nanai in the Bikin valley, the tiger's targets had, thus far, all been Russian. And this posed another problem for Yuri Pionka: by entering into this conflict, he risked drawing that dangerous energy onto himself and his family. The story of Uza and the egule offered a possible solution, but no one alive had what it took to master such a creature the way Uza had. However, since the days of Uza, a new and powerful magic had become available, and it had done more to change the relationship between humans and tigers in the Russian Far East than anything except the attitude of the people who introduced it. Pionka had some of this magic in the form of an SKS semiautomatic rifle, a gun that was invented to kill humans, but which worked on tigers, and which gave those who wielded it an unprecedented—one could say heroic—confidence.

In most places, including Russia, there is an inverted correlation between the rise of firearms and the fall of traditional beliefs. Firearms, especially those like the SKS, made certain kinds of shamanic intervention obsolete, and they did so by functioning much as shamans do—that is, by harnessing powerful natural forces and concentrating them into a supernatural form, which can then be channeled through the hands of a human being. It is no coincidence that the rifle combines the elemental mastery of the shaman with the superhuman might of the hero. Hunters and warriors have always dreamed of this and, in this sense, the SKS was a dream come true. After making its debut in the Russian army at the end of World War II, it was replaced by the simpler and more versatile AK-47. However, the SKS remained available as military surplus and, over time, it became the weapon of choice for serious Russian hunters and game wardens; everyone in Field Group Taiga had one, and the same went for Inspection Tiger. Armed with such a weapon, any man could be an Uza.

————

On the night of December 16, there were eight armed men packed into the back of Trush's Kung. In addition to Schetinin, Trush, Lazurenko, and Gorborukov were Vitaly Timchenko, an inspector from Vladivostok, Andrei Kopayev, leader of the neighboring Kirovsky Inspection Tiger unit, as well as Shibnev and

Pionka from Field Group Taiga. Smirnov and Gorunov had gone home for the night, as had Denis Burukhin. Lazurenko cooked dinner on the Kung's wood stove. With images from the Pochepnya site roaming through their minds and conversation, they made their plan of attack. "Everyone was quite agitated," recalled Trush. "Everyone was emotional. We all agreed that the tiger had to be destroyed and the discussion boiled down to what would be the fastest and most efficient way of doing it."

Initially, Schetinin and his men had to decide whether to proceed with an aerial hunt via helicopter, set cage traps, or stick with a more traditional tracking operation. Within the intimate confines of the Kung there existed a kind of democracy. Each participant had an opportunity to voice his opinion, and pros and cons were weighed on their relative merits. Even so, it wasn't a long conversation. The helicopter hunt was dismissed quickly, not just because of expense, but because of the dense forest cover in the Bikin valley. The chances of spotting a tiger from the air were slim, and even then it would have to be the right tiger, a difficult determination to make from a hundred yards above the ground. Steel cage traps didn't make sense for this situation either; they were available, but it would take days to truck them into the valley and put them in place. Traps of this kind ran the added risk of catching the wrong tigers and injuring them, and thus adding more dangerous tigers to the population. Lazurenko recalled a trapping incident in which a tigress had fought so hard to escape that she had broken her canines on the bars.

The options continued to narrow steadily: the terrain was too steep and the ground cover too thick here for skis, or snowmobiles, both of which were far better suited to river travel and the surrounding swamps. Someone threw out the idea of a bulldozer, which went nowhere. Weighing heavy on the men's minds was the fact that, with every passing day, the chances of another attack increased exponentially, and it was soon agreed that the fastest and surest method for finding this tiger would be to hunt him the same way the Yankovskys had more than a century earlier—on foot with dogs. Such was the nature of this tiger and his "operating environment" that, even though the people hunting him had access to air and ground support, lethal weapons, radios, maps, and centuries of accumulated hunting experience, they were forced to proceed on the tiger's terms. This wasn't the fault of the hunters; it was because effective predators excel at engineering situations that skew the odds in their favor, and this is what the tiger had managed to do, even though he was injured and, most likely, in unfamiliar territory.

That evening, it was determined that they would hunt the tiger using two four-man teams. The strategy was simple, involving a kind of roving pincer movement: while one team tracked the tiger step for step, exerting steady pressure from behind, the other team would drive the surrounding logging roads, searching the edges for signs of the tiger as well as humans who could be at risk. Shibnev was correct in that tigers can cover huge distances in a short period when they need to, but this is rare; major relocations are usually caused by natural catastrophes like fires and plagues. War can cause this, too, and so can a concerted hunt, but on December 16, the tiger was close by, and he was the one who was hunting.

———

A strange feature of the ordeal in Sobolonye was that although the village was well populated with hunters, many of them professionals, only one of them volunteered to assist Inspection Tiger in the hunt. This was striking for a couple of reasons, the first being that it was they and their neighbors who had already lost the most to this tiger, and who had the most yet to lose. But another, more ironic, is that among these reluctant hunters were men who may have had more tiger hunting experience than anyone in Inspection Tiger. Sasha Dvornik had actually admitted to shooting a tiger once "long ago," but, if Trush's information was correct, there were others as well; Zaitsev, for one, was a prime suspect. Unlike Andrei Onofreychuk, Zaitsev had the skill, drive, and discipline for such a task, and also the means to get a dead tiger out of the forest. One reason he may not have stepped forward is because of his history with Yuri Trush, who had busted him once under rather comical circumstances: after luring Zaitsev out of hiding by imitating the call of a rutting elk, he added insult to injury by confiscating his gun and ammunition.

When asked why they didn't participate in the hunt, or initiate one themselves, Zaitsev, Lopatin, and others said, variously, that they weren't invited; they didn't have the right kind of guns; the guns they had were illegal and would have been confiscated; that they couldn't hunt the tiger themselves because it was a protected species. There were grains of truth in all of these claims, but underlying them was a lack of collective morale, distrust of authority, and an ingrained passivity that is one of the enduring legacies of State-enforced disempowerment. But one cannot discount the villagers' well-founded fear and common sense. This tiger was not some geriatric livestock killer; he was a highly motivated man-eater that weighed as much as three men and seemed to specialize in killing hunters just like themselves.

In the end, the only villager to step forward and offer his services was Andrei Pochepnya's best friend, Denis Burukhin. Burukhin's gun was illegal, like just about everyone else's, but this didn't stop him, and Trush wisely let it go, not least because he sympathized deeply with Burukhin's wish to avenge his friends. From a team-building point of view, Burukhin, young as he was, was a fortuitous addition: not only was he a war veteran with more high-stakes shooting experience than most of the older men on the team, but he knew this stretch of river inside and out. Furthermore, as a friend of both victims, he was highly motivated to track this tiger down.

With the checkpoints in place, Inspection Tiger took a head count, trying to determine who from the village might still be in the taiga. There was a real urgency to this task because the tiger was doing the same thing. The tiger clearly understood—had probably always understood—the relationship between humans and their cabins, but they had a new significance now, a new place in the tiger's umwelt. Until two weeks ago, human settlements, which advertised themselves from far away with their outhouses, woodstoves, vehicles, and barking dogs, would have been places to avoid. Now, despite a lifetime of training and a virtual eternity of instinct, the tiger was actively seeking them out.

On two out of three occasions the tiger had experienced success by waiting near a cabin—like a cat at a mousehole only on a grand and sinister scale. His terrible patience had paid off: two kills out of three attempts is a phenomenal success rate for a tiger. This tiger, disabled in the dead of winter during a reportedly bad year for his traditional prey, was staring death in the face. Under the circumstances, he had no choice but to make an extraordinary accommodation. Despite the fact that he had been taught to hunt wild game and had been using those methods and prey species to feed himself ever since leaving his mother, the tiger had, in only a matter of days, developed an entirely different hunting strategy and killing technique, both of which were perfectly suited to a food source with which he had no prior experience as prey. Apparently, necessity is the mother of invention for tigers, too.

Hunger and revenge are not desires that human beings usually experience at the same time, but these primordial drives appeared to merge in the mind and body of this tiger such that one evolved almost seamlessly into the other. The killing and consumption of Markov may have accidentally satisfied two unrelated impulses: the neutralizing of a threat and competitor, and an easy meal. But tigers are quick studies and they are, in their way, analytical: there is no doubt that they absorb and remember relevant data and learn from their experiences, accidental or otherwise. If they produce successful results, the tiger will seek to re-create those circumstances as closely as possible. Humans, this tiger had discovered (or perhaps had always known), were as easy as dogs to locate and kill. If the wind was wrong and the tiger couldn't smell them, he could still hear them, and that sound carried a compelling new message. Now, a person stepping outside to split a few sticks of kindling might as well be ringing a dinner bell. As he proceeded systematically from dwelling to dwelling, the tiger was, in essence, running a trapline of human beings.

20

If [the tiger] is in state y at time n, then the probability
that it moves to state x at time $n + 1$ depends only on
the current state.

"Markov's Theory of Connected Events,"
ANDREI MARKOV, mathematician

If you're afraid of the wolf, stay out of the forest.

Russian Proverb

THE MEN SPENT THE NIGHT IN THE KUNGS, ON THE ROAD ABOVE THE
confluence of the Takhalo and Bikin, inside heavy cloth sleeping
bags that might have been state-of-the-art during the Great Patriotic War. Once the fire in the little stove burned down, the Kung
itself had little in the way of insulation to fend off the all-
consuming cold. There was a stable high pressure system hanging
over Primorye that week and the weather was, for the most part,
clear and dry; at night, the temperatures were bottoming out in
the negative forties. When it gets this cold, things we take for
granted start behaving in strange ways: eyelids can freeze shut; a
truck's cast iron transmission housing can shatter like a china dish.
Under these circumstances, warmth takes on a significance closer
to oxygen, becoming a crucial ingredient for life that must be carefully monitored and conserved. This only served to underscore the
extraordinary fortitude of the animal these men sought.

If the tiger slept at all, he did so alone, never seeking shelter
beyond the cover of tree boughs. Many days would pass between

feedings, and water simply did not exist as such; liquids would be taken in via the blood and meat of prey, when available, or by eating snow. At these temperatures, an animal's fur and fat take on the properties and importance of a space suit; like a polar bear, this tiger was a solitary and self-sufficient vessel designed to withstand the harshest elements in a remote pocket of a frozen world. In such a context, it is easy to see how the combination of extraordinary beauty, total self-containment, and apparent imperviousness to just about everything sets this animal at a godlike remove.

Because of the latitude and the approaching winter solstice, dawn held off until eight or so in the morning, which left only about eight hours of daylight for tracking. In this situation, daylight, too, became a crucial ingredient—if not for life, exactly, then for safety. As brave and eager for a resolution as these men were, no one considered hunting the tiger after dark; the odds were too badly skewed in the tiger's favor. But this is the way it has always been, and so Trush and his men sheltered in the Kungs until the sun made it safe to come out again.

When at last it did, on the morning of December 17, Andrei Pochepnya's best friend and hunting partner showed up on horseback, armed with a double-barreled shotgun and accompanied by a small pack of mongrel dogs. Pictured from a distance, in a grainy black and white photograph, it could have been 1910 with Yuri Yankovsky just outside the frame. "Denis was in an aggressive mood," recalled Sasha Lazurenko. "He wanted revenge."

Andrei's funeral was going to be held the following day. Denis Burukhin's world had changed and he had changed with it. "Somehow, I felt no fear of that tiger anymore," he said later. "I followed his tracks but felt no fear."

Burukhin's role in the hunt came to resemble that of a local fixer, and he was valuable, not just for his determination, his knowledge of local roads, and his access to hunting dogs. "He was the only one from the local population who went with us," explained Lazurenko, "because nobody wanted to show the location of their cabins."

It was around these clandestine hunting bases that multiple

agendas collided. Trush knew that there could still be hunters, trappers, and cone pickers out in the forest, but it seemed many locals would rather risk an attack than betray their neighbors. Trush needed to know where these cabins were because the tiger certainly did and he wanted desperately to avoid another tragedy. But only Burukhin was willing to break this unspoken pact with his neighbors, and his motivation was clear. "He was angry," recalled Yuri Pionka, "and his intention was to 'have a meeting' with that tiger."

The road out to the Pochepnyas' apiary lay between the river and Sobolonye, and Trush knew that, at some point, the tiger would have to cross it. "As we drove, I was asking the guys to look carefully to the right and to the left," Trush explained, "and yes, we found the tiger's tracks crossing the road. He had crossed over and did not come back."

The tiger's tracks ran almost due west of Tsepalev's tarpaper shelter, and when they studied them that afternoon, their edges were already hard and slightly rounded, a natural progression of aging snow tracks. Yuri Pionka judged them to be nearly two days old, which meant the tiger had crossed over almost immediately after leaving Pochepnya on the 15th. From here, it was roughly three miles to Sobolonye as the crow flew, and about twice that overland. The tiger could have been there and gone by now, but so far there had been no sign of him around the village. Team members were posted there just in case, and among them was Yegeny Smirnov from Field Group Taiga.

The terrain between this point and Sobolonye was steep and convoluted, laced with creeks and interrupted repeatedly by steep rocky bluffs. It was perfect habitat for Amur tigers, but very hard on humans. This was where the two tracking teams would be spending their days until the situation resolved itself, one way or another. Should the driving team find a fresher track, they could contact the other team by radio and let them know. Although their radios were Japanese and of decent quality, they only worked line-of-sight. If either party was in a valley or over a hill, there was no way they could communicate with each other.

———

Denis Burukhin, his short, sturdy horse antsy and blowing in the cold, took the first tracking shift with Trush, Shibnev, Pionka, and Gorborukov. He led the way, breaking trail, while the dogs, including Trush's Gitta, ran ahead. The scent trail was cold, so for them this was just a jaunt through the woods; nonetheless, they knew hunters, and they knew something was up. Winter is killing season in the taiga and the dogs were primed. The snow was about knee deep and between that, the fallen trees, and the steep ground, it was hard going for man and horse alike. "You can't really walk in the taiga like they do in the movies: fanned out like Germans hunting resistance fighters," Shibnev explained. "If we'd done that it would have taken two hours to go half a mile."

Instead, they walked single file. It was a more efficient way to cover ground, but it could cause serious problems if the tiger were to attack. There had been the same problem at Markov's: lined up like that along the trail, they ran the risk of shooting each other instead of the tiger. But there was no alternative in this terrain, so they walked in line, each man about two body lengths behind the other, the dogs barking, bolting ahead and then orbiting back to check in. Unless the tiger was laid up somewhere—or waiting for them—they probably wouldn't be catching up to him that day anyway.

Given the temperature, the men wore surprisingly light clothes, and it was so cold and dry that there was no need for rubber or nylon. Some wore camouflage, but Trush chose more traditional clothing—homemade pants and jacket fashioned from gray blanket wool called *sukno*. Hunters like this material because it is quiet in the bush and, when it is this cold, it sheds snow easily. On his feet, Trush wore ordinary boots, but Pionka wore fleece moccasins like Andrei Pochepnya's. Besides their rifles, a belt knife, and a handful of extra shells, the men carried little on the trail. Between them, they shared a rucksack containing a few snacks, a Thermos or two of tea, a radio, and a compass. They brought no maps. Burukhin was their map, and the tiger was their guide.

Like this, the men walked all day, stopping to rest only briefly. Every half hour or so, one of them would pause and study the tiger's tracks, just to make sure they were as old as they had originally thought. Trush and his men had suspected the tiger would head to high ground after crossing the road and then angle southward toward Sobolonye, but the tiger had other plans. He appeared to be heading northwest, following a steep, tight ravine up into the thickly wooded hill country. There was a lot of Korean pine up there, which meant a strong likelihood of wild boar, but there were hunters' cabins up there, too. In any case, the tiger did not travel in a linear fashion and nor did he choose paths that a man or horse would, so his pursuers found themselves weaving through the forest, plowing through underbrush and scrambling over deadfall and rock. Often, Burukhin's horse would be forced back and have to find another route. By the end of that exhausting first day, it would be clear that there was no place for a horse on this hunt.

The sun was well on its way down by the time the five men approached the head of a little stream the locals called Third Creek, and it was up there, about three miles northwest of Sobolonye, that the tiger's tracks began to trend southward toward the village. With the light failing, the men noted their position, checked the tracks one last time, and headed back the way they had come. All around them were low tree-covered mountains about 2,500 feet high. From the right angle, backlit by the sun, one could see through the forest to the stark outlines of the mountains themselves, the trees standing out on the ridges like stubble on a scalp. As the sun fell beyond the treetops, the upper branches seemed to gather mass, coming into high relief like the leading in a stained glass window. Briefly, the slivered voids between were lit in church glass shades of vermilion and purple, soon deepening to indigo and black.

The tracking team arrived back at the Kung after dark having covered, all told, only around ten miles. Still, they were beat. "After following his tracks for a day, we were getting a picture," said Trush. "It was easy to see what the tiger was doing. He was hungry, and he was hunting Manchurian deer and roe deer. The tracks showed where he had pounced at them, but failed to catch them."

"I wouldn't say that he was weak," said Pionka. "His wound was not serious. It was difficult for him to lift that leg, but he wasn't going to die because of the injury. He didn't seek out the easiest routes, and he didn't lie down that often."

Nonetheless, more than two weeks after being shot, the tiger still wasn't able to hunt normally. He was going to need alternative food sources, and this meant livestock, dogs, or humans. There was no livestock in the back country so that left only two options, unless he was able to poach another tiger's kill.

That evening, Burukhin rode home alone on the snowy road with his dogs trailing behind, now much subdued. Up above, the stars seemed to wink and pulse as they often do on particularly cold winter nights. In the village, smoke rose above the sheet metal chimneys as straight as a pencil. Further down the road in the graveyard, a few plots over from Markov's, a coffin-shaped pile of embers glowed among the snow-covered graves, as startling as a wound. In the Pochepnyas' little house, there was a coffin far too big for what it held, but no container big enough for the grief that went with it. It filled the place, and Andrei's father was being slowly crushed beneath its invisible mass.

————

The village was in mourning and the danger was real, but even so, some continued to ignore the warnings from Inspection Tiger and their own families. Trush had seen the tracks of those who dodged the roadblocks, tempting fate. On one hand, he was sympathetic: "You have to remember that these were difficult times," he said. "People were desperate. Wages weren't being paid and, there, money was lying on the road: all you had to do was bend down and pick it up and sell the cones to China. You'd be paid right away."

But at the same time, he was frustrated and deeply hurt. "In a situation like this, how can you blame Inspection Tiger? How can they accuse us of not taking any measures? How can we restrain the local population? And then there were all these negative sensational articles claiming that we were not doing anything. Where is the logic?"

When confronted, these diehards would inevitably repeat the tayozhnik's mantra: "If I don't touch her . . ."

"I'd say to them that they were wrong," said Trush. " 'The tiger doesn't care if you're only out there picking cones.' Some kept quiet, others said, 'God will be merciful.' And they carried on."

In this way, armed with talismanic prayers, the villagers' survival strategy had much in common with those of Korean peasants a century before. When Schetinin encountered an armed man named Andrei Oximenko from the neighboring village of Yasenovie, he confiscated his weapon on the spot, promising to return it only after the tiger had been killed. He then urged Oximenko to go home and stay there, which he didn't. These were headaches Trush and Schetinin didn't need. Each additional body in the forest was like another wild card, making the aggregate situation that much more dangerous. It also raised the question of how Inspection Tiger should be allocating its resources—trying to protect people who refused to cooperate with them, or staying focused on the tiger.

That night, Trush, Schetinin, and the others went over all this in the Kung. The next tracking shift would be Lazurenko's; Burukhin would be off that day because of Andrei's funeral. On the morning of the 18th, Lazurenko's team headed up into the hills behind Sobolonye to pick up the trail. Meanwhile, the second funeral procession in less than two weeks made its way down the road to the cemetery. When it is extremely cold there is an almost frangible quality to the air; even the trees seem frozen hard as crystal, so sounds move differently, becoming sharper and more percussive. There, at the gravesite, surrounded by a hatchwork of forest, the people of Sobolonye gathered close around that hard dark hole. Friends and family threw in ceremonial handfuls of dirt and, when they landed on the lid of that all but empty box, those clods of frozen earth rang like drumbeats through the woods.

Sobolonye was on its knees. To make matters worse, another man was missing. A villager named Kostya Novikov had gone out a day earlier in the direction of Siptsy Creek, and hadn't returned.

Siptsy was the next watershed over from Third Creek, where Trush's team had tracked the tiger on the first day. Given how close he was, the tiger could easily have circled back if he had picked up sound or scent of someone. Perhaps this is what had kept him from heading directly to the village. Further complicating matters was the fact that a group of hunters from Sobolonye had gone out to search for the missing man themselves. Markov's friend Sasha Dvornik was among them: "We all went searching for him," he told the filmmaker Sasha Snow in 2004. "When he was still out there the second day, we thought the tiger had eaten him."

Trush was of the opinion that the tiger wouldn't backtrack on himself and felt strongly that the teams should stay focused on Sobolonye and the tiger. But Schetinin wasn't taking any chances and he ordered Trush's team to go back to Siptsy and make sure Novikov had been accounted for. The following morning, December 19, while Lazurenko's team picked up the tiger's trail, Trush's team, along with Schetinin, drove over to Siptsy. "There was an old logging road there," Trush recalled, "and we saw a truck with three men inside. It turned out that the man had been lost in the forest and spent the night out there."

"He was walking like he was wounded," Dvornik recalled, "falling every fifty yards. He just had no strength left."

It wasn't clear whether Novikov was truly lost, drunk, or both, but there is no doubt he was lucky and, after his friends recovered him, he did not leave the village again. Trush continued on with Schetinin, following logging roads in a great circle around Sobolonye. They wanted to make sure the tiger was still in the immediate area, and to see if any other tigers might be in there with him. "We covered a large territory, about a hundred miles," said Trush, "and we determined that there were five tigers within that circle. But the tiger we were looking for was in the center."

This confused matters somewhat. No one had assumed the tiger would be the only one in the area, but they hadn't counted on there being that many others. None, however, had paws the size of the tiger they were seeking. Although no one could be positive, Trush believed that this area, large as it was, could be the tiger's home territory, and that the neighboring cubs and females were there by his grace.

During the 19th and the 20th, the pattern of stalking and driving repeated itself, and during that time the tracking teams occasionally lost the tiger's trail and found the tracks of another. "The tracking took an awful lot of time," said Trush. "The snow was deep. His wound was restraining him, and the dragging of his right paw on the snow got bigger and worse. The tiger got tired and so did we—that was the whole idea."

"He always walked," recalled Burukhin, who rejoined the hunt on the 19th. "He walked and walked, but he did not walk normally. He was making small jumps all the time. He never lay down." Burukhin wasn't sure if the tiger knew he was being hunted: "I don't know," he said. "He could not tell us what he knew and what he didn't."

Pionka believed the tiger was always too far ahead of them to know he was being tracked, but Trush wasn't so sure. "We would be checking the tracks fifteen to twenty times a day," he said, "and, over the course of a day, the distance between us and the tiger would decrease. I don't doubt that at times the tiger would have heard us, but I don't think he was afraid of us."

Ever since leaving the Pochepnya site on the 15th, the tiger remained in the high country, hunting behind the village. Perhaps he was trying to return to his old hunting methods and prey, or he may have been staying close to Sobolonye in the hope of discovering a stray hunter. As circuitous as his route was, he got closer to Sobolonye every day. On the evening of the 20th, Lazurenko's team reported that the tiger had crossed First Creek, which ran just north of the village. There was sign of a small boar herd there and the tiger had been hunting them—again, without success. However, a second, smaller tiger was in the area, too, and it had managed to catch a young one. Lazurenko and his men found the young boar's remains with the wounded tiger's prints overlaying those of the other tiger. Perhaps he had run the smaller tiger off. In any case, he had eaten what was left of the boar, but it wasn't nearly enough to sustain him. Meanwhile, there was Sobolonye, barely a quarter of a mile away. They continued following the tracks, and they led directly to the village. This was the moment Trush had been fearing all along. The teams immediately relocated the Kungs and notified the residents, but there was no need to: the dogs had already sounded the alarm.

"We could see Sobolonye," said Trush. "We could hear the dogs barking; we could smell the smoke from the chimneys. We were very close—two or three hundred yards away. The tiger stopped, listened, sniffed, and looked directly at the town." And then, inexplicably, the tiger turned away. "Maybe it was us," Trush said. "Maybe he heard us coming into the village and retreated because of that."

The tracks bore off to the west, skirting the village, but it had grown too dark to follow them. There was every reason to suppose the tiger was doing reconnaissance, trying to determine the most advantageous point of entry. "We couldn't be sure he wasn't coming back," said Trush. "We figured he was probably going to hunt dogs because he'd been hungry for a long time."

The tiger had arrived at midwinter, and the coming nights would be the longest of the year. The moon was waning, in its last quarter, and its paltry light cast shadows that were ragged and confused. They had the same fragmenting effect on the gardens and barnyards of the village as stripes have on a tiger: nothing held together but the blocky forms of the houses themselves. Under such conditions a tiger could pass as formless as a ghost, leaving only tracks to betray it. In the village, there was no sign of human activity whatsoever. "As soon as it got dark, I got everyone inside," Dvornik said later. "Water, firewood—we left that for the daytime. Nobody moved."

Fear had hardened into certainty: the tiger was among them, hunting beneath their very windows. In response, the people of Sobolonye battened themselves down like the Danes at Heorot braced for Grendel's final assault. At midnight, the generator was shut down, and then there was no sound but the dogs: a series of shrill and urgent calls and responses that ricocheted between the houses, each one trailing a faint echo behind it like a sonic shadow. Together, these sentinels formed a kind of predator positioning system: when one of them reached a certain pitch, or stopped transmitting altogether, dogs and humans alike would know, if only for a moment, where the tiger was. But this ancient and time-tested network of alarms was only that; it was no defense against the tiger. The night belonged to him. The dogs could bark and growl all they liked, but in the end they were helpless in the face of this creature they could sense but could not see. And this made the long night seem longer still. Around the village, tree-lined ridges rose up against the deeper dark beyond and, along that wavering verge, stars moved imperceptibly in the treetops, encircling man and animal alike. Altogether, those cross-hatched branches wove a spangled basket against the sky and somewhere inside it was the tiger, hunting.

21

He who has suffered you to impose on him, knows
   you....
The tygers of wrath are wiser than the horses of
   instruction.

WILLIAM BLAKE,
The Marriage of Heaven and Hell

WAITING FOR A TIGER TO ATTACK IS LIKE WAITING FOR A BOMB TO GO off. Nobody slept much. Trush was on tenterhooks, but there was nothing he or his men could do until the sun rose on the shortest day of the year. When it finally did, it was so cold out that it took them nearly an hour just to get the trucks running. Once they were mobile, Trush's team drove into the village proper where they discovered that no dogs or livestock were missing. Besides the barking of their dogs, the cautiously emerging villagers had neither heard nor seen anything out of the ordinary. Meanwhile, Lazurenko's team picked up the tiger's trail where they had left off at dusk the previous afternoon. It was evident from the tracks that the tiger had bypassed the village altogether. "I can't explain why," said Trush, "but he did not go in."

For some reason, despite the presence of a variety of easy prey, the tiger had left the village alone, a decision that, under the circumstances, would have taken extraordinary restraint, or caution. Perhaps he sensed the Kungs and the men who were hunting him. Perhaps the village was too crowded with evidence of man and guns. Perhaps the tiger was looking for an easy, isolated kill.

The tiger headed west, back into the hills, following the bed of

First Creek. Burukhin was with Lazurenko and, when they saw where the tracks were going, and how direct the tiger's line of travel was, Burukhin had a chilling realization: about four miles to the west, just over a low ridge at the head of another stream called Svetly (Bright) Creek, there was a cabin belonging to a neighbor named Grisha Tsibenko. In the Bikin valley, people rarely lock their cabins; hospitality is one resource there is still plenty of, and friends and travelers drop in all the time. Burukhin believed that people could be staying up there. Furthermore, Andrei Oximenko, the same man Schetinin had disarmed three days earlier, was known to hunt in that area, and he was nowhere to be found.

By now, the tiger had not rested or eaten well in a week. This would not have been quite so serious had it been a different season, but the temperature was ranging from twenty-five to forty-five below zero. The amount of meat required to keep something the size of a tiger as much as *150 degrees* hotter than the world around it is prodigious—on the order of forty pounds per day. Between his injuries, the brutal cold, the hunger gnawing in his gut, and the hunters' steady pursuit, the tiger was being pressured from all sides. In his compromised state, he also ran the risk of being challenged by another tiger and either killed or driven from the area. But at that moment, as Lazurenko conferred with Burukhin and radioed the tiger's probable destination back to Trush, meat would have been foremost in his thoughts. Winter was only just getting started in the taiga and, without a significant kill, the tiger's thermal clock was in grave danger of running down. He could freeze to death before he starved.

In a sense, Markov had succeeded in bringing the tiger down to his level: now, the tiger was a poacher, too. In order to feed himself, he was once again going to have to violate his own laws. Burukhin had been right: the tiger was headed straight for Tsibenko's cabin. When the tiger arrived there, sometime in the early dark of December 21, it scouted the place for dogs, a meat cache, the owner. Failing to find any of these, he started knocking things off the cabin's outer walls. When he got to a set of large bowls, he chewed them to scrap metal. From his experiences at Markov's cabin, the road workers' camp, and Tsepalev's shelter on the

Takhalo, the tiger had learned many things about the world of men and, here, he brought them all to bear. When the possibilities of the cabin's exterior had been exhausted, the tiger located a window and forced his way in.

To say that a tiger is an "outside" animal is an understatement that is best appreciated when a tiger is inside. Cabins are small, of necessity, and the tiger filled this one the way a cat would a fish tank. Much to the tiger's irritation, Grisha Tsibenko was not at home. In the course of searching for something—anything—made of meat, the tiger destroyed the place. When he got around to the mattress, which smelled richly of Tsibenko, his habits and afflictions, the tiger tore it apart and then lay down on its harrowed remains. Perhaps by chance, or perhaps by synthesizing his recent experiences hunting for humans, the tiger had arrived at a more efficient method: building on his success with cabin stake-outs and with mattresses, he combined the two here in a way that also warmed him in the process. Waiting for prey *inside* was the tigrine equivalent to a better mousetrap. Now it was only a matter of time.

It is not known how long the tiger waited for Tsibenko to show up, but it is a small mercy—in a place notably short on mercy—that he didn't. The image—arriving home to find a tiger in your bed—is one worthy of a folktale, and there are Udeghe and Nanai stories in which exactly this occurs. In any case, at some point that morning, the tiger got up and left. It may have been because he got impatient, or it may have been because he sensed Andrei Oximenko coming up the Svetly Creek road.

———

Vladimir Shibnev knew this road intimately because he had helped build it back when he worked for the logging company. It was a dead-end spur that followed Svetly Creek for about three miles before petering out in a steep tree-clad bowl. Unless one hiked over the ridge behind Sobolonye, the only way to get there was by driving south out of Sobolonye for five miles to Yasenovie, and then turning west onto the main road back to civilization. From there, it was another couple of miles to the Svetly Creek turnoff. The spur followed the creek northward, almost all the way to Tsibenko's cabin, which was set back discreetly in the forest beyond. While Lazurenko, Burukhin, Smirnov, and Kopayev followed the tiger's tracks on foot, Trush, along with Shibnev, Gorborukov, and Pionka, drove the Kung over to Svetly Creek, where they hoped to intercept the tiger. The net was closing: "We had a feeling," said Burukhin, "that we would come over that ridge and he would be there."

It was only a ten-mile trip, but between one thing and another Trush and his men didn't get over to Svetly until shortly before noon. In the back of the Kung, there was a gun rack where the rifles were usually stored, but the rack was empty now. That morning, everyone kept their rifles by their sides. Because it was 1997, and chaos had become the norm in Russia, these men had access to all manner of military surplus at discount prices. As a result, Shibnev's and Pionka's rifles were loaded with bullets that had been designed to kill soldiers inside armored personnel carriers. These rounds, called BZs, can penetrate a slab of steel three quarters of an inch thick, at which point they explode. Trush, because he actually had a budget for ammunition, was using more traditional hunting bullets called dum-dums. Made of lead, as opposed to steel, these will mushroom inside the body as they carom around, tearing up everything in their path. While there are some bullets made to stop a charging man in his tracks; neither BZs nor dum-dums can stop a charging tiger. The impact of an attacking tiger can be compared to that of a piano falling on you from a second-story window. But unlike the piano, the tiger is designed to do this, and the impact is only the beginning.

Lazurenko's team was still hiking up First Creek when Gorborukov turned the Kung onto the Svetly Creek road. By then, the tiger had emerged from the forest at the far end and was walking south, directly toward them. Between the tiger and the Kung was Andrei Oximenko. Oximenko was on foot, heading north, on a collision course with the tiger. If he had a gun, it was because he had found a replacement for the one Schetinin had confiscated—not that guns had been much of a deterrent to this tiger. Trush and his men were not aware of Oximenko's presence there, so they proceeded slowly, the Kung's huge tires churning through the knee-deep snow, smoke billowing from the woodstove in the back. Shibnev and Pionka were riding in back, too, and they couldn't see much out the narrow side windows.

Trush sat in the passenger seat of the high two-man cab with Gitta, scanning the roadside for tiger tracks. It wasn't long before he spotted some. Trush hopped out with his rifle to examine them, and Shibnev and Pionka got out, too. They could tell immediately that the tracks belonged to a different tiger. By now, these men knew this animal's prints almost as well as they knew their own hands. The men climbed back in and they continued northward. The weather was holding: brilliant sun, minus thirty, the snow as fine as confectioners' sugar. Here and there, along the road, were birch trees bent double by heavy snow, their forked branches plunging earthward like lightning bolts frozen in mid-strike. There were more tracks and Trush jumped out to check, as did Shibnev and Pionka. These ones were old and, again, it was the wrong tiger—probably the same one whose tracks they'd crossed earlier. By now, they had covered about a mile and a half at this careful, stop-and-go pace.

Trush and his men had been at this for a week now; they were tired, unwashed, and wanting to be done. Nonetheless, there was a charge that day; this empty road in the back of beyond was full of possibility. The tiger, hungrier than ever, made the most of the easy traveling it offered, and so did Oximenko. Each was making good time toward his respective destiny. But the Kung added a new wrinkle: as it labored up a steep rise, man and tiger alike heard the engine grinding through that perfect silence, and both of those seasoned tayozhniks had the same reaction: they got off the road and hid. As fate would have it, each turned to his right, so they ended up on opposite sides of the road, listening and watching for the Kung. Only three hundred yards stood between them. Had the Kung not disturbed them, they would have met in less than two minutes. Oximenko was oblivious. What the tiger knew had been answered best by Denis Burukhin: "He could not tell us what he knew and what he didn't." Who would live and who would not was equally unclear.

Trush, still scanning the unbroken snow on the roadsides, spotted Oximenko's exit tracks immediately. They stopped again. The tracks were clearly fresh, and their presence there was beyond Trush's comprehension: "We had warned absolutely everyone," he said, still aggrieved. "These people *knew* we had two corpses on our hands, and yet they went into the forest anyway." Trush couldn't be sure who it was, but he had to decide immediately whether to chase this moron down, or continue on after the tiger. Schetinin wasn't around so it was Trush's call. He was fed up with poachers and disobedient locals, and he had a feeling the tiger was close, so he signaled his wheelman to drive on. Less than a minute later, Trush spotted tiger tracks off to his left. Again, they stopped. It was shortly after noon. By now, Trush had been in and out of the Kung many times and he was tired of taking the rifle with him, so he left it in the cab. Shibnev and Pionka climbed out of the back, and Shibnev remembers thinking, "What is it *this* time?" They left their weapons behind as well.

Together, the three of them made their way over to the road's edge. It was clear, even from a distance, that this was their tiger. The tracks led into a clearing that was about fifty yards deep and half again as long. The visibility was unobstructed, and the tiger, wherever he was, was nowhere nearby. It was starting to seem like he was never going to be nearby. Pionka proceeded a short way into the clearing and bent down to test the edge of one of the tracks: it crumbled like powder. Pionka is a fairly quiet man so it surprised everyone when he said, "Motherfucker, it's hot!"

As one, the men hustled back to the Kung for their rifles. Gitta was racing around now, barking, hackles up. This was it, and everyone knew it. Before them lay the clearing, which angled slightly up and to the west. It was a former loading deck for logs so it had been stripped of vegetation and graded. It was empty now save for the pristine snow that covered it. Poking through here and there were a few holdovers from the summer: bare stalks of wormwood and crowfoot, stray canes of raspberry, and blades of tall, golden grass. The tiger's tracks appeared to be angling southwest across this virtually empty canvas and into the forest, which was a chaotic mixture of cedar, pine, aspen, and elm with a tangled understory that would make for hard going.

Gitta started down the track and raced back, yipping wildly, and the men flipped off the safetys on their rifles. Trush unfastened his knife sheath as well, but for some reason he carried his rifle on his shoulder, marching style. Shibnev had his slung off his left shoulder, trigger up, and Pionka held his like he was about to charge a bunker. Meanwhile, Gorborukov, the team's designated driver, was locking up the Kung as he always did when they might be gone for a while. Under other circumstances it might have been comical, but in this case it evoked a different sensation when he said, "You guys go ahead, I'll catch up."

They didn't wait for him but headed down the tiger's limping track; the right forepaw wasn't even clearing the snow now. Though the ground was wide open, they were so used to walking single file that they fell into this formation out of habit. Trush led the way, breaking trail, followed closely by Shibnev and Pionka. They were affected—and irritated—by Gitta's manic barking and their eyes darted across the clearing and then to the forest edge, which stood like a dark wall before them.

The sun shone brilliantly on the undisturbed snow; the only shadows there were those cast by the men themselves—long, even at midday. Gitta continued darting up the trail and then back to Trush, barking incessantly, but she gave no clear indication of the tiger's whereabouts. She didn't know. As they walked, the men scanned the clearing, an expanse in which it would have been difficult to conceal a rabbit, and then they focused their attention on the forest ahead, which was beginning to look like one enormous ambush. With the exception of the dog, everything was calm and nearly still. Behind them, smoke rose lazily from the Kung's chimney, drifting off to the north. Gorborukov was still standing there by the back door, holding his rifle like a broom. In the clearing, the slender stalks and blades nodded reassuringly, as if everything was unfolding according to plan. The men had gone about twenty yards when Shibnev, picking up some kind of ineffable, intuitive cue, calmly said, "Guys, we should spread out."

A moment later, the clearing exploded.

The first impact of a tiger attack does not come from the tiger itself, but from the roar, which, in addition to being loud like a jet, has an eerie capacity to fill the space around it, leaving one unsure where to look. From close range, the experience is overwhelming, and has the effect of separating you from yourself, of scrambling the very neurology that is supposed to save you at times like this. Those who have done serious tiger time—scientists and hunters—describe the tiger's roar not as a sound so much as a full-body experience. Sober, disciplined biologists have sworn they felt the earth shake. One Russian hunter, taken by surprise, recalled thinking a dam had burst somewhere. In short, the tiger's roar exists in the same sonic realm as a natural catastrophe; it is one of those sounds that give meaning and substance to "the fear of God." The Udeghe, Yuri Pionka, described the roar of that tiger in the clearing as *soul-rending*. The literal translation from Russian is "soul-tearing-apart." "I have heard tigers in the forest," he said, "but I never heard anything like that. It was vicious; terrifying."

What happened next transpired in less than three seconds. First, the tiger was nowhere to be seen, and then he was in the air and flying. What the tiger's fangs do to the flesh its eyes do to the psyche, and this tiger's eyes were fixed on Trush: he was the target and, as far as the tiger was concerned, he was as good as dead. Having launched from ten yards away, the tiger was closing at the speed of flight, his roar rumbling through Trush's chest and skull like an avalanche. In spite of this, Trush managed to put his rifle to his shoulder, and the clearing disappeared, along with the forest behind it. All that remained in his consciousness was the black wand of his gun barrel, at the end of which was a ravening blur of yellow eyes and gleaming teeth that were growing in size by the nanosecond. Trush was squeezing the trigger, which seemed a futile gesture in the face of such ferocious intent—that barbed sledge of a paw, raised now for the death blow.

The scenario was identical: the open field; the alert, armed man; the tiger who is seen only when he chooses to be seen, erupting, apparently, from the earth itself—from nowhere at all—

leaving no time and no possibility of escape. Trush was going to die exactly as Markov and Pochepnya had. This was no folktale; nonetheless, only something heroic, shamanic, magical could alter the outcome. Trush's semiautomatic loaded with proven tiger killers was not enough. Trush was a praying man, and only God could save him now.

But in that clearing, there was only Yuri Pionka and Vladimir Shibnev. If divine intervention occurred, Shibnev was the vehicle: it was he who had been visited with the sudden impulse to reposition the men, which had placed him and Pionka broadside to the tiger and out of each other's line of fire. Because there was no time for thought, or even fear, Shibnev's and Pionka's collective response was mainly one of instinct and muscle memory. And yet, somehow, both of these men found the wherewithal to think; they stole it out of time and space the same way gifted athletes wrest opportunities from inches and fractions of seconds. Even in the face of a flying tiger and a man about to die—a scene that would leave most people staring in dull surprise, as Gorborukov was from beside the Kung—both Shibnev and Pionka understood they could not shoot when the tiger was on top of Trush because their hyper-lethal bullets would kill him, too. They had to kill the tiger in the air. In that moment, those ungodly di ex machina became Trush's gifts from God.

Shibnev and Pionka brought their rifles to their shoulders in the same reflexive way Trush had, and Pochepnya and Markov had before him. "I fired and fired and fired and fired," said Shibnev. "I remember seeing him fly through the air, the right paw was out like this."

In that sliver of time between registering the tiger's presence and his airborne collision with Trush less than three seconds later, Shibnev and Pionka fired eleven times between them; Trush fired twice. In spite of this barrage, the tiger hit Trush at full speed—claws extended, jaws agape. The impact was concentrated on Trush's right shoulder, and his rifle was torn from his hands. Trush, now disarmed with the tiger upon him, threw his arms around his attacker, grasping fistfuls of his fur and burying his face in the animal's chest. He was overcome in every sense: by the inexorable force of the tiger; by the point-blank blast of Pionka's and Shibnev's rifles; by the impossible softness of the tiger's fur, the muscles taut as cables underneath. Like this, man and beast went down together, bound in a wrestler's embrace.

No bird flies near, no tiger creeps;
alone the whirlwind, wild and black,
assails the tree of death and sweeps
away with death upon its back.

ALEXANDER PUSHKIN,
"The Upas Tree"

THE TIGER'S ROAR ECHOED AWAY, AND SO, TOO, DID THAT FUSILLADE of rifle shots. The steady south wind carried off the gun smoke, and the crowfoot and wormwood nodded to themselves as if all was well. Svetly Creek flowed on, silent and invisible beneath its carapace of ice, and Alexander Gorborukov took a step forward. Later, he would say that it had been like watching a movie in slow motion, one in which he was powerless to intervene. Shibnev and Pionka would agree that the events in that decisive moment were as vivid as a film, but that there was nothing slow about them. Less than a minute had passed from when they first set foot in the clearing to when they stopped shooting.

———

The first thing Trush remembers is someone saying, "Yurka! Are you alive?"

With his friends' help, the dead man stood. He said, "Oh!" several times in succession. His eyes were big and round and, for a moment, he did not know if they were gazing on this world or the next. After colliding with Trush, the tiger's momentum had caused it to somersault over him and now the tiger lay in the snow, pawing blindly in its death throes. Pionka fired a final control shot. The tiger was dead, perhaps many times over, and Trush was alive, feeling himself for injuries and proof of existence. It is still not clear whether it was a symptom of shock or an example of extraordinary sangfroid, but Trush's first impulse after standing and taking inventory of himself was to get it on film: "I said, 'Guys, stay where you are!' and I ran to the Kung and got my video camera. I filmed footage of where the tiger was and where Yuri Pionka was standing; I filmed his hiding place from where he had pounced at me. I filmed it all."

It is a frantic and scattershot piece of work and the soundtrack plays like a crash course in *mat* (short for "Fuck your mother"), a form of Russian profanity that is the bastard child of *gulag* and criminal slang. It is visceral, violent, and anatomically explicit, and for five or ten minutes after the tiger's death and Trush's resurrection, it poured forth undiluted as the men stormed around the clearing, replaying those death-dealing, life-saving seconds.

Conspicuously absent in all this was Trush's rifle. "I kept wondering," said Trush, "why the tiger hadn't grabbed me by the neck. It was a riddle to me. When I came up to the dead tiger, this was what I saw":

Trush's rifle had gone down the tiger's throat, all the way to the stock. The stock itself was cracked, and pocked with teeth marks, and the gas tube, which runs along the top of the barrel, had been crushed. This explained why Trush took the impact of the tiger on his right shoulder, and it may explain why he is alive today. In the end, the margin between Trush's life and death came down, literally, to millimeters and fractions of seconds; down to Shibnev's uncanny—one could say "animal"—intuition, and to his and Pionka's equally instinctive and precise responses. It is safe to say that nothing but the superhuman powers of those weapons, in conjunction with Shibnev's and Pionka's heroic skill and presence of mind, could have effected such an outcome under those circumstances. Odysseus and Ahab would have been impressed. But these are the tolerances the predator must routinely operate within; the line is always deadly fine.

Trush radioed the other team, but they were still on the far side of the ridge so he could not get through. He then thanked his men and shot triumphal footage of them with the dead tiger, including close-ups of the tiger's face and teeth. Gorborukov noted the time: 12:35 p.m. Though seriously underweight, the tiger was an otherwise impressive specimen with huge paws and magnificent fangs. The head was enormous—in Sasha Dvornik's words: "as big as a basin." Its fur was a russet brown laid over with broad black bands; around its chest, the shaggy white of the underbelly carried on up across its ribs. Its eyes appeared exceptionally slanted, even for a tiger; they were set in the face at an angle approaching forty-five degrees, and further accentuated by the mascara-like striping that ran up from their outside corners.

Trush managed to get Schetinin on the radio, and he was told to bring the tiger directly to the village. Schetinin wanted the people to see it in the flesh—to know that it was dead so they would no longer be afraid. As emaciated as the tiger was, it took all four of them to wrestle it into the back of the Kung. Shibnev and Pionka rode in back with the body, and it covered the floor. Trush rode in front with Gorborukov and, although he does not smoke, he asked Gorborukov for a cigarette. "When he was handing me the cigarette," Trush recalled, "he said, 'Has it finally sunk in?' I said, 'Yes.' And then he noticed my trembling hands."

It took him longer to notice that Trush was bleeding. Between his long underwear and the heavy *sukno,* much of the blood had wicked away, but eventually Gorborukov realized that the obvious rips in Trush's clothes had been caused by the tiger and were deeper than they appeared. Trush had claw wounds on his back, arm, and thigh; the latter was deep, and needed to be stitched, but they had no thread in their first-aid kit. When they got to Sobolonye, the men applied a field dressing that was in common use during the Afghan War, and it offers an insight into the appalling conditions under which Russian soldiers served there. Trush was put back together with a "herring," a name derived from the cans from which these improvised staples were often made. The method is simple, if unsanitary: with a knife, slice a short strip of steel out of a handy can; after pinching the wound together, bend the strip in half, place it over the wound, and clamp it down. Repeat as necessary. Trush was never seen by a doctor. They sterilized the wound with vodka. He kept his herrings in for a week and pried them off himself.

———

After Trush conferred with Schetinin, who had since called in Lazurenko's team, Gorborukov drove the Kung to a snowy crossroad by the village well and parked. When they opened the back door, the news traveled fast and, soon, a semicircle of villagers had gathered around. Baba Liuda was there along with Denis Burukhin's mother, Lida; so were Zaitsev and Dvornik. With the bare trees and the dilapidated houses in the background, the scene had a strangely timeless quality: it was as if these people had come to view a dead outlaw, or a witch. As Schetinin smoked his pipe and went over the details with the villagers, Trush stood by the door with his mangled rifle, ushering people in and out of the back of the Kung. Some thanked him or congratulated him; others glared.

Pionka and Shibnev sat inside on the bunks while the tiger lay at their feet, bleeding on the floor. It was still warm, and its paws made the men's boots look small. Tigers, at the best of times, have a potent smell, and this one exuded a rank and musky, postcoital funk. Combined with its old and improperly healed wounds, the fresh blood, and the unwashed men, it made for an almost palpable atmosphere in the tight confines of the Kung. It would have been striking, and possibly informative, to juxtapose the Russians looking at that tiger with the Russians who regularly file through Lenin's tomb. Viewers are not allowed to touch Lenin, but there were no such restrictions on the tiger. By turns, people patted it, kicked it, swore at it, and spat on it. Some simply stared impassively through the door. Most of them had never been so close to a tiger before, and so were struck by its size. "He was so big and beautiful," said Irina Peshkova, the gas man's wife. "Looking at him there, I didn't feel sorry for those two guys [who were killed]; I felt sorry for the tiger: I think that people did something to him to make him kill."

Lida Burukhina had a different reaction. Recalling her feelings that day, she said, "I wanted to have it killed again."

Meanwhile, Trush, who had just come as close to death as one possibly could and still walk away, and who had been holding himself and his team together for more than two weeks under extraordinarily difficult circumstances, reached a kind of breaking point. With the tiger finally dead, and his boss and the villagers there to witness it, the stress and horror of the past two weeks came rushing home to him: "Andrei Pochepnya's mother and sister came," he said, "and that meeting touched my heart—touched my soul very deeply. When the two of them saw the tiger, they cried, and I could not restrain myself in that situation. I felt so sorry for that guy, Andrei."

———

When the villagers had seen enough, and Trush and Schetinin had been able to tell their side of the story to those willing to listen, Schetinin ordered his men to close up the Kung. "What are you going to do with it?" a woman asked.

"We're going to make dumplings out of him," came the deadpan reply from a local man standing next to her.

Schetinin took Trush aside and instructed him to take the tiger out of the village and skin it. After driving a couple of miles up the road in the direction of the Pochepnyas' apiary, Trush told Gorborukov to pull over. They were followed by Lazurenko's team and Schetinin, and here, by the side of a logging road, the tiger was hauled out. There was a slender rope around its neck, like a leash, and by this, two legs, and its tail Trush's team ran the tiger across the snow about twenty yards away from the vehicles. According to Sasha Lazurenko, they were preparing to cut into it when Denis Burukhin approached Schetinin: "Vladimir Ivanovich," he said, respectfully, "may I kick the tiger for my friend?"

Schetinin granted him permission, and Burukhin wound up and kicked the tiger for Andrei Pochepnya.

A small fire was built, and the men set to work skinning the tiger, starting at the paws and working their way toward the center. Although Schetinin had burned dozens of tiger pelts over the years in order to keep them off the black market, he wanted this one to be removed "carpet style" and preserved. The sun was now in the trees, and it was bitterly cold, but most of the men worked barehanded while Schetinin stood by, puffing on his pipe, observing their progress. All of these men were seasoned animal skinners; nonetheless, as they worked, they commented often on the smell and on how amazingly tough the tiger's hide was. When they opened the chest cavity, the heart was steaming.

Trush, Pionka, and Shibnev did most of the work and, as they went along, they had the opportunity to study the tiger's wounds in detail. In addition to the deep flesh wound in its left forepaw, it now appeared that the tiger had been shot twice in the right leg at point-blank range with weak loads of buckshot. One cluster had only gone skin deep into the foreleg while the other had penetrated the joint above, and many of the balls were still in place. Only one of Trush's bullets had actually gone into the tiger, and most of Pionka's and Shibnev's had passed right through. But as the men went over the tiger's body, carefully flensing the skin away with their hunting knives, they came to understand that it had been shot an extraordinary number of times—not just by them and Markov; this tiger had absorbed bullets the way Moby-Dick absorbed harpoons. In addition to their and Markov's wounds, they found a steel bullet from another rifle and many pieces of birdshot. The end of the tiger's tail was also missing, and had been for a while—either shot off or frozen. There were no plans for a formal autopsy, but it was clear already that during its short life in the traumatic aftermath of perestroika, this tiger had been shot with literally dozens of bullets, balls, and birdshot. Markov may not have been the beginning but rather the last straw. Denis Burukhin said, "Maybe after someone fired that birdshot into him, he got angry with the whole world."

"It was men who were responsible for the aggression of this animal," said Trush, "and the incident with Markov was a sort of quintessence of all those cases."

The tiger dismantled was a disturbing sight. The skinned head—all white muscle and fangs—was terrifying: an egule in the flesh. The legs, extended, were as long as a man's. The stomach was empty. The skin lay as it had come off the body, inside up. How strange it would have been to see it there—so recently alive with unimaginable fury—now as flat and lifeless as a shroud, being folded first in half along the spine, then in quarters, eighths, and sixteenths, like the carpet it had now become. All these disparate parts, laid out neatly at sunset on the bloodstained road, were as hard to relate to a tiger as a crashed plane is to flight.

> Pursuant to the permission for the period December
> 16th–31st, 1997, an Amur tiger has been killed under
> the supervision of Y. A. Trush. The killing has been
> carried out in accordance with Permission No. 731
> issued on December 8, 1997, by the State Ecology
> Committee of Russia.
>
> YURI TRUSH, Final Report

CHRISTMAS AND THE NEW YEAR CAME AND WENT QUICKLY AND QUIETLY.
It was a somber time made more so by the introduction of the
New Ruble, a devastating, if effective, reset of the nation's currency. Already broke, the residents of Sobolonye were minimally
affected and limped on much as they had before. If nothing else, it
had been a good year for pine nuts and now, at least, it was safe to
search for them again. But it wasn't safe for everyone; in Alexander Pochepnya's heart and mind, the tiger was alive and hunting
still. One night in January, it caught up to him. Shortly after
returning to work as the night watchman at the village school, he
was found there, dead by his own hand. The father was buried
beside the son in an anonymous grave.

Today, Sobolonye has the feel of a time capsule in which the
most damaging effects of perestroika have been preserved. What
is so haunting is the fact that this time capsule contains people,
and it is clear from the faces and the material poverty that many
of them remain trapped in 1995, which could have been
Appalachia in 1935, a time when life in the resource-dependent
hill country was particularly desperate and bleak. In the interven-

ing years, Pyotr Zhorkin has died, along with Boris Ivanovich, the boss of the Middle Bikin National Forest Enterprise. Ivan Dunkai was next. Sasha Dvornik moved away after his wife died, and Leonid Lopatin has done the same. With no prospects in Sobolonye, Denis Burukhin moved to Luchegorsk where a friend helped him get a job at the power plant. The trapper-poet Tsepalev left, too, saying that if he stayed, he would drink himself to death. Andrei Onofreychuk stayed in Sobolonye; unemployed and debilitated by alcoholism, he hanged himself in the fall of 2007. That winter, the village administrative offices burned down. Baba Liuda, Irina Peshkova, Lida Burukhina, and the Pochepnya and Onofreychuk families have all stayed on, captives of inertia and the comfort of the known. Danila Zaitsev, alone, seems to have remained of his own volition. A model of stoicism under duress, he continues to keep the village generator running, and also works as a heavy equipment mechanic for a private logging company where he is held in high regard by his co-workers.

Vladimir Markov's wife, Tamara Borisova, has remained as well, but she has never fully recovered from Zaitsev's terrible news that evening, so many years ago. Her sons have stayed by her, and they see to her needs, but her face is a mask of grief, and her loss seems to replay itself daily in her mind. She spends her days fishing on the Bikin in all weather, often alone. Her husband's caravan is gone now, and so are his beehives, but her boys have built a cabin of their own a hundred yards to the west. In the eyes of the law, they are poachers, but there is nothing else and, in the Panchelaza, poaching isn't what it used to be. "They've logged a lot of the forest," said Markov's son, Alexei. "The ecology has deteriorated. The Bikin used to be a deep river, but now, you can walk across it. They've built roads all over the taiga, and a lot of people are coming here now [for hunting and fishing]."

Alexei wears boots identical to those his father died in, and he labors over a motorcycle of the same make and color his father once had. Many of Alexei's happiest memories are of working with his father at his apiary and, even as he approaches thirty, one can see in his eyes the sad vacancy left by the man from whom he learned to love the taiga. Alexei has since planted a Korean pine at the site where his father's remains were found, and surrounded it with stones. There is a cup there, as there is by his grave, so that visitors can remember him with a vodka toast. "Whenever we're at the graveyard," explained Markov's neighbor Irina Peshkova, "we always visit his grave. We'll bring flowers, candy, and a shot of vodka. Who knows who would drink it, but we leave it there anyway."

To this day, Tamara Borisova maintains her husband's innocence, as do his closest friends. Andrei Onofreychuk and Sasha Dvornik were adamant to the last that he had done nothing to the tiger. As evidence they cited Markov's choice of ammunition: "He never shot cartridges,"* Onofreychuk insisted, "because he was hunting with dogs. He only used bullets."

"I hunted with Markov for several years," said Dvornik in an interview with the filmmaker Sasha Snow, "and he never used buckshot. Everyone will tell you: he shot birdshot or bullets."

Danila Zaitsev felt sure the tiger had been wounded before it encountered Markov. Denis Burukhin, who did not know Markov as well, said, "God knows where those bullets came from."

When the tiger was skinned, six balls were recovered from its foreleg and sent to a forensics lab in Ussurisk, near Primorye's principal border crossing with China. There, they were analyzed and compared with the homemade buckshot found in Markov's cartridge belt. According to Trush, the lead composition was identical, and the formal determination made by the ballistics analyst was that the buckshot was Markov's. "Clearly, he thought that he was strong enough to kill the tiger," said Trush, "and he accepted the tiger's challenge."

Vasily Solkin, the leopard specialist, understood it the same way. "Markov couldn't go back to the village. He had to stay and resolve the situation. Try to understand this," he said. "Markov was a tayozhnik—a man of the taiga—and if he were to run away, he would not be able to come back here—ever. For a tayozhnik, there was no other choice: he had to finish this battle. Otherwise,

* This refers to shotgun shells, which Onofreychuk claimed would put dogs at risk of getting hit due to the spreading nature of buckshot.

for the rest of his life, he would be afraid of every tree. The taiga would never let him in again."

Drawing on seventy-five years of experience on the Bikin, Ivan Dunkai made sense of the tragedy this way: "It has never happened that a tiger attacked to kill and eat a man here. In the past, when a tiger attacked a man, it was only because the man was aggressive to the tiger: who would like to be wounded—to get a bullet? These were the only cases. So, it was Markov's destiny to be eaten by a tiger. If he had stayed overnight at my place, it would have been a different story."

———

Lingering on in Trush's mind was the question of what exactly happened on the night Markov was killed—had Markov shot at the tiger then as well? Trush knew little beyond the fact that the gun had been taken from the scene, most likely by Onofreychuk. In March of 2007, Onofreychuk stated that, when he arrived, Markov's gun was lying open in the snow. "There was an empty shell in the barrel," he explained. "Apparently, he shot once, opened the gun to reload it, but he didn't make it and the tiger got him."

Sasha Dvornik had a vivid memory of the scene as well: "Markov's gun was lying open in the snow by the print of his body," he recalled in 2004. "There were two cartridges in the snow: one was empty; the other was full. He had managed to take the fresh cartridge from his belt, but had no time to reload the gun."

Markov's cartridge belt held twenty shells and, when Trush recovered it, three of them were missing. None were found in his caravan. It is conceivable then that the first shell was fired sometime around December 1 or 2, the second shell was fired on the night of December 3, and the third was dropped in the snow moments later. As was the case with Pochepnya and Trush, Markov would have had two or three seconds between hearing the tiger's roar and being attacked. His shotgun would have been loaded, and there is every reason to suppose he would have tried to defend himself. It has never been clear where that shot went, but, based on Inspection Tiger's field autopsy, it now looks as if Markov managed to shoot the tiger twice in the right foreleg—once from his caravan (or in the woods) and, again, just before he was killed. The fact that he was attempting to reload in the midst of the attack implies desperation, but also extraordinary presence of mind: Markov died while trying to fit a small, slippery shotgun shell into a narrow gun barrel, in the dark, at thirty below zero—with a tiger bearing down on him from ten yards away.

Today, only the tiger remains. When Vladimir Schetinin returned to Vladivostok after the hunt, he delivered the tiger's skin to the Arseniev Museum, which occupies a historic building downtown, on Aleutskaya. There, the tiger has been stuffed and put on display for all to see. Safely contained in a glass case, it has been caught forever, out of its element and visible to all.

————

Yuri Trush hoped, at the very least, that these events could serve as a kind of cautionary tale to deter careless hunters and would-be poachers; if laws and warnings failed, he reasoned, maybe graphic images would get the point across. "During the investigation, I sent video footage of Khomenko, Markov, and Pochepnya to the local TV station," he said. "They aired it, and there was a lot of negative feedback. People called saying, 'Why are you broadcasting such horrors?' They thought it was some kind of video montage; they didn't understand that the footage was real. In my opinion, people who hunt—who have guns—really needed to see those images. They have to think about things like that."

There seems to be no question that, in Primorye, human-tiger relations have entered a new era in which the potential for scenarios like Markov's is increasing. Vasily Solkin attributes this to four factors: a simultaneous increase in the availability of powerful hunting rifles, Japanese four-wheel-drive vehicles, and access via logging roads, combined with a breakdown in traditional hunting values. "The biggest problem for a tiger these days," Solkin explained, "is the New Russians who buy good foreign guns with good optical devices, who trample on hunting rules, written or traditional, and who hunt without leaving their jeeps, firing at any animal without even bothering to check whether they killed it or not. Those people bring the most harm to tigers. The situation today is very different from the situation ten years ago because, if I encounter a tiger in the taiga these days, I am encountering an injured tiger more often than not."

According to Galina Salkina, a tiger researcher at the Lazovski Zapovednik and one of only two women working full-time in the testosterone-heavy world of Amur tiger research, about 80 percent of the tigers she autopsies have been shot at some point in their lives, many of them more than once. Sometimes, these situations end like this one did: In May of 2004, three poachers negotiated access to a restricted border zone in a tanklike GTS. Because they were hunting at night with lights, the hunters were aiming at eye-shine alone without being sure what they were shooting at. One of the men managed to hit a tiger, which then charged the massive vehicle, jumped aboard, and fatally mauled one of the hunters before his partners killed it. The crime was discovered, but the commanding officer in charge of the border area refused access to investigators. In cases where the tiger survives, it may hold the memory in mind, and retaliate against the next vehicle or person who fits that sensory profile.

———

There have been no attacks on humans reported in the Bikin valley since 1997, but there is conclusive evidence that tigers are being poached there—by Russians and natives alike. In spite of this, tigers remain a relatively common sight, and the age-old tensions between them and the pastoralist Russians with whom they share the taiga persist, exacerbated by diminishing game populations and loss of habitat to logging. The range of attitudes seems directly related to personal experience: Sergei Boyko, who clearly respects his local tigers, has almost lost his patience with them. At the bridge maintenance camp where he works, five of the six dogs they kept there were killed by tigers during the winter of 2007–2008. "I am sick and tired of them," he said bitterly. "They don't leave me alone. I had made arrangements to get a horse, but then had a change of heart: I can't get a horse because it will get eaten. I can't raise a pig because it will get killed. My neighbor brought a horse to his apiary, and a tiger killed it."

Never a fan of tigers to begin with, Sasha Dvornik was seriously traumatized by the Markov incident. "I'm probably too sensitive," he told Sasha Snow, "but I still have nightmares in which I'm collecting pieces of Markov's body. If I'd known what I would see there, I'd never have gone to his cabin. Now, I won't let a tiger get away alive. I will exterminate that vermin everywhere."

The huntress Baba Liuda's feelings are more philosophical: "If they want to walk around, let 'em walk around. If they want to roar, the hell with 'em—let 'em do it."

———

Long after the paperwork was completed, this incident continued to haunt Yuri Trush, and it does so to this day. Although he managed to survive, Trush has been scarred in a variety of ways: "The native people tell me that I'm now marked by the tiger," he said. "Some of them won't allow me to sleep with them under the same roof."

The notion that Trush now bears some ineffable taint, discernible only to tigers, was put to the test at the tiger catcher Vladimir Kruglov's wildlife rehabilitation center in 2004. Trush had gone there with Sasha Snow in order to get some live footage of a tiger in a forest environment. One of Kruglov's rescued tigers, a particularly impressive male, is named Liuty, which is an efficient word combining vicious, ferocious, cold-blooded, and bold. It is a good descriptor for Ivan the Terrible, but it seemed an odd name for this tiger, which was leaning against the compound fence, getting his neck scratched by Kruglov, who had raised him from a cub. Kruglov then stepped away to attend to something else, leaving Trush, Snow, and a few other visitors spread out along the fence, watching and taking pictures. Liuty, who was used to this kind of attention, appeared content and relaxed until he spotted Trush, at which point his demeanor changed suddenly. Liuty fixed his eyes on him and then, with no warning or apparent motive, he growled, accelerated to a run, and leaped at the fence as if trying to clear it. It was too high, and five hundred pounds of tiger piled into the wire, striking it with so much force that the fence bowed outward ominously, directly in front of Trush. Trush recoiled and fell over backward as if he had been knocked down solely by the projected energy of the tiger. Snow was nearby and went to help him up. "His face was ashen," he recalled.

Remembering the incident, Trush touched his chest and said, "I felt cold in here."

There was no obvious explanation for why this well-fed, well-socialized tiger would do this, or why it would have picked Trush out of a group. "Maybe some sort of a bio field exists," Trush suggested afterward. "Maybe tigers can feel some connection through the cosmos, or have some common language. I don't know. I can't explain it."

Such an interpretation would not have surprised anyone in the Dunkai or Pionka clans, and it is one of the principal reasons those who maintain traditional beliefs avoid tigers. Lubovna Passar, a fifty-year-old Nanai psychologist who uses a combination of shamanic practice and Western psychology to treat patients addicted to drugs and alcohol, describes it as "a centuries-old taboo that's held in the genes."

Yuri Pionka was concerned about this kind of postmortem fallout as well. While skinning the tiger in Sobolonye, he had hit a blood vessel that caused some of the tiger's blood to spatter on him. He reacted, at the time, as if he had been burned with hot embers, and he used his knife blade to scrape the blood off as quickly as possible. "I can say one thing about the tiger," said Pionka, "he is definitely a very smart animal. He has an intellect, and he will go after a specific person who offended him. My father came back [from upriver] for the New Year and, when he learned that I'd been involved in hunting a tiger, he said to me, 'Throw away the clothes you were wearing, and throw away the knife you used to skin him.'"

That the tiger was physically dead didn't seem to matter. In the elder Pionka's view, this tiger was an Amba, and so may have existed beyond mortal containment. Whether there was additional cleansing required, Pionka declined to say. In any case, he suffered a serious illness afterward that lasted a number of years, but he appears to have recovered.

Trush is a man for whom law and order represent not just a job description but a personal code of conduct. As a backcountry lawman, facts and logic—the observable and the provable—form the bedrock of his thought processes. However, his personal experience, along with his exposure to native beliefs, has opened his mind to the supernatural capabilities of the tiger. "I've often heard from hunters and villagers that strange things happen in the presence of a tiger," he said. "It can be compared to a snake looking at a rabbit and hypnotizing him: it has some inexplicable influence on objects and humans and, in his presence, magical phenomena can occur."

Trush sees his own survival as all the more extraordinary because of this, and he considers December 21, 1997, to be his "second birthday." For years afterward, members of his squad, including Pionka, would phone him on the anniversary to acknowledge his survival and rebirth. "Sometime after all this happened," said Trush, "I met Andrei Oximenko [the man who nearly walked into the tiger on the last day], and I said to him that he was born under a lucky star. He admitted it, and said, 'Yes, I heard your truck and turned off the road. Thank you for showing up at the right time.' I said, 'You probably have a guardian angel, just as I do.'

"There was a period after these events when I had unpleasant sensations if I went to the forest alone, or saw a tiger track," Trush explained. "And now, when I see tiger tracks, I still feel fearful and cautious. I don't believe anyone who says, 'I'm not afraid of tigers.' A man must have a sense of fear; it's only normal. Since then, I have encountered tigers in the forest, but I have never lost self-control. Maybe more encounters lie ahead, God forbid."

———

In 2000, Vladimir Schetinin, Inspection Tiger's founding chief, was forced into retirement, and with him went much of his hand-picked staff, including Trush. Shortly afterward, Trush's squad mate, Alexander Gorborukov, committed suicide. Subsequent "reorganizations" at all levels of government have led to staff and funding cuts that have left the agency's future in doubt. In 2008, Sasha Lazurenko was the only member of the team still affiliated with Inspection Tiger, but since the shake-up in 2000, its power to effectively enforce the law in the forest has been steadily whittled away, and undermined by allegations of corruption under the new chief (he was replaced in 2009). Salaries and morale have diminished accordingly. The current state of things becomes clear after a visit to their offices. When it was first created, Inspection Tiger was based in downtown Vladivostok with the State Committee of Ecology; after 2000, it was banished to the second floor of an obscure housing project, two bus connections and an hour's travel away.

"That's why I left," said Trush. "That's why I came to work in a federal national park. Here, we have the status of state inspectors: I have the authority to write a report and follow it through. If I catch someone, I have the authority [as he once had in Inspection Tiger] to push the matter to the very end."

Talking to Inspection Tiger's alumni now is kind of like reminiscing with a successful rock band or sports team that has broken up and fallen on hard times. Those years, 1994–2000, were glory days. They had good training, respectable salaries, high morale, a strong media presence, and real power. With the necessary equipment—uniforms, vehicles, guns, cameras, and fuel—to do their job properly, the public respected them, and so did poachers. They even had a community outreach program through which they visited schools to talk about their work and the importance of a healthy, intact environment (Trush continues to do this). At a time when cynicism and corruption seemed to be the order of the day in Primorye, Inspection Tiger offered an alternative and, for the most part, its members took pride in being part of something that was having a tangible, positive impact on the territory. For many of these men, their work with Inspection Tiger represents one of the best, most empowered moments in their lives. The thought of it, and the demise of it, are bittersweet for Trush, and they elicit strong feelings to this day. But it is clear that what he and his former colleagues are mourning is not simply the job, but their youth. "My only regret," said Trush, "is that I didn't get into conservation work ten or fifteen years earlier."

Now Trush seems to be making up for lost time. In 2007, two new federal parks were created in Primorye, Zov Tigra ("Call of the Tiger") and Udegheyskaya Legenda ("Udeghe Legend"). It is strangely appropriate that Trush would have been made the deputy director of Udeghe Legend, and that has been his title since 2008. However, there is currently no salary for this position and so Trush must rely on Phoenix Fund, a Vladivostok-based conservation group affiliated with the Wildlife Alliance in Washington, D.C., which also funds a number of inspection teams throughout Primorye. The park is medium-sized, totaling five hundred square miles*; currently, Trush's duties are focused on protection and enforcement, the work he loves. In spite of its protected status, a powerful logging company gained access to the Zov Tigra park and ransacked it; they attempted this in Udeghe Legend as well, but Trush intervened. "They thought that if they got caught, they would just pay a bribe and be done with it," Trush explained. "But the case received good coverage in the media. I must admit I was very pleased. Because they logged in a national park, the fines and damages were five times higher than usual."

Trush is an almost relentlessly positive person, and he is exhilarated by this new challenge. "We are truly starting from scratch," he said. "There is nothing there right now, no buildings or anything, and there is still a lot of lawlessness. We have to do enforcement work in order to create a place for recreation, civilized fishing and hunting in the indicated areas. We also have to create an infrastructure; we have to find a team of people who would be genuinely interested in the job. We have to develop tourism, create an ecological trail system, create ecological education programs, etc. It will all happen."

That said, funding remains a serious concern and tigers are still being killed. Some things have changed in Primorye, but one thing hasn't and that is the hazardous business of dealing with

* In 2009, the park's areas was reduced dramatically.

poachers. In November of 2008, Trush was on a raid in the new park when he and his team confronted a group of Nanai poachers, one of whom fired three shots at Trush's squad mate. The shots missed, and Trush chased the shooter down. He managed to catch him and disarm him, but during the struggle, Trush was stabbed in the hand. Ultimately, he managed to handcuff the man, who turned out to be drunk. Shortly afterward, Trush had a heart attack; in August of 2009, he underwent triple bypass surgery. Trush is nearly sixty, and this kind of high-stress, high-impact field enforcement is a young man's job. If anything, the working environment is only growing more dangerous, but within weeks of his surgery, Trush was back on patrol in the taiga. "Nature has decided there should be a tiger here," he said. And Trush's vocation, as he describes it, is to see that it remains. Summoning a Russian proverb, he added, "Hope dies last."

Epilogue

AS OF 2008, THERE WERE AN ESTIMATED FOUR HUNDRED AND FIFTY tigers living in Primorye, southern Khabarovsk Territory, and their adjacent border regions—down from a postwar high of roughly five hundred in the late 1980s. (By comparison, the state of Texas, a place that has no natural history of tigers, has more than two thousand of them living in various forms of captivity.) This may sound like a lot of tigers, but it is nothing compared to what the wild population was a hundred years ago. At the beginning of the last century, it is estimated that there were more than 75,000 tigers living in Asia. Today, you would never know; within the fragile envelope of a single human memory 95 percent of those animals have been killed—for sport, for beauty, for medicine, for money, for territory, and for revenge. Looking at distribution maps of tigers then and now is like looking at maps of European Jewry before and after World War II: you simply cannot believe your eyes. It is hard to imagine such a thing is possible, especially when you consider that tigers have accompanied our species throughout its entire history on the Asian continent and have been embraced for their physical, aesthetic, and iconic power. Because of its beauty, charisma, and mythic resonance, the tiger has been adopted as a kind of totem animal worldwide. There is no other creature that functions simultaneously as a poster child for the conservation movement and as shorthand for power, sex, and danger. Like a fist, or a cross, the tiger is a symbol we all understand.

Of the eight commonly recognized tiger subspecies, three of them—the Balinese, the Javan, and the Caspian—have become extinct in the past two generations, and a fourth, the South China tiger, has not been seen in the wild since 1990. No reliable tiger sightings have been reported from the Koreas since 1991. Today, the tiger has been reduced to isolated pockets of relic populations scattered across the vast territory over which it once roamed freely. Current estimates indicate a total wild population of around 3,200 and falling.

Making this situation more upsetting, especially for conservationists, is the fact that this cascading trend could be reversed tomorrow. Left alone, with enough cover and prey, there are two things tigers do exceptionally well: adapt and breed. In nature, versatility equals viability, and in this, tigers rival human beings. Until around 1940, tigers could be found almost anywhere on the Asian continent from Hong Kong to Iran and from Bali to Sakhalin Island—and at any habitable altitude: tigers have been sighted in Nepal at 13,000 feet, and they are still somewhat common in the semi-amphibious mangrove swamps of the Sundarbans. Nor are they terribly choosy: as long as quantities are sufficient, tigers take their protein where and how they find it. And this is precisely where the tension lies: *Panthera tigris* and *Homo sapiens* are actually very much alike, and we are drawn to many of the same things, if for slightly different reasons. Both of us demand large territories; both of us have prodigious appetites for meat; both of us require control over our living space and are prepared to defend it, and both of us have an enormous sense of entitlement to the resources around us. If a tiger can poach on another's territory, it probably will, and so, of course, will we. A key difference, however, is that tigers take only what they need. This is why, given the choice, many Russian hunters and farmers would rather have tigers around than wolves. The former are much less prone to surplus killing.

What is happening to tigers now is analogous to what happened to the Neanderthals twenty-five thousand years ago, when that durable, proven species found itself unable to withstand the competitive force and expansion of *Homo sapiens* and was backed into a corner of southwestern Europe. There would have been a point when their numbers, too, began to visibly shrink, and falter, and finally disappear. There would have been a last one. Many human tribes have met the same fate since then, and many more are meeting it now. Today, it occurs not so much by death as by dilution: through resettlement, religious and economic conversion, and intermarriage, gradually the skills, stories, and languages fade away. Needless to say, once sheltered by a roof, carried in a car, and fed from a can, very few humans willingly return to sleeping on the ground, walking cross-country, and foraging with hand tools. The same is true of tigers: once they have been habituated to zoo conditions, there is no going back. To date, there has been no case of a captive tiger being successfully introduced, or reintroduced, to the wild. Captivity is a one-way trip. There is a poignant irony in this because, at one time or another, all of us have been in the tiger's situation. The majority of us live how and where we do because, at some point in the recent past, we were forced out of our former habitats and ways of living by more aggressive, if not better adapted, humans. Worth asking here is: Where does this trend ultimately lead? Is there a better way to honor the fact that we survived?

———

From a distance, saving wild tigers is an appealing idea, but for many of the people who live alongside them, these animals might as well be members of an enemy tribe. Powerful, frightening, and unpredictable, tigers often represent competition in the quest to meet basic needs, whether it is for timber, game, farmland, or simply peace of mind. What exactly do you say to the cell phone-wielding, Toyota-driving dacha owner when she complains that tigers—*tigers!*—have eaten all her dogs, and now she's afraid to walk in the same woods where she used to pick mushrooms with her grandmother? What do you say to the farmer whose cow has just been killed, or to the hunter who believes tigers are scaring away all the game? These are some of the conversations people are having in Primorye in the post-perestroika age—along with why a local masseur is considered a serious candidate for mayor of Vladivostok, when the former mayor will be caught and sent to prison, why bread costs twice as much as it did last year, and how it seems like the Chinese are the only ones willing to work a farm anymore. This is the environment that people concerned about the future of the Amur tiger must work in.

Meanwhile, across the border in Harbin, the second largest city in Manchuria, one could find—just months before the 2008 Summer Olympics—Tibetan street vendors openly selling the paws and penises of tigers. From where they crouch on the sidewalk, a stone's throw from the central train station, it is a thirty-minute bus ride to the Harbin Tiger Park. Jammed between an army base, a housing estate, and a railroad line, this euphemistically termed "breeding and rehabilitation center" is one of a dozen or so privately owned factory farms dressed up as theme parks in which tigers are kept and bred like so much livestock. The stated goal of the Harbin Tiger Park is to release these animals into the wild, but one only needs to see these cats' ineptitude when presented with a live cow to understand that this is impossible. There is virtually no doubt that, eventually, these animals will find their way into the wide variety of folk remedies still sold by many Chinese apothecaries. Whether or not to legalize the breeding of tigers for this purpose is a matter of acrimonious debate. The general feeling among conservationists and those knowledgeable about the industry is that if it is legitimized, the killing of tigers will also be legitimized and products made from "wild" (poached) tigers will become even more highly prized. Furthermore, distinguishing between farmed and wild tigers would be next to impossible.

The trade in tiger-based products has been officially banned in China since 1993, but it is lackadaisically enforced, and blatant evidence of this greets every visitor to the Harbin Tiger Park: in the center of the ticket lobby stands a huge glass vat filled with "tiger wine." Immersed in this transparent liquid like a piece of provocative modern art is the full skeleton of a tiger, shreds of flesh still hanging from the bone. Around its feet are strewn more bones from other tigers. Visitors may have some of this morbid elixir decanted for 1,000 yuan (about $140) per liter. It is in the presence of things like this that one can better appreciate Far Eastern Russians' anxiety and confusion—the feeling that they are perched precariously on the rim of an alien world.

But as easy and tempting as it is to vilify the trade in tiger-based products, it has a long and honored history in Asia. As the Plains Indians were reputed to have used every part of the buffalo, so, in Asia, is there a use for every part of the tiger. Even the scat was used to treat gastric ailments, and Korean mandarins especially prized robes made with the skins of unborn cubs. This may seem repugnant, but in every culture, the wealthy and, increasingly, the middle class have sought products that are exotic, precious, and rare, often at great cost to the environment. Alligator handbags, tropical woods, waterfront property, caviar, and diamonds are just a few examples of this. In terms of its impact on nature—and on us—our appetite for oil is infinitely more damaging than our appetite for tigers.

An unanticipated side effect of our ravenous success is that we have found ourselves in charge of the tiger's fate. This is not a burden anyone consciously chose, but it is ours nonetheless. It is an extraordinary power for one species to wield over another, and it represents a test of sorts. The results will be in shortly. In the meantime, the tiger will not survive as an ornament hung on our conscience. In order to appreciate the true value of this animal— the necessity of this animal—humans need reference points that mesh with their own self-interest. Probably the most compelling of these, beyond the sublime image of a tiger in the wild, is the fact that an environment inhabited by tigers is, by definition, healthy. If there is enough land, cover, water, and game to support a keystone species like this, it implies that all the creatures beneath it are present and accounted for, and that the ecosystem is intact. In this sense, the tiger represents an enormous canary in the biological coal mine. Environments in which tigers have been wiped out are often damaged in other ways as well: the game is gone and, in many cases, the forests are, too.

A vivid example of what is left behind after the tigers go can be seen from a train window between the Russian frontier and Beijing. Should a passenger turn her attention from the seatback instructional video demonstrating how to make a cell phone lanyard from her own hair, she would see a landscape in which the Marxist vision of nature has been fully realized. With the exception of a swathe of forest along the Chinese-Russian border, what used to be the *shuhai*—Manchuria's ocean of trees—has been largely stripped away. Every square yard of arable land appears to have been made useful with a vengeance—scraped off, plowed up, altered in one way or another. There is virtually nothing left in the way of animal or bird life. A magpie is an event. Every wild thing larger than a rat appears to have been eaten or poisoned. Stunted scrub oak still grows in russet waves on crags above the scoured plain, but down below, as far as the eye can see, spread the works of man.

Beyond the train window, this anthroscape continues southward until one is about an hour outside Beijing proper. Here the factories start and one passes into a Turneresque "miasm in brown"—part pollution and part dust from the encroaching Gobi Desert. China is the putative birthplace of the tiger and, prior to the advent of communism, Manchuria—the vast area north and east of Beijing—was a source of prime tiger habitat. Today, with the exception of a few transients along the Russian border, it is as barren of tigers as the Gobi. Judging from the highways being built there now, tigers won't be back any time soon. A Confucian road sign proclaims the new status quo: "Car Accidents Are More Ravenous than Tigers." But not as ravenous as pollution: in November 2005, a devastating benzene spill in Jilin City, 120 miles south of Harbin, killed virtually everything downstream in the Songhua River. The Songhua is a major tributary of the Amur, and the effects of this catastrophe are still being felt as far away as the Sea of Japan. This is but one of many such accidents, and their impacts reach far beyond the country's borders.

It is safe to say that had Czar Alexander II not annexed Outer Manchuria a century and a half ago, no wild tigers would remain there today and Primorye would be as unrecognizable as the neighboring provinces in China. Were Yuri Yankovsky, Vladimir Arseniev, or Roy Chapman Andrews to return to Manchuria now, they would be completely disoriented. And so would a tiger. Primorye and its borderlands now represent the last hope for tigerdom in Northeast Asia. Completely cut off from any other subspecies, the Amur tiger's nearest wild neighbors are in Cambodia, two thousand miles away.

Looked at from this perspective, Russia's conservation efforts have been a resounding success. The presence and current viability of tigers in the Russian Far East may have begun as an accident of history, but it has been maintained by human intention, often at considerable personal risk. And now it may require more: in October 2009, the international Siberian Tiger Monitoring Program reported a precipitous drop in tiger sightings in its sample areas. The decrease—approximately 40 percent below the averages recorded over the previous decade—has been attributed to several factors, but chief among them is poaching. Even though the fine for killing a tiger in Russia is severe—approximately $20,000—the vicissitudes of Russian law make it nearly impossible to convict tiger poachers. In order to succeed in court, one must be able to produce a dead tiger, a suspect, and two witnesses—a hard combination to come by in the deep forest. Some of the details may differ, but in terms of the collective impact on Amur tigers, it is the early '90s all over again.

While Inspection Tiger and its sister agencies have been "reorganized," disempowered, and starved for funding over the past decade, the responsibility for wildlife protection in Primorye has been shifted from the federal government to the territory. The territorial government has, in turn, handed this job to the Committee for Hunting Management, which oversees sixty thousand registered hunters. The results are analogous to privatization: a job requiring objective oversight has been given to an entity with conflicting interests. Hunting managers don't, as a rule, like tigers very much because a single tiger can kill scores of deer, boar, or elk in a year, thus depriving hunters of game they feel is rightfully theirs. Add to this the fact that, since 2000, the number of active wardens in Primorye has been slashed and slashed again to the point that one warden may be responsible for overseeing thousands of square miles of forest, and the new data, though inconclusive, begin to make more sense.

As of this writing (December 2009), fewer than four hundred tigers may remain in the Russian Far East. Elsewhere in Asia, tiger populations continue to slip as well. If the tiger is permitted to go extinct in the wild, it would be the largest carnivore to do so since the American lion (*Panthera leo atrox*) died out at the end of the Pleistocene, approximately ten thousand years ago. The extinction of the American lion happened to coincide with the dawn of our current era, which some scientists have taken to calling the Anthropocene. It is characterized by increasingly dense concentrations of human beings living in permanent settlements on a landscape that has been progressively altered and degraded in order to support our steadily growing population.

The difference between the extinctions at the close of the Pleistocene and the bulk of those taking place today is one of consciousness: this time, however passively they may occur, they still amount to voluntary acts. Simply put: we know better. This is not an opinion, or a moral judgment; it is a fact. And yet, just as the tiger has not evolved to understand that contact with modern humans and their possessions is generally fatal, we have failed to grasp the fact that we can no longer behave like small bands of nomads who simply move on to the next valley—or oil field, or foreign market—when the current one is exhausted. It is in this context—the meeting of immediate needs versus long-term self-preservation—that the inherent similarities, and limitations, of tiger nature and human nature reveal themselves most starkly. In the case of the tiger, this is less surprising.

To be fair, ten thousand years is an astonishingly short time for a species to fundamentally remake its relationship to the systems that keep it alive. But humans *are* astonishing, and that is precisely what we have done: by mass-producing food, energy, material goods, and ourselves, we have attempted to secede from, and override, the natural order.* Now with the true costs of this experiment becoming painfully apparent, we must remake this relationship yet again. In this, the tiger is a bellwether—one of thousands of similarly vulnerable species, which are, at once, casualties of our success and symbols of our failure. The current moment is proof of our struggle to evolve (perhaps "mature" is a better word) beyond outmoded fears and attitudes, to face the fact that nature is neither our enemy nor our slave.

——

So how does one remake this relationship in the Russian Far East—with a tiger?

One could start by restoring oversight in the form of well-trained and well-funded agencies like Schetinin's Inspection Tiger. In addition to protecting tigers and leopards, these agencies would protect the prey base, not just for big cats, but for human hunters, too. One might then propose the creation of jointly managed wildlife preserves on the Russian-Chinese border. If this was agreed to, one would assemble an international team to assess forest cover in the border region to see if it could, given sufficient quantities of prey, support a viable population of tigers. If this was found to be the case, one would go a step further and initiate a program to start removing the thousands of snares and other trapping devices that plague Manchuria's remaining forests like so many landmines. A system of protected corridors could then be created, allowing predators and prey to migrate naturally and safely across the border as they always have, while increased pressure is brought to bear on the cross-border tiger trade.

With China engaged as an active participant in the effort to revive one of its most revered and potent symbols, there would be

* The only other warm-blooded creature that rivals us in number is chickens. After that, you must go to rats and mice to find a comparably numerous species. In terms of our collective impact on the planet, one would have to look to asteroids and supervolcanoes in order to find a comparison.

the opportunity to move beyond the defensive posture that country has so often taken toward foreign initiatives and begin to share the wealth of knowledge that Russians, Indians, Americans, and others have accumulated with regard to tigers and related matters of wildlife conservation and management. In order to herald this new era, an international tiger conference could be convened in a Far Eastern border city, showcasing the Amur tiger and celebrating the renewed spirit of cooperation between these two enormous and sometimes tigerish countries. With any luck, this event might coincide with the Chinese Year of the Tiger, which comes around every twelve years.

Such scenarios may look like pipe dreams, but, in fact, all of these things have either recently occurred or are currently in the works. In 2002, the four-hundred-square-mile Hunchun Nature Reserve was created in China's Jilin province, adjacent to the North Korean and Russian borders. Between 2002 and 2007, Chinese volunteers removed *thousands* of snares and traps from the Hunchun Reserve. In that same period, reports of tiger sightings increased by roughly 2,000 percent—from about five per year to nearly a hundred sightings annually. In 2004, an active cross-border migration route was discovered on the Ussuri River, and researchers have concluded that roughly a dozen more tigers are living in that area. Another viable conduit exists between the Sikhote-Alin and China's Wandashan Mountains in Heilongjiang Province, and the possibilities of a preserve are being explored there as well.

In 2008, Tatyana Aramileva, one of the most competent policy makers in the region and well-versed in conservation issues, was put in charge of Primorye's Committee for Hunting Management. Her appointment represents the potential for a sea change in wildlife protection across the region. In June 2009, the Global Tiger Initiative, an international alliance that includes the Smithsonian Institution, the World Bank, and the World Wildlife Fund, among others, announced the creation of a generously funded new program dedicated to training game wardens in the interdiction of tiger traffickers. In the fall of 2009, China—for the first time ever—actively solicited the advice and opinions of NGOs on matters of tiger conservation, the tiger bone trade, and that country's central role in the rapid decline of tiger populations across Asia. In October 2009, at the Khatmandu Global Tiger Workshop, Russia announced that it would host an international conference on tiger conservation to be held in Vladivostok in the fall of 2010. Because 2010 is the Chinese Year of the Tiger, the conservation community has adopted it as a slogan and rallying cry to draw attention to the critical state of the world's wild tigers. The commitments made and the actions taken in this pivotal year will likely determine whether or not tigers remain viable in the wild.

What these agencies and the millions of private citizens who support them are ultimately seeking is what Dale Miquelle calls "The Coexistence Recipe," an enlightened and multifaceted approach to mediating the complex, and sometimes conflicting, needs of the humans and tigers who share a common landscape. This recipe is elusive, costly, and time-consuming to prepare, but one thing is clear: its active ingredients are not grief or guilt, but vision and desire. John Goodrich, the longtime field coordinator for the Siberian Tiger Project, said it best: "For tigers to exist, we have to want them to exist."

Now more than ever.

Acknowledgments

Sine qua non is not usually used in the plural, but in this case, it is the only way to describe the contributions made by the following people:

Dr. Dmitri Pikunov, director of the Laboratory for the Ecology of Large Mammals at the Far Eastern Institute of Geography in Primorye, is the veteran tiger researcher who first documented these tragic and signal events. I am grateful for his passion, and for his time.

Sasha Snow is the British filmmaker who brought this story to a wider audience in the form of the multiple award-winning drama-documentary *Conflict Tiger*. His vision, generosity, friendship, and enthusiasm emboldened me to go to Russia, and have nourished me ever since.

Yuri Trush, of course, is the linchpin of this story. His patience, kindness, and willingness to explain in detail a series of events that are, at times, almost unbearable to contemplate gave me a life-changing window into one Russian soul. On a daily basis, Trush manifests the verity that faith is a physical act. It is my fervent hope that this book reflects that fact.

Josh Stenberg accompanied me on every step of my journeys through Manchuria and Primorye. Josh speaks eight languages, including Mandarin and Russian, and his contributions went far beyond those of an ordinary translator, at times including those of fixer, minder, cultural advisor, counselor, and historian. In short, Josh was my Dersu; I can safely and proudly say that, without him, this book would be a different and lesser thing, if it had come to be at all.

I am continually amazed by—and grateful for—the generosity of strangers. The residents of Sobolonye and Yasenovie were welcoming and helpful in spite of all they have endured. In particular, I wish to thank Alexander Borisov, Tamara Borisova, Sergei Boyko, Denis Burukhin, Lida Burukhina, Ludmilla Gvordzik (Baba Liuda), Viktor Isayev, Leonid Lopatin, Sergei Luzgan, Alexei Markov, Irina Peshkova, Irina and the late Andrei Onofreychuk, Yevgeny Sakirko, Igor and Tatyana Sedykh, Anatoly Sukhanov (Kopchony), and Danila Zaitsev.

In Krasny Yar, Vasily and Natalya Dunkai were gracious hosts of strangers as were their daughter, Olga, and her husband, Lyanka. Thanks also to Mikhail Dunkai, Nikolai Gorunov, Alexander Konchuga, and Natalya Pionka.

In Luchegorsk, Yuri Trush's wife, Lyubov, welcomed and fed us day after day while putting up with marathon interviews.

A number of current and former rangers, wardens, and inspectors from various hunting and wildlife protection agencies took the time to share their memories, opinions, and documents, among them Anatoli Khobitnov, Alexander Lazurenko, Yuri Pionka, Vladimir Shibnev, Yevgeny Smirnov, Vitaly Starostin, Anatoli Tarasenko, Yevgeny Voropaev, and Sergei Zubtsov. I am especially grateful to Vladimir Ivanovich Schetinin, founding chief of Inspection Tiger, for his refreshing candor and profound dedication.

There is a distinguished legacy of conservation in Primorye, and the fact that it has persisted so vigorously, against all odds, is a key reason there are still tigers and leopards living wild in the Far East. The courage, determination, and sacrifice of these individuals cannot be overstated and, collectively, they have given this book a larger purpose beyond mere storytelling. In particular, I wish to thank Sergei Bereznyuk and his colleagues at Phoenix Fund,

Vasily Solkin of the Far Eastern Institute of Geography, Sergei Sokolov of the Primorye Institute for Sustainable Resource Management, Sarah Christie of 21st Century Tiger, Michiel Hötte of the Tigris Foundation, and John Goodrich of the Wildlife Conservation Society. I am grateful to Aleksandr Laptev who generously granted me permission to visit the Lazovski Zapovednik, and to Linda Kerley, Vasily Khramtsov, and Galina Salkina, who shared their deep knowledge of that beautiful place. I am equally grateful to Anatoli Astafyev for granting me permission to visit the Sikhote-Alin Zapovednik, and to Vladimir Melnikov and Nikolai Rybin for sharing their extensive knowledge of the Sikhote-Alin tigers. Thanks also to Viktor Yudin for his time and tigers, and to Yevgeny Suvorov for sharing his remarkable collection of data on human-tiger conflict in Primorye. Namfou Rutten and Alex von Kemenade were generous hosts in Beijing, as was Audrey Perestyuk in Khabarovsk.

I owe a special debt of gratitude to Dale Miquelle, director of the Wildlife Conservation Society's Siberian Tiger Project, whose generosity, hospitality, and openness to all manner of questions and requests served as a touchstone and reality check throughout this process.

A portion of the proceeds from this book are being donated to several organizations working on the front lines of the tiger protection effort in Primorye:

In addition to supporting Yuri Trush's work in Udeghe Legend National Park, Phoenix Fund, www.phoenix.vl.ru, based in Vladivostok, is currently assisting more than a dozen inspection teams in Primorye.

The Tigris Foundation, www.tigrisfoundation.nl, based in Amsterdam, and 21st Century Tiger, www.21stCenturyTiger.org, which is affiliated with the London Zoo, are both supporting the work of inspection teams in Primorye.

In addition to its ongoing work studying the tigers of the Sikhote-Alin, the Wildlife Conservation Society, www.wcs.org, is focused on refining and implementing the all-important "coexistence recipe" in an effort to meet the needs of the Amur tiger and the humans who share its habitat.

Conservation of tigers and their habitat is not a priority in Moscow, so foreign funding is crucial to the efforts of these worthy organizations. Even modest donations are greatly appreciated.

Patricia Polansky, Russian bibliographer at the University of Hawaii's Hamilton Library; Nina Semenovna Ivantsova, head of the Regional Bibliography Section at the Gorky Library in Vladivostok; Cheryl Hojnowski at the Wildlife Conservation Society's Vladivostok office; and Michael Zwirn at Wildlife Alliance in Washington, D.C., were helpful allies in ferreting out obscure source material. In Vancouver, Peter and Rosa Stenberg provided a great translator and generous assistance with research materials. Bree Bacon, Mike Bakst, Karin Elliot, and Roma Sidortsov were generous with their insights into all things Russian. Walt Cressler and Shelly Rosenblum waded through the manuscript, offering many helpful comments and suggestions.

A number of experts in various disciplines shared their advice, research, and encouragement at crucial points along the way, among them Clark Barrett, Rock Brynner, C. J. Chivers, Donald Clark, Amir Khisamutdinov, Geoff Mann, Frank Mendel, Lubov Passar, Chris Schneider, Galina Titorova, Kira Van Deusen, Ed Walsh, and Ron Ydenburg. The late Valery Georgevich Yankovsky offered a vivid glimpse of a time and place now all but lost to history.

In addition to being classics in their respective fields, George Schaller's *The Deer and the Tiger*, John Stephan's *The Russian Far East*, and Matt Cartmill's *A View to a Death in the Morning* are solid base camps from which many students have launched their own expeditions into these fascinating realms. That the authors are generous and personable is a bonus to those following in their tracks. Some other key sources were Charles K. Brain's *The Hunters or the Hunted?*, Donna Hart and Robert W. Sussman's *Man the Hunted*, David Prynn's *Amur Tiger*, and Elizabeth Marshall Thomas's *The Tribe of Tiger*. For those wanting a rich and readable one-stop source on everything tiger, I would heartily recommend *The World of the Tiger* by Richard Perry (sadly, out of print).

Finally, I want to thank Sonny Mehta, Louise Dennys, and

Marty Asher for their potent enthusiasm, and Stuart Krichevsky for his expert guidance through the urban forest. I am especially grateful to my editor, Andrew Miller, whose sharp eye, light touch, and good company kept this beast from getting out of hand. My deepest gratitude goes always to Nora, and to our children, whose love makes all things possible.

J.V.

Oaxaca, Mexico
December 17, 2009

A Note on Translation

This is a book about Russians and their tigers, and much of the information in it comes from Russian sources, including many interviews. I cannot speak Russian, so with a few exceptions all of these interviews were conducted by Josh Stenberg and recorded by me during March 2007 and May 2008. They were transcribed by Igor Levit and Asta Mott, two court-certified translators whose skill and insight gave me a much better appreciation for the material. Beyond a handful of common words, Russian bears virtually no resemblance to English, so literal translations often read like chimeras of grammar and syntax. Therefore, of necessity, all the translated quotes in this book have been retooled to flow in English. I have done this while making every effort to preserve the sense, mood, and character of the speaker and, where possible, their slang and idiomatic usage. That said, Russian is a rich, colorful, and nuanced language, and there is no substitute for the real thing.

Several interviews, specifically those with Sasha Dvornik, the late Ivan Dunkai, and the late Vladimir Kruglov, were graciously shared by Sasha Snow and Dale Miquelle. They have enriched this book tremendously. I also wish to thank Misha Jones for his translations of key Russian texts. Monica Hong and Si Nae Park supplied valuable assistance with Korean translations and sources.

Notes

Epigraphs:

vii   Arseniev, p. 70.

vii   Heaney, tr., *Beowulf*, lines 2415–16.

Chapter 2

19   Epigraph: Chehkov, p. 41.

20   "The area around these harbors": Khisamutdinov, pp. 133–34.

20   "There are several kinds": James, p. 545.

22   "If you stand with us": Personal communication, March 3, 2007.

23   "Manchurian and Sakhalin-Hokkaido Provinces": A.L. Takhtadzhian, ed. Problemy paleobotaniki: sb. nauch. tr. ["Problems of Paleobotanists: A Collection of Scientific Works"]. Leningrad: Nauka, Leningr. otd-nie, 1986.

25   "The general appearance of the tiger": Heptner, p. 98.

29   "Now I felt afraid of nothing": Arseniev, p. 100.

30   "The prohibition on shooting": Ibid., p. 335.

30   "My . . . landmarks had vanished": Ibid., p. 340.

30   "Arseniev had the good sense not to live to be old": Ibid., p. viii.

30   the total elapsed time: Khisamutdinov, p. 91.

Chapter 3

32   Epigraph: Jeffers, p. 204.

38   "Terminal Modernism": Hudgins, p. 150.

39   "So, what brings you to this asshole of the world?": Personal communication, May 6, 2008.

41   "Siberian conversation": Landsdell, Vol. 2, p. 247.

Chapter 5

56   Epigraph: Gogol, p. 226.

59   "Each Siberian would be confronted": *Izvestia,* Science section, June 8, 2004, http://www.inauka.ru/english/article47379.html.

61   "Maybe it's near Iran": Personal communication, July 12, 2008.

62   "You came here alone?": Irina Peshkova, March 21, 2007.

63   "absorb no less than one-third": R. Craig Nation, *Black Earth, Red Star: A History of Soviet Security Policy, 1917–1991* (Ithaca: Cornell University Press, 1992), p. 267, quoted in Goldstein.

Chapter 6

64   Epigraph: Coxwell, p. 122.

69   200,000 people were imprisoned: Interview with Roy Medvedev on Ekho Moskvy Radio, March 5, 2003.

Chapter 7

73   Epigraph: From "The Book of Rites"; translation by Josh Stenberg, 2008.

75   Party slogans like "Rob the Robbers!": Valery G. Yankovsky.

75   *"It is precisely now":* Pipes, *The Unknown Lenin,* pp. 152–54.

75   In 2008, nineteen of the world's one hundred richest people were Russians: Luisa Kroll, ed., "The World's Billionaires," *Forbes,* March 5, 2008.

77   "There's no government here": Personal communication, March 21, 2007.

77   "People don't live in Sobolonye, they survive": Vasily Dunkai's daughter, Olga, personal communication, March 17, 2007.

83   "The truth of Necessity, therefore, is Freedom": G. W. F. Hegel, *Logic, The Encyclopædia of the Philosophical Sciences,* Part 1. Translated by William Wallace. Oxford: Oxford University Press, 1975, p. 220.

Chapter 8

88   "The entire winter life of a solitary tiger": Kaplanov, 1941.

88   "Its massive body and powerful skeleton system": Baikov.

90   "must have belonged to an animal that measured 14 feet": Sowerby, *The Naturalist in Manchuria,* Vol. 2, pp. 30–31.

91   tigers have killed approximately a million Asians: Matthiessen, p. 89.

91   "When the majority of people have no means": Personal communication, April 6, 2009.

92   "Father's first two kills were immediately discredited": Caldwell, pp. 36–37.

93   "Those who missed": Neff, April 18, 2007.

93   "Before long we came upon a startling scene": Taylor, p. 77. In 1907, shortly after the Japanese occupied Korea, the Tiger Hunters Guild was ordered to disarm. According to Kim Young-Sik, the former editor of the South Korean Internet journal *Koreaweb Weekly,* the guild's response to this command was to assassinate the magistrate who issued it and launch a guerrilla war against the invaders. Despite being hopelessly outnumbered, this band of charismatic patriots, led by the famous tiger hunter and general Hong Pomdo, carried on a deadly campaign against the Japanese for more than ten years. Finally, in the fall of 1920, after a series of particularly savage battles in which the Japanese suffered heavy casualties, the high command in Tokyo assembled three armies to crush the independence movement once and for all. Hong and his allies were forced to take refuge in Manchuria and Primorye where they found sympathy with the Russians, who had suffered devastating losses against the Japanese while fighting for control of Korea and coastal Manchuria in 1904–1905.

    With the Kremlin's support, Hong's army was able to make cross-border raids for another decade until the new Soviet leadership, wishing to normalize relations with Japan, finally forbade them. Not long afterward, Stalin's increasingly repressive policies and paranoia caught up with the Korean rebels and many were forcibly relocated to Kazakhstan along with the leader of the Tiger Hunters Guild, who languished there until his death in 1943. A reported side effect of the Tiger Hunters' shift to freedom fighting was an increase in the incidence of tiger attacks in the Korean countryside. However, this problem—and its cause—was short-lived: the Japanese took the same approach to tigers that they had to their hunters and, by the time the Japanese were forced to abandon Korea in 1945, the tiger was effectively extinct there.

    Today, Hong Pomdo is considered a hero in South Korea.

93   Apparently, this is a timeless: Defense Department photo (Marine Corps) No. A373217: "This was the largest tiger ever killed within the 1st Marine Division TAOR," http://www.footnote.com/image/51219707/.

94   "A cornucopia!": Eric Miller, "The Fifth of April, 1793," in *The Reservoir* (Victoria, BC: Ekstasis Editions, 2006), p. 23.

94   The Maharaja of Udaipur . . . (one thousand one hundred fifty only)": Schaller, p. 226.

95   "No, the *bogatyri* have not died out in Russia": Vsevolod Sysoev, in Troinin, p. 122.

96   "When I got it it was in a paroxysm of rage": Sowerby, Vol. 1, p. 69.

96   "There were cases": Baikov.

100   "the most precipitous peacetime decline": Pipes, *Communism,* p. 53, from Alec Nove, *An Economic History of the USSR,* p. 208.

100   "We cannot expect charity from nature": Feshbach and Friendly, p. 43.

100   "Let the fragile green breast of Siberia": Pearce, "All Polluted on the Eastern Front."

101   " 'universal values' such as avoiding war": Keller, p. A1.

Chapter 9

110   "It's more of a silence": Sergei Boyko.

111   "it killed nothing": Schaller and Lowther, p. 329.

112   "that under similar conditions": Ibid., p. 328.

112   "If among all the members of our primate family": Ardrey, p. 8.

113   "Never blame the man": Jeffers, p. 433.

114   "We heard the sound of voices": Thomas, *The Old Way*, p. 101.

114   "All of the seven lion groups": Schaller and Lowther, p. 328, fn.

114   Schaller later speculated that this may have been due: Personal communication, August 7, 2009.

116   "a web of socially transmitted behaviours": Thomas, *The Tribe of Tiger*, 1994, p. 111.

116   "The lions around here don't harm people": Ibid., p. 157.

116   "Beyond our fire": Ibid., p. 131.

Chapter 10

119   Epigraph: Gogol, p. 128.

Chapter 11

129   Epigraph: Thomas, *The Tribe of Tiger*, p. 17.

131   ". . . The male strode slowly": Strachan, pp. 244–45.

138   "Usually animals shot and wounded": Heptner, p. 194.

138   "I'd wear different hats": Personal communication, June 16, 2009.

140   "In January 1941": Kaplanov.

142   "Once upon a time": Lopatin, p. 208.

143   "They are semi-savages": Fraser, pp. 221–22.

145   "Some years ago": Shreider, pp. 42–44.

147   "It is heavy going": Chekhov, p. 31.

148   "Sixty-five tigers": Landsdell, Vol. 2, p. 324.

149   "The Russians were probably": Correspondence with the author, May 15, 2008.

150   "God be with you, children!": Trofimov, p. 209.

151   "All of a sudden": Rooney, pp. A-1, A-2.

152   "None of us had ever heard of anything": Personal communication, July 7, 2009.

153   "Will the tigress leave the area": Energiya TV, Luchegorsk, December, 9, 1997.

Chapter 12

154   Epigraph: Fontenrose, p. 254.

159   "like a tiger": Nikolaevna, p. 163, fn.

Chapter 13

161   Ludwig Wittgenstein, *Philosophical Investigations* (London: Blackwell, 1953/2001), p. 190.

161   Charles Darwin, *The Descent of Man, and Selection in Relation to Sex,* Vol. 1 (London: John Murray, 1888), p. 193.

161   Dersa Vzala epigraph: Arseniev, p. 19.

161   "To do so, we must first": Uexküll, p. 5.

163   "The eyeless tick": Ibid., p. 7.

163   "These different worlds": Ibid., p. 6.

163   "we have no means of describing cognitive processes that do not involve words": Budiansky, p. 192.

164   "All species have been shaped": Page, p. 116.

165   *anywhere but here* principle: Barrett, "Adaptations to Predators and Prey," p. 219.

173   "I've read a tiger's not dangerous": Vladimir Solomatin via Suvorov.

173   "entirely ordinary occurrences": Suvorov.

173   "Give me a company of soldiers and I'll conquer China": Stephan, p. 57.

176   "Our clothes, always stiff with blood and sweat": Martin, p. 158.

177   "Using towels as loin-cloths": Ibid., p. 157.

177   "My paleolithic soul feels at home here": Ibid., p. 135.

177   "They were like people you meet": Ibid., pp. 98–99.

177   "We learnt to recognise": Ibid., p. 116.

177   "The longer we lived with animals": Ibid., p. 222.

178   "Animals began to play an increasing part": Ibid., p. 276.

178   "Perhaps this was the origin": Ibid.

Chapter 14

181   Epigraph: Budiansky, p. 33.

182   "I hid inside the cavern": Brain, p. 271.

184   "But whence came the race of man?": Jeffers, pp. 432–33.

185   "If a man-eater continues to kill and eat people": Rushby, p. 183.

185   "The baboons were apparently too terrified": Stevenson-Hamilton, p. 262.

188   "When the lion sees the zebra": Barrett, "How Do We Understand the Behavior of Others?," Slide 28.

188   "The lion wants to chase/bite/kill the zebra": Ibid., Slide 28.

188   "When the lion catches the zebra": Ibid., Slide 29.

188   "The lion hurts/kills/eats the zebra": Ibid., Slide 29.

189   "Jurassic Park syndrome": Barrett in Grimes; see also Barrett, "Cognitive Development and the Understanding of Animal Behavior."

190   "the results herein implicate": New, p. 16603.

190   "People develop phobias": Bryner.

Chapter 15

195   Epigraph: Coxwell, p. 114.
195   "It became a bit of a joke": Anatoly Sukhanov (Kopchony).
199   "Those folks are tougher than nails and hardened from horrors": Karin Elliot, personal communication, June 5, 2009.

Chapter 16

212   Epigraph: Van Deusen, p. 176.

Chapter 17

218   Epigraph: Herman Melville, *Moby-Dick; or the Whale* (University Park: Pennsylvania State University, Electronic Classics Series, 2001), p. 203.
222   "Optimists study English": Mike Bakst and Josh Stenberg, personal communications.
223   "What went wrong": Stephan, p. 3.

Chapter 18

229   Epigraph: Herman Melville, *Moby-Dick; or the Whale* (University Park: Pennsylvania State University, Electronic Classics Series, 2001), p. 389.
233   "as with a razor": Troinin, p. 117.
237   "you learn to read the writing": Martin, p. 123.
240   "There is a high demand for artistry here": Chekhov, p. 41.
242   "Don't ever assume anything with tigers": Via Linda Kerley, personal communication, May 7, 2008.

Chapter 19

244   Epigraph: Peter H. Lee, editor and translator, *Poems from Korea* (Honolulu: University of Hawaii Press, 1974), pp. 128–29.
249   "But when the blast of war blows in our ears": William Shakespeare, *Henry V,* III, 1.

Chapter 22

277   Epigraph: Pushkin, p. 121.

Epilogue

306   "For tigers to exist": Goodrich, p. 29.

Selected Bibliography

Alexievich, Svetlana. *Zinky Boys: Soviet Voices from a Forgotten War.* Translated by Julia and Robin Whitby. London: Chatto & Windus, 1992.

Andrews, Roy C. *Ends of the Earth.* Garden City, NY: Garden City Publishing Co., 1929.

Applebaum, Anne. *Gulag: A History.* New York: Doubleday, 2003.

Aramilev, Ivan. *Beyond the Ural Mountains: The Adventures of a Siberian Hunter.* Translated and adapted by Michael Heron. Chicago: Rand McNally, 1961.

Ardrey, Robert. *The Hunting Hypothesis: A Personal Conclusion Concerning the Evolutionary Nature of Man.* New York: Atheneum, 1976.

Arseniev, V. K. *Dersu the Trapper.* Translated by Malcolm Burr. Kingston, NY: McPherson, 1996.

Baikov, N. A. "The Manchurian Tiger." Harbin: Society for the Study of the Manchurian Region, 1925. Translated by Alex Shevlakov, 1999.

Barrett, H. Clark. "Adaptations to Predators and Prey," in *The Handbook of Evolutionary Psychology,* David M. Buss, ed. New York: Wiley, 2005, pp. 200–23.

———. "Cognitive Development and the Understanding of Animal Behavior," in *Origins of the Social Mind,* B. Ellis and D. Bjorklund, eds. New York: Guilford, 2004, pp. 438–67.

———. "How Do We Understand the Behavior of Others?: The Agency System" (lecture with PowerPoint presentation), from "Human Cognitive Adaptations to Predators and Prey" (Ph.D. Diss.: University of California at Santa Barbara, 1999). UMI Microform number 9986870.

Becker, Jasper. *Hungry Ghosts: China's Secret Famine.* London: J. Murray, 1996.

Bloch, Alexia, and Laurel Kendall. *Museum at the End of the World: Encounters in the Russian Far East.* Philadelphia: University of Pennsylvania Press, 2004.

Brain, C. K. *The Hunters or the Hunted?: An Introduction to African Cave Taphonomy.* Chicago: University of Chicago Press, 1981.

Bryner, Jeanna. "Modern Humans Retain Caveman's Survival Instincts." *LiveScience,* posted September 24, 2007, http://www.livescience.com/health/070924_ancestors_eyes.html.

Brynner, Rock. *Empire and Odyssey: The Brynners in Far East Russia and Beyond.* Hanover, NH: Steerforth, 2006.

Budiansky, Stephen. *If a Lion Could Talk: Animal Intelligence and the Evolution of Consciousness.* New York: Free Press, 1998.

Caldwell, John C. *China Coast Family.* Chicago: Henry Regnery, 1953.

Canda, Edward R. "The Korean Tiger: Trickster and Servant of the Sacred." *Korea Journal* (November 1981): 22–38.

Cartmill, Matt. *A View to a Death in the Morning: Hunting and Nature Through History.* Cambridge: Harvard University Press, 1993.

Cha, Kai-Ching. "Can the Convention on Biological Diversity Save the Siberian Tiger?" *Environs* (Environmental Law and Policy Journal) 24, nos. 2:3 (2000/2001): 3–28.

Champion, F. W. *With a Camera in Tiger-Land.* London: Chatto & Windus, 1927.

Chekhov, Anton. *A Journey to Sakhalin.* Translated by Brian Reeve. Cambridge: I. Faulkner, 1993.

Corwin, Julie, et al. "The Looting of Russia." *U.S. News & World Report,* March 7, 1994.

Coxwell, C. F. *Siberian and Other Folk Tales.* London: C. W. Daniel, 1925.

Dart, Raymond. "Australopithecus africanus—The Man-ape of South Africa." *Nature,* no. 2884, vol. 115 (February 7, 1925): 195–99.

Davie, Lucille. "Who Killed the Taung Child?" City of Johannesburg: January 13, 2006, www.southafrica.info/about/science/taung-skull-130106.htm.

Deer, Bryan. "Nature's Prey." *Sunday Times Magazine* (London), March 9, 1997.

Diment, Galya, and Yuri Slezkine. *Between Heaven and Hell: The Myth of Siberia in Russian Culture.* New York: St. Martin's, 1993.

Doeker-Mach, Gunther, ed. *Forgotten Peoples of Siberia.* Zurich: Scalo, 1993.

Dunishenko, Y., and A. Kulikov. *The Amur Tiger.* Khabarovsk: The Wildlife Foundation, 1999.

Eliot, John L. "Hard Times Put Siberian Tigers Out in the Cold." *National Geographic* 182, no. 4 (October 1992).

Erofeyev, Victor. "Letter from Moscow: Dirty Words." *The New Yorker,* September 15, 2003.

Feshbach, M., and A. Friendly. *Ecocide in the USSR: Health and Nature Under Siege.* New York: Basic Books, 1992.

Fontenrose, Joseph. *Orion: The Myth of the Hunter and the Huntress.* University of California Publications in Classical Studies, Vol. 23 (1981): 1–315, Berkeley: University of California Press.

Formosov, A. N. "Pamiati L. G. Kaplanova ["To the Memory of L. G. Kaplanov"], 1948, reprinted in *Okhotnick'I,* Vol. 4 (2000): 164–86.

Fraser, John F. *The Real Siberia—Together with an Account of a Dash Through Manchuria.* New York: D. Appleton, 1902.

Galster, Steven R., et al. *Russia's Final Roar: Criminal Threats to the Siberian Tiger and Local Communities.* Washington, D.C.: Investigative Network, 1996.

Glick, Daniel. "Can Russia Save the Endangered Siberian Tiger?" *Newsweek,* January 18, 1993, p. 51.

Gogol, Nikolai. *Dead Souls.* New York: Vintage, 1997.

Goldstein, Lyle J. "Return to Zhenbao Island: Who Started Shooting and Why It Matters." *China Quarterly* 168 (December 2001): 985–97.

Goodrich, John, et al. "Time for Tigers: Paving the way for tiger conservation in Russia." *Wildlife Conservation* 105, no. 1: (Jan.–Feb. 2002): 22–29.

Gorokhov, G. F. "The Tiger and Other Carnivores." *Okhota i okhotnich'e khoziaistvo* 9 (1973): 16–17.

Grant, Richard. "Siberian Tigers—The Hunted Ones." *The Telegraph* (London), December 1, 2007.

Grew, J. C. "Hunting the Cave-Dwelling Tiger of China." *Outing* 44, no. 6 (September 1904): 737–45.

Griffin, Donald R. *Animal Minds.* Chicago: University of Chicago Press, 1992.

Grimes, Ken. "Hunted!" *New Scientist* 174, no. 2338 (April 13, 2002).

Hart, Donna, and Robert W. Sussman. *Man the Hunted: Primates, Predators, and Human Evolution.* New York: Westview, 2005.

Hawes, Charles H. *In the Uttermost East; Being an Account of Investigations Among the Natives and Russian Convicts of the Island of Sakhalin, with Notes of Travel in Korea, Siberia, and Manchuria.* New York: Harper & Brothers, 1903.

Heaney, Seamus, translator. *Beowulf.* London: Faber & Faber, 1999.

Heptner, V. G., et al. *Mammals of the Soviet Union*, Vol. 2, Part 2. Washington, D.C.: Smithsonian Institution Libraries and National Science Foundation, 1988.

Hiatt, Fred. "Even Rangers Prey on Russia's Parks." *Washington Post*, June 12, 1994.

Ho-gŭn, Kim, and Yun Yŏl-su. *Hanguk horangi = The Korean Tiger*. Seoul: Yŏrhwadang, 1986.

Hornocker, Maurice, ed. *Track of the Tiger*. San Francisco: Sierra Club, 1997.

Hötte, Michiel. "Amur Leopard Conservation Update." Tigris Foundation; Amsterdam, August 2004.

Hudgins, Sharon. *The Other Side of Russia: A Slice of Life in Siberia and the Russian Far East*. College Station: Texas A&M University Press, 2003.

Iskyan, Kim. "Selling Off Siberia: Why China Should Purchase the Russian Far East." *Slate*, posted July 28, 2003.

Jackson, Peter. "The Status of the Tiger in 1993." *The World Conservation Union*, pp. 1–12.

James, H. E. M. *Proceedings of the Royal Geographical Society and Monthly Record of Geography*. New Monthly Series 9, no. 9 (September 1887): 531–67.

Jeffers, Robinson. *The Collected Poetry of Robinson Jeffers*, Vol. 3. Tim Hunt, ed. Stanford: Stanford University Press, 1991.

Kaplanov, Lev G. "The Tiger in the Sikhote-Alin" (in *Tigr, izyubr, los*. Moscow: 1948). Translated by K. Lofdahl and A. Shevlakov.

Kattoulas, Velisarios. "Russian Far East: Crime Central." *Far Eastern Economic Review*, May 30, 2002.

Keller, Bill. "Key Soviet Aide Recommending Freer Economy." *New York Times*, October 6, 1988, p. A1.

Kerley, Linda, et al. "Effects of Roads and Human Disturbance on Amur Tigers." *Conservation Biology* 16, no. 1 (February 2002): 97–108.

Khatchadourian, Raffi. "The Stolen Forests: Inside the Covert War on Illegal Logging." *The New Yorker*, October 6, 2008.

Khisamutdinov, Amir. *The Russian Far East: Historical Essays*. Edited by Patricia Polansky. Honolulu: Center for Russia in Asia, 1993.

Knight, Danielle. "Russia: Corruption, Trade, Illegal Logging Threaten Far East Forests." InterPress Service, August 6, 2000.

Kruuk, Hans. *Hunter and Hunted: Relationships Between Carnivores and People*. Cambridge: Cambridge University Press, 2002.

Landsdell, Henry. *Through Siberia*, Vols. 1 and 2. New York: Houghton Mifflin, 1882.

Laptev, A., and Y. Chistyakov. *Taiga at the Ocean: Red Book Endangered Species of Primorye*. Translated by Yevgeny Kovtun and Alexandra Tsuranova. Vladivostok: Dalpress State Publishing Complex, 2000.

Lattimore, Owen. "The Gold Tribe, 'Fishskin Tatars' of the Lower Sungari." *Memoirs of the American Anthropological Association*, No. 40, Menasha, WI, 1933.

Lee, Richard B., and Irven DeVore, eds. *Man the Hunter*. Chicago: Aldine, 1968.

Levy, A., and C. Scott-Clark. "He Won, Russia Lost." *The Guardian* (London), May 8, 2004.

Liebenberg, Louis. *The Art of Tracking: The Origin of Science*. Claremont, South Africa: D. Philip, 1990.

Linden, Eugene, et al. "Tigers on the Brink." *Time*, March 28, 1994, pp. 44–51.

Lopatin, Ivan A. *Gol'dy amurskie, ussuriiskie i sungariiskie: opyt etnograficheskago izsliedovaniia* ["The Golds of the Amur, Ussurii and Sungarii: Results of Ethnographic Research"]. Vladivostok: 1922. (Series: *Zapiski* Obshchestva izucheniia Amurskogo kraia, t. 17.)

Loukashkin, A. S. "The Manchurian Tiger." *The China Journal* 28, no. 3 (March 1938): 127–33.

Marean, Curtis W. "Sabertooth Cats and Their Relevance for Early Hominid Diet and Evolution." *Journal of Human Evolution* 18. no. 6 (1989): 559–82.

Martin, Henno. *The Sheltering Desert*. Johannesburg: Donker, 1988.

Matthiessen, Peter. *Tigers in the Snow*. New York: North Point, 2000.

Matyushkin, Yevgeny, ed. *The Amur Tiger in Russia: An Annotated Bibliography, 1925–1997*. Moscow: Russian Nature Press, 1998.

Matyushkin, Yevgeny. ("Man, Achievements, Faith, and a Clearly Recognized Goal: In Memory of L. G. Kaplanov"). *Okhota i okhotnich'e khoziaistvo* 7 (1995): 36–38.

Meier, Andrew. *Black Earth: A Journey Through Russia After the Fall*. New York: Norton, 2003.

Miquelle, Dale, Igor Nikolaev, and John Goodrich, et al. "Searching for the Coexistence Recipe: A Case Study of Conflicts Between People and Tigers in the Russian Far East," in Seidensticker et al. *Riding the Tiger*. Cambridge: Cambridge University Press, 1999, pp. 305–22.

Montefiore, Simon S. *Stalin: The Court of the Red Tsar*. New York: Vintage, 2007.

———. *Young Stalin*. New York: Alfred A. Knopf, 2007.

Morell, Virginia. "Can the Wild Tiger Survive?" *Science* 317, no. 5843 (September 7, 2007): 1312–1314.

Nagishkin, Dmitri. *Folk Tales of the Amur*. New York: Harry N. Abrams, 1980.

Neff, Robert. "Westerners No Match for Korean Tiger Hunters," April 18, 2007, www.english.ohmynews.com (Korea).

———. "When Tigers Stalked Korea." Ibid., May 6, 2007.

New, Joshua, et al. "Category-Specific Attention for Animals Reflects Ancestral Priorities, Not Expertise." *Proceedings of the National Academy of Sciences* 104, no. 42 (October 16, 2007): 16598–603.

Nikolaev, I. G., and V. G. Yudin. "Conflicts Between Man and the Tiger in the Russian Far East." *Bulletin Moskovskogo obshchestva ispytateley Prirody* 98, no. 3 (1993).

Nikolaevna, Irina, et al. "Udeghe (Udihe) Folk Tales." *Tunguso Sibirica*, No. 10, Wiesbaden: Harrassowitz, 2002.

Nowak, Ronald M. *Walker's Carnivores of the World.* Baltimore: Johns Hopkins University Press, 2004.

Okladnikov, A. P. *Ancient Art of the Amur Region.* Leningrad: Aurora, 1981.

———. *The Soviet Far East in Antiquity.* Toronto: University of Toronto Press, 1965.

Packer, Craig. "Rational Fear." *Natural History,* May 2009.

Packer, Craig, and Jean Clottes. "When Lions Ruled France." *Natural History* 109, no. 9 (November 2000).

Page, George. *Inside the Animal Mind.* New York: Doubleday, 1999.

Pearce, Fred. "All Polluted on the Eastern Front" (book review). *New Scientist,* October 3, 1992.

Pearce, Fred. "How the West Is Attacking Russia: As Tropical Rainforests Disappear, Logging Companies Move into the North." *The Independent* (London), March 28, 1993.

Perry, Richard. *The World of the Tiger.* New York: Atheneum, 1965.

Pikunov, Dmitri G. "Please Don't Shoot the Tigers!" Translated by Misha Jones. *Zov Taigi,* No. 1 (January–February 1998): 6–11.

Pipes, Richard. *Communism: A History.* New York: Modern Library, 2001.

———. *The Unknown Lenin: From the Secret Archive.* New Haven: Yale University Press, 1996.

Possehl, Suzanne. "Russia and America Team Up to Try to Save Endangered Tiger." *New York Times,* August 31, 1993, p. C4.

Prynn, David. *Amur Tiger.* Edinburgh: Russian Nature Press, 2002.

Pushkin, Alexander. *Verses and Versions.* Translated by Vladimir Nabokov. Boston: Harcourt, 2008.

Quigley, Howard. "Saving Siberia's Tigers." *National Geographic* 184, no. 1 (July 1993).

Raeburn, Paul. "Scientists See Threat to Life in Siberian Wilderness." *Seattle Times,* February 14, 1991.

Remnick, David. "Letter from Moscow: Echo in the Dark." *The New Yorker.* September 22, 2008, pp. 36–43.

Rooney, Carole. "Attacked Green Lake Man Kills Bear with Stick." *100 Mile House Free Press,* October 8, 2008, pp. A-1, A-2.

Rosencranz, A., and A. Scott. "Siberia's Threatened Forests." *Nature* 355 (January 1992): 293–94.

———. "Cutting Down Siberia." *The Washington Post,* August 18, 1991.

Rostov, I. D., et al. *Oceanographic Atlas of the Bering Sea, Okhotsk Sea and Japan/East Sea.* Vladivostok: V. I. Ilichev Pacific Oceanographic Institute, 2003, www.pacificinfo .ru/data/cdrom/2/start_english.htm.

Rushby, G. G. *No More the Tusker.* London: W. H. Allen, 1965.

Salmin, Yuri A. "K rasprostraneniiu, biologii i promyslu amurskogo tigra Felis tigris longipilis Fitz. v gornoi strane Sikhote-Alin" ["On the Biology and Commerce of the Tiger in the Mountains of the Sikhote-Alin"]. *Nauchno-metodicheskie zapiski* Glavnogo upravleniia po zapovednikam, No. 7 (1940): 251–54.

Schafer, Kevin, and Martha Hill. "The Logger and the Tiger." *Wildlife Conservation* 96, no. 3 (May–June 1993): 22–29.

Schaller, George B. *The Deer and the Tiger: A Study of Wildlife in India.* Chicago: University of Chicago Press, 1967.

Schaller, George B., and Gordon R. Lowther. "The Relevance of Carnivore Behavior to the Study of Early Hominids." *Southwestern Journal of Anthropology* 25, no. 4 (Winter 1969): 307–41.

Schemann, Serge. "Vladivostok, Russia's Wild Far East." *New York Times,* September 12, 1993, Section 6, p. 40.

Seidensticker, J., S. Christie, and P. Jackson, eds. *Riding the Tiger: Tiger Conservation in Human-Dominated Landscapes.* Cambridge: Cambridge University Press, 1999.

Selvinski, Ilyia. "Fur Trade." Moscow-Leningrad, 1929 (in Russian).

Shahgedanova, Maria, ed. *The Physical Geography of Northern Eurasia.* Oxford: Oxford University Press, 2002.

Sharma, Charu. "Chinese Endangered Species at the Brink of Extinction: A Critical Look at the Current Law and Policy in China." *Animal Law Review,* Lewis & Clark Law School, 2005.

Shipman, Pat. "Scavenging or Hunting in Early Hominids: Theoretical Framework and Tests." *American Anthropologist,* New Series 88, no. 1 (March 1986): 27–43.

Shreider, Dmitri I. *Nash dalny vostok: try god a v ussuriakom uraie* ["Our Far East: Three Years in the Ussuri Region"]. St. Petersburg: A. F. Devrien, 1897.

Shtilmark, Feliks. *History of Russian Zapovedniks, 1895–1995.* Edinburgh: Russian Nature Press, 2003.

Siegel, Marc. "The Emotions of Attack." *San Francisco Chronicle,* January 1, 2008, p. B-5.

Smirnov, E. N. *Sto vstrech s tigrom* ["One Hundred Meetings with Tigers"]. Vladivostok: Zov Taigi, 1997. Excerpts translated by O. Zyrina, A. Shevlakov, 1999.

————. "Tracking the Striped Cannibal." *Terney News,* No. 5883, January 15, 1997.

Snow, Sasha. "To Catch a Killer." *The Independent* (London), November 28, 2004.

Sowerby, Arthur de Carle. *The Naturalist in Manchuria,* Vols. 1–3. Tientsin: Tientsin Press, 1922.

————. "A Tiger Hunt in Manchuria." *China Journal* 34, no. 4 (April 1941): 184.

————. "The Tiger in China." *China Journal* 18, no. 2 (February 1933): 94–101.

Specter, Michael. "Siberia: 5 Million Miles of Frozen Dreams." *New York Times,* August 21, 1994.

————. "A Too-Free Enterprise Endangers Siberian Tigers." *New York Times,* September 5, 1995, pp. A1, 2bw.

Stephan, John J. *The Russian Far East: A History.* Stanford: Stanford University Press, 1994.

Stevenson-Hamilton, James. *Wild Life in South Africa.* London: Cassell, 1947.

Strachan, Arthur W. *Mauled by a Tiger: Encounters in the Indian Jungles.* Edinburgh/London: The Moray Press, 1933.

Suvorov, Evgenii A. *Zapovednoe Primor'e* ["Zapovedniks of Primorye"]. Vladivostok, 2003.

————. *Zapovednye khroniki* ["Forbidden Chronicles"]. Vladivostok: Izd-vo DV univ-ta, 2004.

Taylor, Mary L. *The Tiger's Claw: The Life-Story of East Asia's Mighty Hunter.* London: Burke, 1956.

Thomas, Elizabeth Marshall. *The Old Way: A Story of the First People.* New York: Picador, 1997.

————. *The Tribe of Tiger: Cats and Their Culture.* New York: Simon & Schuster, 1994.

Trofimov, Vladimir. *Towards the Sun: The History of Development of the Far East.* Vladivostok: Utro Rossii, 1998.

Troinin, Vladimir. "The Year of the Tiger." Translated by Lise Brody. *MĀNOA,* University of Hawaii 6, no. 2 (Winter 1994): 113–124.

Uexküll, Jakob von. "A Stroll Through the Worlds of Animals and Men: A Picture Book of Invisible Worlds," in *Instinctive Behavior: The Development of a Modern Concept,*

Claire H. Schiller, editor and translator. New York: International Universities Press, 1957, pp. 5–80.

Underwood, Horace. "Hunting and Hunters' Lore in Korea." *Transactions of the Korea Branch of the Royal Asiatic Society* 6, no. 2 (1915).

Van Deusen, Kira. *The Flying Tiger: Women Shamans and Story-tellers of the Amur.* Montreal: McGill-Queen's University Press, 2001.

Vrishch, Alexander. *Fauna of the Ussuriyskii Taiga: A Field Guide to the Animal World of the Southern Russian Far East.* Vladivostok: Dalpress, 2004.

Wall, David. "Shaking Up Russia's Far East." *Japan Times,* April 5, 2007.

Watts, Jonathan. "Bred for the Freezer: How Zoo Rears Tigers like Battery Hens." *The Guardian* (London), April 13, 2007.

Weiner, Douglas R. *Models of Nature: Ecology, Conservation, and Cultural Revolution in Soviet Russia.* Bloomington: Indiana University Press, 1988.

Winchester, Simon. "Black Dragon River." *National Geographic* 197, no. 2 (February 2000).

Yang, Yang. "A China Environmental Health Project Factsheet: Pesticides and Environmental Health Trends in China." Woodrow Wilson International Center for Scholars, China Environment Forum, February 28, 2007.

Yankovsky, Valery G. *From the Crusades to the Gulag and Beyond.* Vladimir, Russia: M. Gorky Scientific Library, 2007.

Yankovsky, Yuri M. *Fifty Years of Hunting Tigers.* Vladivostok: 1990 (in Russian).

Youth, Howard. "Russia's Tough Tigers." *Zoogoer* 37, no. 1 (January–February 2008).

Permissions Acknowledgments

Grateful acknowledgment is made to the following for permission
to reprint previously published material:

Stanford University Press: Excerpt from untitled poem from
The Collected Poetry of Robinson Jeffers, volume 3, 1939–1962
edited by Tim Hunt, copyright © 1954, 1963 by Garth and
Donnan Jeffers. All rights reserved. Reprinted by permission of
Stanford University Press, www.sup.org.

University of Hawaii Press: "Sunset" by Yun Sŏn-do from
Poems from Korea, edited and translated by Peter H. Lee,
copyright © 1974 by University of Hawaii Press.
Reprinted by permission of University of Hawaii Press.

A Note About the Author

John Vaillant's first book was *The Golden Spruce*. He has written for *The New Yorker, The Atlantic, Outside, National Geographic,* and *Men's Journal,* among others. He lives in Vancouver, British Columbia, with his wife and children.

A Note on the Type

This book was set in a typeface called Walbaum. The original cutting of
this face was made by Justus Erich Walbaum (1768–1839) in Weimar in
1810. The type was revived by the Monotype Corporation in 1934.
Young Walbaum began his artistic career as an apprentice to a maker of
cookie molds. How he managed to leave this field and become a
successful punch cutter remains a mystery. Although the type that bears
his name may be classified as modern, numerous slight irregularities in
its cut give this face its humane manner.

Composed by North Market Street Graphics,
Lancaster, Pennsylvania

Printed and bound by Worldcolor Fairfield,
Fairfield, Pennsylvania

Cartography by Mapping Specialists, Ltd.,
Madison, Wisconsin

Designed by Maria Carella